With the Grain

With the GRAIN

Raymond Sokolov

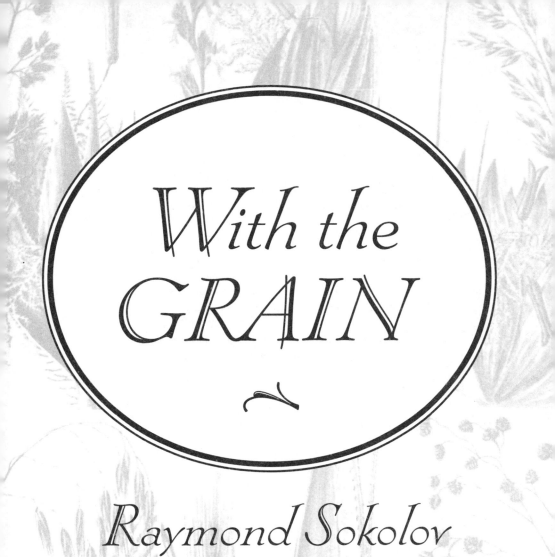

Alfred A. Knopf   NEW YORK   1996

THIS IS A BORZOI BOOK
PUBLISHED BY ALFRED A. KNOPF, INC.

Copyright © 1995 by Raymond Sokolov

Some of the material in this book was originally published in
Natural History magazine.

Library of Congress Cataloging-in-Publication Data

Sokolov, Raymond A.
With the grain / by Raymond Sokolov. — 1st ed.
p. cm.
Includes index.
ISBN 0-679-42561-6
1. Cookery (Cereals) 2. Grain. I. Title.
TX808.S66 1996
641.6'31—dc20   95-14617
CIP

Manufactured in the United States of America
FIRST EDITION

For Matilda and Rosemary

Contents

Acknowledgments

Many thanks again to Johanna Hecht, Kathy Robbins, Judith Jones, Jenny Minton, and the staff of the New York Botanical Garden Library. They know why.

Introduction

Everyone in the world except unweaned infants has eaten grains, and everyone who cooks at all has prepared rice, or at least oatmeal. Most people consume grains every day and think of them as plain stuff, a starchy filler that sits beside the protein point of the meal. This book takes the opposite position, or rather it proposes an alternate view of the matter. It puts grains at the center of the meal and lets the other elements of the menu trail along behind.

Why? My aim is not to be perverse, not even to be original. Most of the recipes that follow are traditional, and some go back to ancient times. As a historian of food, I hope to entice you to look at eating in an old-fashioned way, as all people did when meat was scarce and grain was in ample supply. This is also the attitude that informs most of today's cuisines outside Europe and her former colonies. Even in Europe, especially northern Europe, the old grain-based dishes persist as an earthy echo of pre-Christian times—a true "roots" cuisine.

At the same time, grain-centered cookery is the answer to the hyper-modern problem of nutrition in a long but sedentary life. Grains are high in fiber and virtually fat-free. So they help us avoid cholesterol and colon cancer.

But I am not advising a medical diet of gruel and porridge. You may have to go to health-food stores to purchase some of the grain products called for here, but this book is not intended as a prescription for disease-free longevity. Some of my recipes are not "healthy" at all. But I think they are all delicious, and they definitely all put grain in the spotlight.

Why? Because I want to change the way you think about what you eat. I want grain—and not meat—to be what first comes to mind when you plan a meal. When this happens to you, as it has for me, you will find it easy and appealing to change your diet in a medically and economically desirable way. Most diets fail because they attempt to compel a dramatic departure from traditional eating patterns. For a time dieters give up something they have grown up thinking was a natural part of eating. But such is the power of culturally engrained ideas and habits that people almost inevitably go off their diets after a brief period of religious commitment.

The grain-centered recipes in this book are not spartan exercises in self-denial. They are drawn from actual cuisines eaten by actual people all over the world. Many contain meat, but if you eat these dishes frequently, you will gradually slough off your meat fixation and begin to adopt a new eating pattern in which healthier grains predominate.

The selection of recipes I am offering as fodder, so to speak, for this experiment is, of course, only a selection. There can never be a complete book of grain recipes. No one could lift it. Nor is this an evenhanded survey of all the world's grains from amaranth to zizania. Attention is paid to the exotics, but they will be left where they belong—at the margins of the enterprise. These recipes are not exhibits in a museum of cereals, but delicious dishes I think everyone will love—and that will encourage people to slip happily into a long life of grain cookery. This is, therefore, my own collection of favorites, basic and traditional dishes with a few original concoctions that I invented while testing the others.

With the Grain

What Is Grain?

When the modern

urban person says that wheat and rice are grains,
she thinks she has said something simple and obvious.
But as a Supreme Court justice once remarked
about obscenity, he knew it when he saw it,
but defining it was the hard part.
The etymologist will tell you that our word "grain" comes
from the Latin *granum,* meaning seed, as in *cum grano salis,*
"with a grain of salt." Which is what you have to take
that definition with, because by no means all seeds
are grains. Think of sesame or poppy seeds,
or potato seeds, et cetera. There is, nevertheless,
a grain of truth in the etymological approach.
Let's try saying that grains contain the seeds of grasses.
At least, they do start that way.
The major grains are, in a botanical sense,
the fruits of true grasses, from the Gramineae
family. There, however, the universality of the
definition comes to an end. Ears of corn and drooping

green rice plants do not seem to have much in common, but that has more to do with their history under cultivation than with any underlying botanical dissimilarities. The useful "grain" parts of these plants, those parts that are fit for human consumption, are the endosperms. These little packets of starch, protein, and other nutrients are meant by Nature to nourish the true seed—called the germ, or embryo—and they grow alongside the seed after the flowers of the parent plant are successfully pollinated.

This starchy packet is many times larger than the seed it accompanies. Like some bloated commissary of carbohydrate, it is properly referred to as the fruit of the grass plant, just as the fleshy orange globe surrounding the seed-containing pit of the peach is its fruit. Both organs are primarily food sources for the seed or for ambulatory frugivorous animals that will eat the seed along with the delicious fruit and then spread the seeds around the landscape in their dung.

Grass "grains," or kernels, are structured rather differently from peaches. No doubt you recall from Botany 101 those diagrams of the parts of a wheat grain with their technical names marked by arrows. I will pass over this nomenclature in virtual silence, mentioning only the features of the grain that matter to us as grain consumers interested in how edible grains grow and how their biology influences the way they are processed on their way to us.

Each major grain varies slightly, but they all share two features: a dry fibrous outer layer and an inner kernel of useful starch. The whole of grain technology after harvest aims at minimizing or removing the outer layer and at making the inner starch packet available for human consumption.

Grain harvests are generally the equivalent of mass mowings. Then comes a threshing stage, which separates the grain from the chaff—the fibrous, grassy part of the plant that ends up, when dried, as straw. Of the major cereal grains, three come wrapped in hard husks formed from leaflike structures: rice, barley, and oats. Corn, wheat, and rye are, as Harold McGee reminds us in *On Food and Cooking* (Macmillan, 1988), "naked," or huskless, fruits. But even they are not ready to eat after harvest.

At this point, the wheat farmer finds himself with millions of grains covered with a fibrous layer known as bran. These so-called wheat berries also still have the germ, or seed, attached. The germ spoils quickly because of its fat content. Nevertheless, wheat berries can be eaten as they emerge from the threshing floor. Indeed, modern health-food stores sell them, and some restaurants do an inventive job of cooking them. But the unpolished brownish wheat berry takes a long time to cook and is an indelicate food, although not without appeal as an occasional item in a modern diet.

In the dawn of grain agriculture, however, storage and convenience were paramount goals. We cannot prove it, but it seems overwhelmingly plausible that a desire to keep the harvest safe led early men and women to exhaust themselves by grinding their wheat or rice between two stones. This loosened the bran and, incidentally, turned the interior starch into a pleasing powder that we call flour, or meal.

Of course, it is possible, when milling, to stop short of pulverization. White rice is the leading example of that. After its bran has been rubbed off, it can easily be steamed or boiled to a wonderful tenderness. Rice can also be pulverized into flour and then used to make rice cakes and noodles.

Today wheat is most often milled into flour, as is rye. But oats and barley are usually not, because their flours lack gluten and can't compete with wheat in elasticity for baking pastry, and most important, they don't rise when combined in a dough with yeast.

Corn is *sui generis*. Its kernels can be eaten whole—steamed on the cob or gently heated in almost any way. On the other hand, the bran, or hulls, can be removed when the corn is exposed to an alkali such as wood ash, yielding a beneficially altered starch called hominy. Or untreated dried corn can be ground into meal. Early Americans prepared corn in all three ways.

Hand-milling techniques have persisted in isolated pockets of traditional American culture right up to the present time. In some Pueblo Indian villages (and in many parts of rural Mexico), there are still people who make flour by grinding grain between two rocks. (The archaic English word for such freestanding millstones is quern.) One rock tends to be concave, the other convex. The mortar and pestle are slightly more efficient tools derived from these primordial hand mills. Such laborious techniques eventually gave way in many places to a modern mill, some sort of permanent machine in which millstones were turned by human, animal, or water power. In industrial societies, electrical power runs giant roller mills, and stone grinding has survived only sporadically. However, educated opinion has set its face squarely against roller-milled pure-white flour.

In her authoritative *English Bread and Yeast Cookery* (Viking, 1977), Elizabeth David campaigns for the preservation of England's historic stone mills. She rhapsodizes about the hard emery stones with their carefully cut grooves. She prints a detailed schematic diagram of a working mill, with its quants and shoes and damsels all neatly labeled. In the end, like proselytizers for stone-ground corn and rice meals, David makes a case for imperfectly pulverized and sieved (the technical term is bolted) flour.

The big machines work so well, she argues, that they remove virtually all the bran and germ—and with them the traditional flavor of bread flour. Gone, too, is the appealing texture of less completely milled wheat.

The Chinese food expert Florence Lin does not say whether the advent of machine grinding of fresh water-ground rice flour yields an inferior product. But even without the hand grinding and stone wheels of her childhood, modern methods (themselves now obsolescent), as she describes them in her *Complete Book of Chinese Noodles, Dumplings, and Breads* (Morrow, 1986), offer an eloquent testimonial to the importance of specific milling methods to the ultimate food on the table:

> In New York's Chinatown there is a factory still making fresh old-fashioned plain rice cakes. It does use machines to speed the process, however. Electric-driven grinders grind the presoaked rice. Then the ground rice, including the water, is put in a muslin bag and the water is pressed out by machine. The result is fresh water-ground rice flour. A powerful steamer then steams the wet ground flour, which is immediately kneaded by machine into a soft dough. The cakes are formed by hand. The only cooking in the process is the steaming of the flour. No seasoning is added.

It was difficult for me to read that as an account of a degraded industrial process. After all, I normally buy anonymous wheat flour in five-pound bags in a supermarket. But that passage got me thinking. I remembered visiting the Hopi villages in Arizona, distant mesas with captive eagles flapping from adobe rooftops. There I bought blue cornmeal from a woman who had ground it by hand at home. It was superbly fresh-tasting and finer than any flour I had ever seen before.

Why not try this with wheat? I could buy wheat berries at a health-food store. True, I wouldn't know what kind of wheat they were, or where they came from, or when they had been harvested. But I could mill them myself with a hand-powered Italian mill now on the market in this country. I could grind them to a satisfying coarseness. I could sift out only as much of the bran as pleased me.

The results were greatly different from supermarket flour. The "grain" of my flour was appealingly un-fine. I also found that bolting flour is an exacting task. I did not have the right cloth, so I ended up with a product flecked with brown specks. This flour was full of personality and made excellent, rustic bread. But hand milling was very hard work, and I already have a full-time career. Fortunately, I have ready access to commercial stone-ground bread flour at a nearby water-powered country mill.

Actually, I don't think there's any reason, except for nostalgia, to prefer that handmade flour to flour sold in supermarkets. The wheat itself, in either case, is the product of faceless agribusiness. In our day the job of growing *Triticum aestivum* is overwhelmingly an industrial business. The world's wheat crop is immense, but almost none of it is grown in gardens by individuals for home consumption. And because of advanced modern forms of storage and transportation, it has been possible to focus wheat production—and the production of other fundamental grains—in those parts of the world that are best suited for it.

As a result, the most crucial and largest part of world food production is now a transnational event run by giants. It also means that wheat is, in principle, available anywhere, at any time, instead of being a crop of limited range that gave way, in more challenging climates, to other staples. In the Old World, wheat was once rivaled by oats, barley, rye, and buckwheat. Nowadays these grains occupy special niches in the human diet. Some people barely consume them at all. And almost no one supplements industrially grown wheat with backyard garden wheat in the way that possibly millions of home gardeners supplement agribusiness's tomatoes with their own vine-ripened crop.

This is a very odd state of affairs, considering how our lives are built on the hybrid grasses of the *Triticum* genus. The origins of wheat, and almost everything important to know about this useful plant, are lost in prehistory or hidden away in today's mammoth prairie fields and behemoth mills. The same could be said of all the other staple grains, but wheat is the preeminent case. Today wheat ranks first in production totals among the world's grains, and it accounts for more than 20 percent of the total calorie consumption of the human race. With the possible exception of corn, more is known about its distant past and its transformation from a wild grass to the staff of life of billions than about any other grain.

❧

We know what we know about the origins of modern wheat—and of other modern food grains—either from genetic research or from that subsection of archaeology called paleoethnobotany.

Archaeological fieldwork in this discipline is not outwardly glamorous. Like all archaeology, it is a learned version of ditchdigging conducted in slow motion and in miniature—sometimes laborious and sunbaked, other times a dank, bone-chilling business pursued in caves colonized by chittering bats.

Human excrement is a central feature of paleoethnobotany, because accidentally preserved feces, called coprolites, often contain traces of undigested food, particularly seeds. For example, as Daniel Zohary and Maria Hopf explain in *Domestication of Plants in the Old World: The Origin and Spread of Cultivated Plants in West Asia, Europe, and the Nile Valley* (Oxford, 1988), when several corpses were pulled from Iron Age sites in Danish peat bogs, they were so well preserved that it was possible to do a "detailed analysis of the last meals still contained in the stomachs."

Other sources of archaeological data about plants include charred or carbonized plant remains (sometimes including whole ears or entire caches of grain that were burned and then left undisturbed for thousands of years) and imprints left on pottery, bricks, and plaster. From such humble relics investigators have reconstructed a complex vision of agriculture in the Neolithic Age, when human societies all over the world were switching from hunting and foraging to farming.

Richard S. MacNeish surveys the current state of research in *The Origins of Agriculture and Settled Life* (University of Oklahoma, 1991). He begins by sketching the history of theories of the origin of agriculture. To the outsider it may come as a surprise to learn how much first-rate theorizing has been done about such an apparently straightforward development as agriculture. But the stakes are high: agriculture seems to go hand in hand with a settled life in villages and then cities, and a settled life is the main prerequisite for civilization.

It matters greatly, then, exactly how the human race evolved from nomadic bands of illiterates into rooted agricultural settlers with the time for and the societal need to keep records. Unfortunately, the physical evidence for this great shift—no doubt the most fundamental advance in human history—is thin and can be interpreted in many ways. Whence the irresistible temptation to theorize.

The British archaeologist V. Gordon Childe and his followers believed that climatic changes at the end of the Pleistocene favored expansion of deserts in the Near East. Human beings as well as plants and animals were forced into close contact around oases. In this relatively stationary setting humans began a sort of primitive biological experimentation that led to the expertise with seeds necessary for true agriculture.

On the other side of the fence was the distinguished Soviet botanist Ivan Vavilov, who sent teams of colleagues out all over the world to gather plant evidence to prove that increased population and new technology were the causes of settled agricultural life rather than the results of an environmental crisis. Vavilov's greatest contribution was not, however, at this high theoretical level, but closer to the ground. His teams gathered an enormous amount of data, and Vavilov fitted that data into a framework of great influence. He concluded that places with the most varieties of a certain domesticated plant were the "hearths" of domestication of that plant, the place from which the original domesticated variety and its offspring radiated outward to the rest of the world.

In the sweaty, feverishly theoretical world of paleobotany, archaeologists continue to sift sites of prehistoric villages and encampments, hoping to establish where and when our forebears first took to eating and planting the edible grasses we call grains. This is a noble undertaking: the birth of agriculture and the settled life marks the beginning of true civilization. But the very nature of archaeological remains is fragmentary, scattered, and hard to interpret, especially if the goal is to determine the patterns of social and economic life that precipitated, or resulted from, the discovery of grain agriculture.

Perhaps the complexity and inconclusive character of agricultural archaeology are intrinsic to social science. By contrast, the answers that the relevant hard science—biology—gives to the same question based on the same data are, comparatively, clear and rational.

For botanists, the problem is clear. What genetic process did human beings bring to bear on wild grasses so as to convert them into grains suitable for agriculture?

There is no doubt that over and over again protofarmers selected appropriate varieties, saved their seeds, and planted them in fields—to the exclusion of less desirable varieties. This is what we do today on a vast scale that merely continues the practice of our remote ancestors. Botanists have no need to speculate about the social backdrop to events that interest them on the supremely logical level of genes and chromosomes.

Put baldly, the grains we have today were engineered by biogenetic tinkerers who somehow came to understand what characteristics were essential for farming grass. The analysis that these late Stone Age people made without any knowledge of formal biology is probably the most revolutionary and profound set of thoughts in human history.

There is no recorded Newton to credit with the theory of agriculture. There were probably dozens of such Promethean culture heroes in different locations and for each of the ultimate cereal grains. But in every case the logic they came to was the same:

1. Agriculture is a deliberate exploitation of seeds. Put them in the ground, tend them until they mature, and then harvest them. None of this is worth the trouble unless it is done in quantity and yields a reliable crop.
2. To produce cereal grass in quantity, these unsung Mendels needed to collect large amounts of seed. And that seed had to yield grasses that, in turn, would yield seeds desirable for the human diet that could be harvested all at once.

This second requirement is the one that demanded the revolutionary human effort, since we can assume that the protofarmers found desirable wild grains in nature through random experimentation and made their selection well before they embarked on bona fide agriculture. What they had to understand—or imagine—was the concept of harvest itself.

What is a harvest? It is a form of industrialized gathering in of a single strain of cultivated plants all at one time. In a true harvest the plants are easily accessible to the harvester (reaper); they can be found in the same place, in neat rows, without other plants (weeds) or physical obstacles to impede or confuse their collection. We call this arrangement a field. The plants growing in a field are a crop.

Plants cultivated in such a field are a true crop if and only if the harvester can pass through them in a single sweep, taking what she wants and as little else as possible. For this to happen, crop plants have to mature uniformly—at roughly the same time—and conveniently.

Consider the reverse, the state of nature found by the Clerk-Maxwells of agriculture. Wild grasses put out seed early and late in the season. And individual grasses put out many seeds on the same blade that mature at different rates. Each mature seed eventually falls to the ground in order to continue its genetic mission and grow into another blade of grass. This falling to the ground is called shattering. It is essential for the propagation of wild grasses but an absolute disaster for cultivated grasses.

Why? Because shattered seeds are difficult, if not impossible, to retrieve. Remember that in the Book of Ruth, Boaz lets Ruth and Naomi "glean among the sheaves," meaning that he permitted them to scavenge in his fields, picking up grain left behind by the harvesters. These dropped seeds weren't worth his time, but the homeless women could have them if they were that desperate.

Boaz and his men had already done what all grain farmers do at harvest. They had moved through their fields, cutting the grain plants with their seeds all ripe and still attached to the plant. Thus plants could be easily and efficiently carried to a threshing ground, where the force of wind or a beating by a flail would winnow out the desirable seed from the undesirable grassy chaff. The next stop was a mill, where the hull and other fibrous parts of the seed would be removed and the rest, the good part, would be pulverized and stored.

In some grains, like rice, barley, and millet, a recognizable seed, not a flour, is the normal end product of the harvest, but the basic requirement of uniformly maturing, nonshattering seeds is universal. At some point in their history, all staple grains were hybridized with this goal in mind.

Try to imagine the situation faced by hunter-gatherers before this pivotal moment. Imagine, for instance, ears of corn whose kernels ripened progressively from the top to the bottom of the ear over several weeks and dropped to the ground as they ripened. This would have serious survival advantages for a wild plant, since it would maximize the chances of some of the kernels hitting the ground on a day when the weather was favorable. But who would harvest such corn? It would never be *ready*. Either most of the ear would be green, or it would have dropped most of its kernels.

Instead, somewhere in Central America long ago, clever people coaxed a grass to evolve into *Zea mays*, creating corn on the cob, which, in turn, made survival possible for millions of people over many centuries.

There is no doubt that this kind of deliberate selection occurred all over the world. I even witnessed the last such miracle of its type myself—in Minnesota, in the late '70s.

Up until then, wild rice was literally wild. Not really a true rice (*Oryza*), but an aquatic grass of the genus *Zizania*, it grew of its own accord (unplanted and uncultivated) in northern lakes. Wild rice was nonuniformly maturing and its seeds fell into the water. Local Indians had learned to harvest it by making frequent passes through the lakes and flailing seeds that were ready to shatter into their canoes. One man would bend the grass over the canoe; the other would beat the seed heads. The same plants were "harvested" again and again. This type of harvest was really no harvest at all, but an organized form of gathering.

Enter some plant scientists and agronomic opportunists who searched high and low for naturally occurring plants with the right characteristics. They found nonshattering wild rice plants, cultivated them, and eventually had enough seed in hand to start "wild" rice agriculture on paddies designed for machine harvesting.

Behind such useful hybridizations lies a basic genetic transformation of the plant. Botanists have analyzed these transformations, and when they can locate the original wild form of the plant, they can trace the change and describe it in formal terms.

In this technical sense, each grain has a story hidden away in its cells that becomes visible in its special adaptation to human needs. In *Domestication of Plants in the Old World*, Zohary and Hopf survey everything from grapes to beets to sesame and pistachios. But the most complex of these plant histories are those of the common grains. And of those, the great saga is that of wheat.

Wheat obviously matters. Our culture began with wheat. Neolithic civilization was based on a reliable supply of wheat (and barley). For the cook and the consumer, wheat distinguishes itself from all other grains because of its high gluten content. Gluten—or to be more accurate, gluten-forming proteins—produces elasticity in bread doughs, captures the carbon dioxide emitted by yeast fermentation, and thereby enables bread to rise. Only one of the four basic genetic varieties of wheat can do this, and it is the result of a happy encounter between a true wheat and a related grass sometime between 6000 and 5000 B.C. near the Caspian Sea. The result was *Triticum aestivum,* which went on to conquer the world. But it was the end of a tortuous process that began with three wild wheat grasses.

T. monococcum, or einkorn, is a single-seeded primitive plant whose hull adheres to the wheat grain unless it is pounded loose. Einkorn, once vital to Neolithic agriculture in Europe and the Near East, barely survives today. It is a so-called diploid wheat, because it has 14 chromosomes—double the basic complement of seven. Wild einkorn is brittle (shattering); cultivated einkorn is nonshattering.

Einkorn will not "mate" successfully with the two other naturally occurring wheat species, which are themselves not mutually fertile and produce sterile hybrids. Both *T. turgidum* and *T. timopheevi* are tetraploid (28 chromosomes, four times the basic seven). *T. timopheevi* grows only in Caucasian Georgia and is of no practical consequence to the outside world, nor has it ever been. *T. turgidum,* on the other hand, is the hero of our tale.

As a wild plant, it is brittle and hulled. The next stage up the ladder is called emmer, a hulled cultivar of *T. turgidum.* As such, it was the ancestor crop of Neolithic agriculture, radiating outward in all directions from the Near East. In time it was supplanted by a naked, or free-threshing, variety that lost its hull during threshing. Old-fashioned hulled emmer survives today as a minor crop in the Balkans, eastern Czechoslovakia, and Iran, and as a common crop in Ethiopia.

Elsewhere, free-threshing *T. turgidum,* usually called durum or macaroni wheat, took over. It is the wheat of choice for pasta and various flatbreads of the Mediterranean and Near East. But it, too, eventually ceded

the field in most places to a genetically more complicated and versatile high-gluten wheat—*T. aestivum,* or bread wheat.

Bread wheat is a hexaploid wheat. It has 42 chromosomes, or six times the basic seven. There is no wild form of hexaploid wheat. Genetic analysis has shown that it is a hybrid of durum wheat and a diploid wild grass of the Caucasus, *Aegilops squarrosa.* This wheatlike plant has never been cultivated, but it thrives as a "colonizer of secondary, man-made habitats and a common weed in cereal fields" (Zohary and Hopf).

As such, it has not migrated west of Iran. So it must have lain in wait for cultivated durum wheat to reach the Caspian region 8,000 years ago, when these two distant cousins linked genomes to produce a primitive hulled form of bread wheat known as spelt. Today, spelt is still cultivated as a minor crop and can even be found in health-food stores in the United States. It is prepared as a whole grain and tastes . . . healthy.

Scientists have repeated this process in the laboratory, crossing durum wheat and *Ae. squarrosa* to yield *T. aestivum.* Such hybridization, between tetraploid wheat and diploid *Aegilops squarrosa,* still occurs spontaneously in wheat fields in Iran today.

The spread of bread wheat nearly everywhere from the site of this obscure and unlikely coupling did not depend on the attractions of high-gluten rising alone. Bread wheat was adaptable to a much wider growing range than tetraploid wheat. This factor, and the usefulness of low-gluten wheat in noodlemaking, explains the lingering importance of durum wheat in its traditional range, with bread wheat spreading far and wide beyond it.

The historic sweep of this paleobotanical vision is immense, but in reality, it collapses into something tangible and small enough to hold in one hand: a loaf of bread. The great irony is that in our day the most refined palates have been returning to this primitive discovery of early man and trying to re-create the "primitive" conditions of the dawn of risen bread. They do it partly because they like the unpredictability of uncommercial "wild" yeasts dropping out of the air, but mostly they like the tangy sourdough bread they get from their efforts. And every time such a loaf comes out of an oven, it is a reminder of the primordial significance of grain in human life and of its continuing fundamental importance to our happy—and healthy—survival.

THE NUTRITIONAL ARGUMENT
or Pyramid Power

More nonsense has been written about nutrition than any other topic so important to the survival of the human race. Fad diets promoted by doctors have cost worried people billions of dollars and millions of hours . . . for nothing. Meanwhile, even the medical-nutritional establishment (MNE, pronounced mo-ney) has flip-flopped enough on this vital topic to erode the confidence of panicked laymen.

As a child, I watched apparently sensible adults go on weight-reduction diets heavily canted toward protein and shunning carbohydrates. My parents' friends would gorge on steak and other red meats loaded with fat and turn their noses up at potatoes and rice and bread. Then the bad news came in about cholesterol, so they dropped all that red meat and began peeling the skin off chicken. They dropped butter altogether, along with eggs, whole milk, and cheese. But what would they replace them with?

By and by, the news came thundering in from the East that Asians with very little fat of any kind in their diets were outliving us self-indulgent Westerners with the same puritanical industry that enabled them to beat us in world commerce. They also had lower rates of colon cancer, because they were happy to eat foods high in fiber—the very carbohydrates my parents' friends had spurned.

These dire facts led more or less directly to the boom in oat bran, which some studies showed not only provided an obvious source of fiber but also reduced cholesterol levels in the blood. (The phrase "high fiber" always makes me think of high five, that exuberant greeting some African-Americans have made popular. After eating an oat bran muffin, I often suppress the impulse to give my wife a high five across the table to celebrate my dietary shrewdness.) No sooner had American cereal producers adjusted to the demand for oat bran than the flighty world of official nutritional dogma came forth with a truly awesome and all-encompassing ukase. In 1992 the United States Department of Agriculture made headlines and waves with the food guide pyramid.

Intended as a simplifying, graphic device for representing modern

thinking about diet, the pyramid confused laymen and infuriated professionals in industry and science alike. Leaving aside the fact that it was not
a three-dimensional pyramid but a two-dimensional triangle, the "pyramid," with its four "tiers" and six "groups" subdivided into 18 categories
of foods, was not a simplifying substitute for the old-fashioned system of
four food groups it was meant to replace.

The old four groups (originally seven, but don't try to keep track; no
nondietitian ever really succeeded) were all created equal, just like people. In a "balanced" diet the educated consumer divided his or her meal
equitably among the groups: 1. milk and dairy products; 2. meat, chicken,
and fish; 3. grains and breads; 4. fruits and vegetables.

From the modern point of view, that was not only a crude system but
a dangerous one. It seemed to advise that we devote half our consumption
to foods rich in fat and low in fiber (groups 1 and 2). The pyramid aban-
dons this innocent policy of apparent nutritional egalitarianism in favor of
a frank elitism favoring carbohydrate sources over protein sources and de-
moting fat to pariah status. At the pyramid's broad base, the bread, cereal,
rice, and pasta group is approved for 6 to 11 daily servings. The next tier
up, narrower and by implication less worthwhile, is split between the vegetable group (3 to 5 servings) and the fruit group (2 to 4 servings). Still
higher up, tier 3 is divided between the milk, yogurt, and cheese group (2
to 3 servings) and the meat, poultry, fish, dry beans, eggs, and nuts group
(2 to 3 servings). At the apex of the triangle are fats, oils, and sweets,
which we are admonished by the USDA to "USE SPARINGLY."

Brief reflection should make it obvious why almost no one liked this
new dietary polygon. Those who took it on its own terms wanted to
know why foods of such different nutritional content as navy beans and
porterhouse steak were put in the same group. The dairy industry won-
dered, with justice, why skim milk and nonfat yogurt should be lumped
together with whole milk and cheese. Olive oil producers didn't think
they should be tarred with the same brush as lard and chocolate fudge.

These were not just sectarian concerns. They raised real questions,
but they did not go to the heart of the pyramid's problem. The pyramid,
by itself, did not directly answer the most fundamental questions it raised
with its own jargon: What is a serving? How many servings from each
group should be combined to make a dish or a meal? The poor, worried
consumer, already bludgeoned by health statistics and doctors into sup-

posing that cheese kills, was now confronted with an ostensible answer to the life-or-death question of what to eat that could not be understood and that did not ever speak to the problem of the well-meaning cook in a real-life kitchen. Just imagine the quandary of someone about to cook, say, spaghetti alla carbonara, trying to calculate how many servings of pasta or unsmoked bacon or sparing amounts of grated Parmesan, et cetera, were in the total recipe and how many forkfuls equaling how many "servings" were consumed by each family member. And did the cook have to ask each one at the table what he or she had eaten at lunch so as to make the amount of noodles on the plate tally with that person's pyramidal goals for the day?

Underlying all of this inevitable confusion was that basic question again: What is a serving?

This is not easy to find out. But if you can locate a USDA publication of August 1992 called "The Food Guide Pyramid," it is clear enough on this crucial point, in its way. "What counts as a serving?" it asks rhetorically. Well, it goes on, a serving of bread is one slice. (Thin, whole wheat, challah? Don't ask.) A serving of ready-to-eat cereal is one ounce, so get out your scale and don't be surprised if the amount seems mingy.

Perhaps I have convinced you that the food guide pyramid is a snare and a delusion. If so, I am not particularly happy about it. In fact, the pyramid makes me sad in the way that every well-meant failure to do good lowers one's spirits. The pyramid, to mix a metaphor, had its heart in the right place. Its bottom line (bottom tier?) was clear and valid: fat is bad; plant-derived foods, especially those made from grain, are good.

Unfortunately, that message was lost in the pseudogeometry and semantic tangle of tiers and groups and servings. But the basic message is, in fact, the nutritional orthodoxy of our day. Most people now accept as common sense that densely caloric, tenaciously storable fats are undesirable for people who typically live long enough in a sedentary manner to acquire cardiovascular and other diseases associated with obesity and the accumulation of cholesterol. "Common sense" also dictates that grains and their derivatives offer a desirable alternative source of nutrition: cholesterol-free and fat-free calories easily put to use and dissipated, and much fiber.

This was not at all the common sense of yesteryear. In 1968, that annus mirabilis of revolutionary thought and action, if I had suggested that a grain-based diet extremely low in animal fat was the way to go, almost everyone including the most radical would have dismissed the idea as unhealthy and dangerous macrobiotic extremism. Now most of us have swung in that direction, at least in our minds. Why? How?

In traditional societies new ideas percolated downward from the elite to a wider public. In our world, where novelty ricochets from all sides at high velocity carried by the mass media, the rate of communication is almost instantaneous, but there is still a vestige of the old top-down dynamic. Serious medical and nutritional research has gradually convinced those capable of rational thought that the low-fat/high-fiber theory is correct.

Why didn't science reach this conclusion sooner? The reason is simple. To discover the nature of optimal diet is not the same as learning to cure a disease. Disease kills dramatically, one person at a time, and it can be studied with efficiency in individuals. Optimal diet reveals itself through statistics and must be studied in many people over long periods of time. The data are notoriously unreliable because people are quick to lie about what they put in their mouths. But these obstacles have been laboriously and tediously overcome. First came the evidence about obesity and cholesterol in the Framingham Heart Study in Massachusetts. Then, decisively, comparative data arrived from China, and the discussion was, in a major sense, over.

Since 1983 a joint Chinese-American project, sponsored by the Academy for Preventive Medicine in Beijing and Cornell University, has investigated the diet of 6,500 rural Chinese. The results show with devastating clarity the superiority of a plant-based diet. The average Chinese diet was only 10 percent animal-based. Less than 15 percent of the calories were derived from fat. The Chinese ate a third less protein than Americans, and only about a tenth of that protein was animal. Americans got about 70 percent of their protein from animals. Chinese fiber consumption was huge compared with American consumption. The Chinese, moreover, typically have about half the blood cholesterol that Americans have. And the incidence of heart disease and cancer is much lower in China than in the United States.

The most impressive—and depressing—statistics are those that show the disastrous effect of modest increases in animal-based food consumption on the Chinese sampling. Heart disease and cancer rates climbed when the study's rural folk began to adopt typical elements of the Western diet.

All of this confirms the theory that animal fat and animal-based foods in general produce the diseases rife in affluent Western societies. (And it supports common-sense doubts about the evidence for the so-called French Connection Theory, which seems to show that French people, wallowing in a diet of animal fat and red wine, somehow escape the cardiovascular consequences of their indulgence.) The negative result of the animal-fat theory leads to a negative course of action: reduce consumption of animal-based foods. But there is also a positive conclusion to be drawn and a positive course of action to be taken: increase the intake of plant-based foods, not just as a desperate alternative, but as a constructive remedy, a restoration of balance in what we eat.

We should be revamping our menus by choosing dishes rich in vegetables and grains, especially grains. Grains supply the food energy and the fiber we must have to survive. They are versatile, and they are already major ingredients in thousands and thousands of recipes people already love. The trick is to put these grain-based dishes at the center of our diet, rather than leaving them at the periphery.

Something like this shift has already been happening. The vogue for pasta is a key example. So is the trend toward Asian stir-fries (despite insidiously high amounts of fat from the oil used in frying) and other dishes in which the central ingredient is rice and in which meat, when there is any, is a superaddition, almost a condiment. As this kind of eating becomes more common, it will be less and less normal or mandatory to plan a meal around a roast or a steak. Such a readjustment of attitude, moderate and gradual, will have the revolutionary goal of returning our meals to a pattern that has been the historical norm for most human beings at all times everywhere. The battle will be won when ordinary Americans ask themselves: What should we have for dinner tonight—risotto or barley with chicken?

⁓⟨

The selection of recipes that follows is an invitation to begin thinking in this way. I have tried to show off the versatility of grains without, however, turning a cold shoulder to other foods. There is plenty of meat here, but grains are always vibrantly present in each dish. Where possible, I have emphasized whole grains, but there are also many recipes in which the grain appears as flour. The idea was to exemplify the spectrum of possibilities available with each grain. On the other hand, I have done very little with flour-based desserts—pastries and cakes and cookies—because they are, while obviously grain-based, as far as possible from the whole-grain focus of the book and also remarkably unhealthy. For the sake of completeness, however, there are a few of these desserts.

Barley

If anyone

is looking for a symbol of the submersion
of traditional values in a trash-filled
sea of modern life, she could do worse
than pick on barley. This wholesome grain
lurks in the background of most cuisines,
a plain wallflower no one asks to dance much
anymore. Yes, there is Scotch broth
and there is mushroom-and-barley soup.
In a few advanced restaurants and cookbooks
barley crops up, so to speak, as a novelty
or a stand-in for better-known grains:
barley risotto is the leading example.
Health-food stores sell barley flour that can be
made into flatbreads and mixed with wheat
flour for leavened breads. Italians eat a pasta that
is really a *faux* barley called *orzo,* a small barley-shaped
"noodle" formed from wheat flour. Meanwhile,
barley itself, Linnaeus's *Hordeum vulgare,*

gets almost no credit for the primeval role it played in the origins of settled human life and civilization.

It is still possible to see barley in its ancient glory as the staple grain of a culture, but only in certain remote places, like the Ecuadorian village that Mary Jo Weismantel described so eloquently in *Food, Gender, and Poverty in the Ecuadorian Andes* (University of Pennsylvania, 1988), or in Tibet. In such bracing climates, where the hard currency necessary to import wheat or rice is not available, barley holds sway. But almost everywhere else, more versatile starch sources have swept the field. Barley's greatest advantage used to be that it could grow where more delicate grains couldn't make it. Oats and buckwheat and rye also filled demanding agronomic niches in the old days.

Cheap modern transportation has all but eliminated the need for these hardy old grasses. North America can supply wheat to most of the world. Rice long ago displaced millet in China. Scotland is not the oat ghetto it once was, so Scots can have airy white wheat bread like the rest of the world instead of flat leaden bannocks.

This process of gramineal dethronement has especially humiliated barley, leaving only a few crucial vestiges behind. Of all major industrial countries, Korea is probably the last to preserve an important visible role for barley. Koreans drink it.

At the end of the lunch hour in the upstairs dining room of Kang Suh at 1250 Broadway in Manhattan's Herald Square, you can see Korean businessmen winding up their meal with little blue bottles of *soju*, a bluish 20–25 percent alcoholic distillation of barley (or rye or sweet potatoes, but not rice). At the even more completely un-Americanized restaurant across the street, they brought me *poricha* one winter night— a decoction brewed from toasted barley that is a constant feature of traditional Korean life.

The taste reminded me at first of hot porridge. This turned out to be a creative misunderstanding, but it did lead me to consider the significance of a whole spectrum of lost or depreciated grain dishes. Porridge is a poor word to describe the category of grain dishes I have in mind, yet it is where we almost have to start, since porridge—hot, thick breakfast cereal—is the most familiar example of all those wet boiled gruels and grits and groats that once fed our ancestors, or formed the core of their alimentary universe.

If the origin of agriculture is the ability to plant edible, harvestable grass seeds, the origin of cooking is the ability to make those seeds palatable. After toasting and milling, the next—and really the most fundamental—culinary step was to moisten the grain product in whatever form it came to the kitchen. Before anyone learned to make bread or cake or noodles, someone discovered how to make mush, with cold and then with hot water. Oatmeal is a link with the most primitive days of subsistence in northern Europe. Barley gruel takes us back to the dawn of all cuisine.

The form in which most of us now experience a survival of prehistoric barley cookery is beer. Beer starts with sprouted barley. The process, called malting, occurs when moistened barley grains are allowed to germinate, thereby converting inborn starches into a fermentable sugar called maltose. No doubt, the primordial malt makers in all the many cultures that fell into wetting barley and letting nature take its course kept at it because sprouted barley was edible as such and didn't have to be hulled or cracked or milled. From there it was but a step—actually more than one—to exploiting the natural fermentation inherent in malting either to make an intoxicating drink (beer) that got its punch from the alcoholic byproduct of malting's yeast fermentation or to produce a solid food (bread) that got an appealing lift from the same process's release of carbon dioxide.

Scholars such as Solomon Katz of the University of Pennsylvania now debate which came first, bread or beer. But the ancestor of both was wet barley (or wheat and all the other grains). And even without waiting for those grains to sprout or ferment, ancient peoples could make them into beverages, porridges, gruels, batters, and doughs—depending on how dilute the mixture of grain and water was.

Today barley is almost always found as a processed whole grain. The full name for what we all know as a delicious, chewy white almost-sphere, about the size of a ball bearing, is pearled barley. It has had its husk completely removed in a grinding process that also leaves it rounded, like a pearl.

Of all the grains, barley is my favorite. It has a good resilient texture, and it picks up flavors from meat and other foods it has been cooked with. It is warming in winter, requires no great finesse to cook well, and is just rare enough in today's diet to add a discreet touch of originality to a menu.

Basic Barley

Almost all whole-grain barley is white, rounded pearled barley. You can find less thoroughly processed barley in health-food stores, but I would rather eat wood.

Yields
about 3½ cups

1 cup pearled barley
1 tablespoon salt
4 cups water, approximately

1. Put all the ingredients into a 6 to 8-cup saucepan. Bring to a rolling boil over high heat. Reduce the heat and simmer slowly until the barley is al dente, tender enough to chew but not mushy. Cooking times will vary according to the age (dryness) of the barley, its size, and how completely it has been processed. Twenty minutes is usually enough, but barley is forgiving and can be cooked for 30 minutes or more in fully boiling water without losing its shape or its point.

2. Drain and serve. Or refrigerate until needed in a closed container. Cooked barley will keep for several days this way, and it can be reheated, with a little water, to almost optimal condition.

Barley Pancakes

Technically, there is no difference between these and wheat-flour pancakes. Mix the batter, pour onto the griddle or skillet, fry into golden rounds, and eat. But the result will be darker and tangier.

Yields about 2 dozen pancakes

1½ cups barley flour, available in most health-food stores
2 teaspoons baking powder
½ teaspoon salt
2 tablespoons oil
2 eggs, lightly beaten
2 cups skim milk

1. Stir together the flour, baking powder, and salt in a mixing bowl.

2. Beat in the oil, then the eggs and milk, taking care to work the liquid completely into the dry ingredients to eliminate lumps.

3. Lightly oil the surface of a skillet or griddle and place it over medium heat. With a soup ladle, pour on enough batter to make a thin pancake. When the surface begins to bubble, flip the pancake over with a spatula and cook briefly to brown the other side (the original top). Remove the pancake to a serving plate and repeat until you have a stack of lightly browned pancakes. Serve with syrup or honey and jam.

～ SOUPS ん

This is one of the most basic food ideas of the Western world—a warming, filling soup made from barley and the liquid it is cooked in. Undoubtedly, the first barley soup, and tens of thousands afterward, were nothing more than barley and water with whatever else was around thrown in the pot, like herbs, seasonings, vegetables, and, in good times, scraps of meat or bones. Even now, plain barley soup is the mainstay of some poor villages in the highlands of Ecuador, which survive on this hardy grain brought to their ancestors long ago from the Old World.

Well made, a pure barley soup (one that is water-based, meatless) can please even First World diners.

Plain Barley Soup

By varying the amount of water, you change the nature of the soup. Simmering barley in twice its volume of water will produce a "dry" soup, like minestrone or Mexican *sopa seca* (see Basic Barley recipe, page 26). More water stretches the recipe into a "soupier" dish, as Spanish and Latino cooks do when they add extra liquid to rice to make *arroces caldosos* (soupy rice) or *asopaos* (a whole category of "souped" rice dishes).

Yields
4 servings

4 cups water
½ cup barley
Salt and pepper
2 tablespoons oil (optional)
2 carrots, scraped and cut into rounds (optional)
1 red bell pepper, trimmed, seeded, and chopped
    (optional)
2 scallions, trimmed and chopped (optional)
Pinch of ground coriander or marjoram or a few
    drops of hot Szechuan oil, to taste (optional)

1. Bring the water to a boil. Add the barley and the salt and pepper. Return to the boil, reduce the heat, and simmer for 30 minutes, or until the barley is al dente.

2. Meanwhile, if you are using the optional vegetables, heat the oil in a skillet and sauté the vegetables until they soften slightly. The order in which they are listed above is also the order you should put them into the skillet. Give the carrots a few minutes more than the pepper, the pepper a few minutes more than the scallions.

3. Add the vegetables (if used) to the barley soup and continue simmering until they reach desired doneness. For me, this would be almost immediately, so that the vegetables could add a texture counterpoint to the softer barley; but still, I would simmer for a minute or two to let the flavors enhance the broth. Without any vegetables added, you will prob-

ably want to perk things up with a spice such as ground coriander or marjoram, or even a few drops of hot Szechuan oil.

Note: If this recipe strikes you as overly spartan, substitute chicken or meat stock for the water. You will be following in the footsteps of earlier cooks who enriched plain barley soup and created the two classics that follow.

Barley Mushroom Soup

This basic combination—barley and mushrooms—crops up in many cuisines in slightly different forms. Eastern Europe is its most ardent sponsor, where originally, one assumes, the addition of mushrooms to the basic barley soup would have given it a meaty richness. Meat itself, or meat broth, is present in most modern recipes, but I've made it optional here as a temptation to try the primordial soup.

Yields
8 servings

1 cup barley
8 cups chicken stock or water
1 bay leaf
1 sprig fresh thyme or ½ teaspoon dried
1 rib celery, chopped
Salt and pepper
2 medium potatoes, peeled and diced
2 cups sliced mushrooms
2 ounces dried Polish or Italian porcini
  mushrooms, soaked for 30 minutes or until
  soft, then cut into thick slices (optional)

1. Put the barley and 8 cups stock or water in a large nonaluminum saucepan with the bay leaf, thyme, celery, and salt and pepper. Bring slowly to a boil over medium heat, then lower the heat and simmer for 15 minutes.

2. Add the potatoes and continue cooking until tender, about 10 minutes.

3. Add the sliced mushrooms and the dried Polish or porcini mush-

rooms and their soaking water (if used). Cook a few minutes more, until the mushrooms are softened. Remove the bay leaf. Serve with dark rye bread.

Scotch Broth

In the cook's bible of the eighteenth century, *The Art of Cookery Made Plain and Easy*, Hannah Glasse offered her large public a recipe for Scotch broth that included a "leg" of beef and a rooster. (She conceded that it was "very good without the fowl.") She also listed a sheep's head as an alternative to the beef. This substitution points the way toward contemporary recipes (and most probably reflected ordinary practice in her own day) specifying cheap, flavorful cuts or scraps of lamb. Here I follow Marion Cunningham's lead in her 1979 revision of *The Fannie Farmer Cookbook* (Knopf) in recommending breast of lamb, a very cheap and very flavorful cut, ideal for soup (and not for most other dishes) because it has many small bones.

Yields
8 servings

1 cup barley
3 pounds lamb breast
8 cups water
2 tablespoons oil
1 clove garlic, peeled and finely chopped
1 medium kohlrabi or turnip, peeled
    and chopped
2 carrots, scraped and chopped
1 medium onion, peeled and chopped
Salt and pepper

1. The day before serving, put the barley, lamb, and water in a large pot. Bring to a boil, reduce the heat, and simmer for 1 hour, or until the meat is tender and separates easily from the bones. Remove the meat from the pot. Cut away and discard any large pieces of fat and discard all the bones. Cut the meat into ½-inch pieces and refrigerate.

2. Let the stock cool to room temperature, UNCOVERED, to prevent

bacterial spoilage. Then cover and refrigerate overnight. When ready to use, remove and discard the layer of fat that has congealed on the top of the broth.

3. Heat the oil in a skillet and sauté the garlic until it begins to brown. Remove the garlic with a slotted spoon and then put in the chopped kohlrabi or turnip, carrots, and onion. Cook until the onion is translucent; then add the vegetables to the barley and broth, bring to a boil, and season to taste with salt and pepper.

Su Farre
(Italian Thick Barley-Flour and Mint Soup)

When Italians talk in glowing, nostalgic terms about *la cucina pòvera*, this primitive and delicious combination of prehistoric grain and wild mint is the kind of thing they have in mind.

Yields　　　6 cups beef stock (see Light Meat Stock recipe,
6 servings　　　page 129)
　　　　　5 cups (1¼ pounds) barley flour, approximately
　　　　　¼ pound grated Parmesan or Romano cheese
　　　　　2 tablespoons chopped mint leaves
　　　　　Salt

1. Put the beef stock in a saucepan, bring to a boil, and reduce the heat to medium. Stir in the barley flour and let the mixture simmer slowly for 30 minutes, stirring regularly.

2. By now you should have a thick soup. If it isn't thick enough, add another cup of flour and simmer until the raw taste disappears. Stir in the cheese, mint leaves, and salt to taste.

Minestra di Orzo Perlato
(Thick Barley Soup with Vegetables)

Here the whole but husked (pearled) grain mixes with the plainest of root vegetables for a most comforting soup, frugally enriched with the unsmoked Italian bacon called pancetta. To an American, this soup may seem like a clamless New England chowder: milk, a taste of pork, and potatoes, with the barley "substituting" for little chunks of quahog.

Yields
6 servings

1¼ cups barley
1 large onion, peeled and finely chopped
2 medium carrots, scraped and diced
4 medium potatoes, peeled
1 rib celery, trimmed and finely chopped
3 quarts water
10 ounces pancetta, diced
2 cups milk
Salt

1. Put the barley, onion, carrots, potatoes, and celery in a large saucepan. Cover with the water, bring to a boil, lower the heat, and simmer slowly for 2½ hours.

2. Mash the potatoes by pressing them against the side of the pan. Add the pancetta, along with the milk. Add salt to taste.

3. Return to a simmer and cook for another 30 minutes.

⤳ FIRST COURSE ⤳

Stuffed Grape Leaves

It's merely an accident that barley has, to my knowledge, never been used as a stuffing for vine leaves. Its nubbly texture and special flavor make it an outstanding choice as an alternative for the customary rice.

(Other grains—wheat, amaranth, buckwheat—also make good substitutes for rice; see recipes on pages 154, 206, and 212. The recipe for Stuffed Grape Leaves using rice can be found on page 110.)

Yields
24 stuffed
grape leaves

2 cloves garlic, minced
¼ cup oil or lard
1 pound mushrooms, finely chopped
1 cup barley
Salt and pepper
2 dozen grape leaves, rinsed if canned or
    blanched if fresh
4 cloves garlic, slivered
1 cup chicken stock or water, approximately

1. In a medium skillet, sauté the garlic in the oil or lard over medium heat until browning begins. Stir in the mushrooms and cook until they yield up their water, and then continue cooking until all the water has evaporated and the mushroom fragments are nicely browned. Stir in the barley and coat with the oil. Remove the skillet from the heat.

2. Stir in the salt and pepper to taste.

3. Stuff the grape leaves. The classic method is to lay the leaf smooth side down on the counter. Put 1 tablespoon of stuffing at the base of the leaf (stem end) and roll the leaf over the stuffing, starting from the base. Fold the sides over the stuffing and continue rolling from the base end until the leaf is completely rolled up. Continue in this manner until all the stuffing is used.

4. In a large saucepan, cover the bottom with flat leaves to keep the rolled-up leaves from sticking. Then arrange the rolled-up leaves, seams down, in alternating layers (one layer north-south, the next east-west), interspersing slivers of garlic as you go. Add the chicken stock or water to cover and set a plate on top of the leaves to hold them in place. Bring the stock or water to a boil, reduce the heat, cover, and simmer for 45 minutes to 2 hours, until the leaves are tender.

Barley Stew

This is the epitome of an all-out grain main course. The barley itself is the anchor. The mushrooms provide a "meat" accent, should you be looking for one. And the three colors of the peppers brighten the look of things.

Yields
8 servings

¼ cup oil
3 carrots, scraped and diced
3 ribs celery, trimmed and diced
1 green bell pepper, stemmed, seeded,
  and diced
1 red bell pepper, stemmed, seeded,
  and chopped
1 yellow bell pepper, stemmed, seeded, and
  chopped (optional)
1 large onion, peeled and chopped
¾ pound mushrooms, preferably shiitake, sliced
2 cups cooked barley (see recipe, page 26)
Salt and pepper

1. Heat the oil in a skillet. Add the carrots and sauté for 5 minutes.

2. Add the celery, peppers, and onion. Sauté until the onion is translucent. Add the mushrooms and sauté until all the vegetables are cooked al dente.

3. Add the barley and stir until heated through. Season with salt and pepper.

Veal Breast Stuffed with Barley

Most butchers or supermarket meat departments sell veal breast with a pocket already cut in it. These pockets can be filled with almost anything, but barley will soak up the richness of the meat as it cooks. The turmeric colors the barley yellow, as if it were saffron rice. Turmeric will also color almost anything else it touches, so be careful or you will have a semipermanently jaundiced kitchen and fingers to match.

Yields
6 servings

One 4-pound veal breast (5 ribs)
1 cup cooked barley (see recipe, page 26)
1 onion, peeled and chopped
2 cloves garlic, minced
1 tablespoon turmeric
Salt
1 tablespoon oil
½ cup red wine vinegar
12 small red potatoes

1. Although veal breast often has a pouch for stuffing already cut in it by the supermarket meat department, it is easy to cut your own slit. Set the veal breast on the counter, meat side up. Cut the slit on the thick side of the breast, keeping the blade close to the bones. The idea is to cut as large and deep a pouch as possible.

2. Combine the barley, onion, garlic, and turmeric. Then stuff the mixture into the pouch and sew it tight with soft kitchen string and a utility needle, or simply tie up the breast so the opening of the pouch is held closed.

3. Salt the breast. Pour the oil into a Dutch oven or heavy enameled cast-iron casserole large enough to hold the veal breast. There should be enough oil to cover the bottom of the pot. Set over high heat until the oil begins to smoke.

4. Reduce the heat to medium and brown the breast in the oil on all sides. Add the vinegar. Cover, reduce the heat to low, and cook for 1 hour. After 45 minutes, preheat the oven to 400° F.

5. Pick up the breast with a large fork, slide the potatoes under it, and then set the pot in the preheated oven. Roast for 30 to 40 minutes.

6. Arrange the roast on a platter with the potatoes and the pan juices. The ribs should be twisted out and discarded, if possible. Then slice the breast parallel to the rib line, so that each person gets the rich turmeric-yellow barley in the center of each slice. Set 2 potatoes on one side and drizzle with cooking liquid.

Variations: You can substitute wild rice, brown rice, or bulgur for the barley, but they should all be slightly undercooked—on the chewy side of al dente rather than fully cooked—before stuffing.

Brisket with Barley Grits and Apricots

Barley grits, cracked like hominy grits and with a similar texture, are sold in health-food stores. This is comfort food that sets off the austere sweetness of the apricots, for which brisket is a natural and traditional partner.

Yields
8 servings

2 cloves garlic, peeled and pushed through a
    garlic press
2 tablespoons salt
1 tablespoon pepper
5 pounds brisket of beef
1 bottle red wine
2 large onions, peeled and sliced
2 cups barley grits
1 pound dried apricots

1. Preheat the oven to 500° F.

2. Make a paste with the garlic, salt, and pepper. Rub the paste all over the meat, then put the meat in a roasting pan, fat side up. Put the pan in the oven, uncovered, and cook for 15 minutes, or until the meat is very brown but not burned.

3. Lower the heat to 350° F. Remove the roaster from the oven, take the meat out, and set it on the counter. Put the roaster over medium heat

and pour in the wine. Bring to a boil and then scrape the brown bits from the surface of the pan with a metal spatula. Remove the roaster from the heat. Spread the onions over the bottom of the pan and set the meat on top of them. Cover the meat with aluminum foil and roast in the oven for 2 hours.

4. Add the barley grits and the apricots. Cover again with the foil and continue cooking in the oven until the barley grits are cooked through, about 20 minutes.

5. Remove the meat and slice it in the kitchen. Place the slices on a serving dish in an overlapping line. Mix the barley grits and apricots together and arrange in a ring around the meat.

Barley and Lamb Casserole

Lamb and barley are a classic combination. So are lamb and eggplant. Here they merge in a warming, old-fashioned casserole that makes a knowing nod to the eastern Mediterranean. Lamb neck is an economical and tasty cut that is available in supermarkets and offers fine lamb flavor. The effect on the plate, because of the bones, is something like that of oxtails. Anyone who thinks it profligate to upend a bottle of wine into this straightforward dish can easily substitute chicken broth or plain water. The taste and nutritional content of the dish will change, but the overall idea will remain serenely uncorrupted and ready for use.

Yields 8 to 10 servings

3 pounds lamb neck, cut into 1-inch chunks
Olive oil
6 carrots, scraped and cut into rounds
2 medium onions, peeled and sliced
2 cloves garlic, minced
1 bottle red wine
3 sprigs fresh thyme, oregano, or marjoram or
    ½ teaspoon dried
2 cups barley
1 large eggplant, trimmed and sliced into ½-inch
    rounds
Salt and pepper

1. Brown the lamb pieces in a 4-quart Dutch oven or other large, heavy-bottomed pot. Try doing this without adding any olive oil, just using the fat that renders from the lamb itself. To brown meat successfully, you want the individual pieces to stick to the pan and caramelize on all sides, but not burn. This improves the taste and color of the eventual dish, but it only occurs at high heat. Therefore, you do not want to slow the process by filling the pan with all the lamb pieces piled on top of one another. Brown a few of them at a time, remove them to a bowl, and then continue with the rest. The job actually goes faster this way.

2. Add a little olive oil to the pan and sauté the carrot rounds. After they have colored nicely, stir in the onions and garlic. Continue cooking over medium heat until the onions are translucent. The carrots do not need to be soft.

3. Deglaze the pan with the red wine, scraping the congealed brown meat juices into the liquid. Let the wine simmer for a minute or two. Then add the thyme, oregano, or marjoram and the barley. Stir all the ingredients together and add water, if necessary, to bring the liquid level up a couple inches over the solid ingredients. Reduce the heat so as to produce a low simmer.

4. Continue cooking, covered, until the barley is al dente, just comfortably chewable. This should take about 40 minutes, during which time the barley will keep absorbing water. Be sure to check every 10 minutes or so and add more water as needed.

5. Array the eggplant slices on top of the other solid ingredients. Make sure the water level extends an inch or so over them. Simmer until the eggplant is soft and the water has been almost completely absorbed, approximately 15 minutes. Season with salt and pepper. This dish can be prepared a day in advance and will reheat nicely, although it will probably be necessary to add some water.

Barley Pudding

Catherine Brown, who writes about food in the Glasgow *Herald*, explains that this pudding is a descendant of the medieval wheat pudding and is eaten with meat in the Lothian region of Scotland, near Edinburgh. It could certainly be served as a dessert, but historically it functioned in the way that candied sweet potatoes or sweet chutneys do today. It is part of a great family of ancient, pre-potato starch dishes invented in Europe's colder places. Jewish kugel (see pages 91 and 221), which can be prepared with a wide number of ingredients from noodles to potatoes, is a distant cousin that illustrates the versatility of this surprisingly toothsome and welcome kind of "pudding." My recipe is adapted from Ms. Brown's *Scottish Regional Recipes* (Edinburgh: Chambers, 1981).

Yields	1 cup barley
4 servings	2½ cups water
	⅓ cup currants
	¼ teaspoon nutmeg
	Sugar
	Cream

1. Preheat the oven to 300° F.

2. Spread the barley evenly across a 4-cup baking dish. Pour the water over the barley and bake for 2 hours and 10 minutes.

3. Stir in the currants and nutmeg and bake for another 20 minutes.

4. Serve with sugar and cream.

Unleavened Bannocks

These are the original flat barley breads of the wheatless North. They are crisp outside, softer within, and they go very nicely with drinks.

Yields
4 servings

1 tablespoon butter
¾ cup milk
1 cup barley flour, approximately
1 teaspoon salt

1. Preheat a griddle or a cast-iron skillet over medium heat until a hand held an inch above will feel warm.
2. In a saucepan, heat the butter in the milk until it melts. Add the barley flour and salt to taste to make a soft dough.
3. Knead lightly on a floured surface and form the dough into a ball.
4. Flour the griddle or skillet. Flour your hands, place the dough on the griddle, and press out into a 9-inch-diameter round that is ⅛ inch thick. Cook until lightly browned on the bottom side, about 10 to 15 minutes, then turn and cook another 15 minutes or longer, until the center has cooked through.

Bannocks

This is a classic flat barley bread, of a type that benefits from modern raising agents but still closely resembles the staff of life, as it once was, for much of northern Europe. Today bannocks can be appreciated for their strong flavor and ease of preparation. Soft in texture, they are somewhere between pancakes and stiff, storable flatbreads.

Yields
4 to 6 pieces

2 cups barley flour
10 tablespoons all-purpose (wheat) flour
1 teaspoon cream of tartar

½ teaspoon salt
1¼ cups buttermilk
1 teaspoon baking soda

1. Preheat a griddle or cast-iron skillet over medium-low heat until a hand held an inch above will feel warm.

2. Mix together in a bowl the barley and wheat flours, cream of tartar, and salt. In another bowl, stir together the buttermilk and baking soda; then beat this into the dry ingredients to make a soft dough.

3. Flour the griddle. Flour your hands, turn the dough out onto the griddle, and press the dough into a 6-inch round that is ½ inch thick. Cook on the griddle for 7 minutes per side. Cut in quarters or sixths. Bannocks are good hot, but they store well and taste good at room temperature.

Leavened Barley Bread

By adding high-gluten wheat, you make it possible to have a fairly light leavened bread with the strong flavor of barley flour. There is a very high proportion of barley to wheat in this recipe, so the "crumb" of the loaf will be a bit denser than an all-wheat loaf, but also denser in personality.

Yields
1 loaf

1 cup all-purpose (wheat) flour, approximately
1 package active dry yeast
1½ cups lukewarm milk
1 tablespoon melted lukewarm butter
½ teaspoon salt
2½ cups barley flour

1. Whisk together the wheat flour and yeast in a bowl. Then whisk in half the milk. Cover with a dishcloth and let stand for about 50 minutes, or until doubled in bulk.

2. Beat in the remaining milk, butter, and salt. Now work in the barley flour with a wooden spoon, a handful at a time, until you have a dough that cleans the bowl. Form into a ball and let rise in a lightly oiled bowl covered with a dishcloth or plastic wrap for 1½ hours, or until doubled in bulk.

3. Turn the dough out onto a well-floured board and knead vigorously. Reshape into a ball, sprinkle with cornmeal, and leave for final rising on a lightly oiled baking sheet, covered with a dishcloth. Let rise for up to 1 hour, or until doubled in bulk.

4. Preheat the oven to 500° F. Bake for 15 minutes, then reduce the heat to 400° F. and bake another 20 minutes, or until the loaf is done. (A finished loaf will be brown on top and will sound hollow when tapped sharply.) Let cool completely on a rack.

Barley Whole-Wheat Bread

Here, as in the previous recipe, wheat gives a lift to low-gluten barley flour. Whole-wheat flour adds its extra bit of personality.

Yields *1 loaf*	1 package active dry yeast 2 cups warm water 2 teaspoons salt 2 cups barley flour 2½ cups whole-wheat flour

1. Stir the yeast into the warm water and let stand 5 minutes.

2. In a large mixing bowl, stir the yeast mixture together with the salt and then work in the barley and whole-wheat flours in alternating handfuls until they are well mixed. When the mixture makes a dough, form into a ball, and turn it out onto a lightly floured surface.

3. Knead the dough vigorously until smooth and elastic, at least 5 minutes.

4. Form the dough into a ball and set it to rise in a warm, draft-free place on a lightly oiled baking sheet. Cover with a moistened dish towel and leave to double in bulk. This will take at least 1 hour, possibly 2 or 3.

5. Preheat the oven to 350° F.

6. Bake 50 to 60 minutes, until the loaf sounds hollow when sharply tapped. Let cool before slicing.

Barley Risotto with Ruby Chard and Mushrooms

Barley is obviously not a pasta, but both orzo and farfel (see pages 186–89) are pastas that are shaped like barley, modeled after it, and named after it. It seems reasonable to suppose that they were actually manufactured substitutes for barley, produced at a time when barley was a normal starch at meals in a Europe less completely won over to wheat and rice and potatoes. So why not turn the tables and treat barley like pasta? This idea has already occurred to several chefs working in the metaphorical and historicizing atmosphere of the nouvelle cuisine. Here is my version.

Yields
6 servings

8 cups chicken stock
Oil
2 cups barley
1 pound ruby chard, washed, with leaves trimmed
    from stems and stems chopped
Salt
1 pound mushrooms, preferably oyster
    mushrooms, coarsely chopped

1. Bring the chicken stock to a boil, reduce the heat, and keep at a very slow simmer, covered.

2. Heat 2 tablespoons of the oil in another large saucepan. Add the barley and cook for a minute or two, stirring constantly, so as to coat all the grains. Pour in 1 cup of simmering stock and continue to simmer, stirring constantly until virtually all the liquid has been absorbed. Add another cup of stock. Continue as before, adding additional stock until it has been totally imbibed by the barley, about 40 minutes. If the barley is still not soft enough for your taste, continue with boiling water, adding 1 cup at a time, as with the chicken stock, until it is. Remove from heat and keep covered.

3. While the barley is absorbing the stock, put the chard leaves with water clinging to them in a saucepan, cover, set over low-medium heat, and cook until the leaves wilt. Timing will vary according to the size of the leaves, the shape of the pan, and so on, but it should happen in a few minutes and well before the barley is finished. Set the chard aside, covered.

4. Meanwhile, heat 2 more tablespoons of the oil in a large skillet and sauté the chard stems with salt, to taste, until they are almost softened. Add the chopped mushrooms and continue sautéing until the mushrooms give up their water and the water evaporates. (The temperature in the pan will rise at this point, and the oil will sizzle.) Cover and set aside, off the heat, until the barley is finished.

5. When the barley is done, stir in the chard-stem–mushroom mixture. Drain the chard leaves and arrange them on a serving platter in a thin layer that covers the entire platter, reserving a couple of leaves for decoration. Spread the barley risotto in a mound over the chard leaves,* leaving a visible margin of chard leaves. Arrange the reserved leaves on top of the barley mound. Perhaps you will want to cut the leaves in strips and make a design with them.

Variation: For the ruby chard, substitute any of the spinachlike greens, such as spinach itself, Swiss chard, beet greens, mustard greens, or kale. Any gilled mushroom will stand in nicely for the oyster mushrooms.

---

* Should you be concerned that either the leaves or the stem-mushroom mixture is not hot enough, reheat gently while the last addition of stock is being absorbed by the barley. Remember that the leaves are still in their cooking water at this point. A minute or two more of cooking will not hurt them, nor will it degrade the quality of the stem-mushroom mixture.

✑ DESSERTS ✑

Elinor Fettiplace's Barley Cream

The British biographer Hilary Spurling adapted this unusual recipe from a family manuscript begun in Elizabethan times. She believes this "suave and subtle" dessert was added to the collection no earlier than the end of the seventeenth century. What follows is an adaptation of the modernized recipe Ms. Spurling published in 1986. The dish itself turned out to be one of Ms. Spurling's favorites. Mine, too.

Yields
4 to 6 servings

3 tablespoons leftover cooked barley (see Basic
    Barley recipe, page 26)
2½ cups half-and-half
3 egg yolks, lightly beaten
1 tablespoon sugar
½ teaspoon vanilla extract
Whole nutmeg

1. In a heavy saucepan, stir the barley together with the half-and-half.

2. In a bowl, beat the egg yolks, then add the sugar and continue beating until smooth and lemony. Add to the barley mixture.

3. Stir in the vanilla and whisk steadily over medium heat. What you are making is a custard, and you must not boil it or the egg will scramble and ruin the dish. Pay close attention, therefore, and when the liquid visibly thickens (this is not a subtle process), remove the saucepan and set it in cold water or on a bed of ice cubes to stop any cooking from the residual heat in the pan. Continue whisking until the mixture returns to room temperature. Then spoon the

custard into wineglasses or glass bowls. Cover each glass or bowl with plastic wrap and refrigerate several hours.

4. Remove the plastic wrap. The puddings should be thick. Grate a bit of nutmeg on top and serve.

Hannah Glasse's Barley Gruel

Mrs. Glasse's *The Art of Cookery Made Plain and Easy* was the most popular English cookbook of the eighteenth century. My recipe is a slightly modernized version of hers, adapted from a chapter containing her idea of convenience foods. No special indication of its place in the meal is given, but the presence of wine, as well as its location amid several dessert recipes (gooseberry fool, apple fritters), makes it clear that this "porridge" was an informal sweet, a hasty pudding. Indeed, on the next page of her book are three hasty pudding recipes—one made with oatmeal, the other two with plain flour.

Yields
6 servings

1 gallon (4 quarts, or 16 cups) water
1½ cups barley
¾ cup raisins
¾ cup dried currants or white raisins
1 cup pitted prunes, chopped
1 teaspoon mace or nutmeg
¾ cup brown sugar or honey
½ cup white wine
½ cup heavy cream, whipped to soft peaks

1. In a 6 to 8-quart saucepan, bring the water to a boil. Add the barley, raisins, currants or white raisins, prunes, and mace or nutmeg. Boil until the water is almost completely absorbed, about 45 minutes to an hour. Toward the end, reduce the heat and stir. The barley should be soft but not mushy.

2. Add the brown sugar or honey and the wine. Cook briefly, until the sugar is dissolved and the alcohol has evaporated. Serve while still hot, if possible. Pass whipped cream separately.

Corn (Zea mays)

is the most important grain of the Americas.
It began as a wild grass in southern
Mexico or Central America long before
the arrival of Columbus. By the time
the Europeans first saw it, this grass
had developed into the ear-bearing giant
we know today, or something much like it.
It is impossible to exaggerate the importance
of corn to traditional life in the New World. During
the early days of European colonization, it was
adapted to new hybrid dishes, and corn continues to be at
the center of all American cuisines (except in the
Arctic), from New England Indian pudding to
Mexican tamales to the Chilean/Quechua
stew called *locro*.
Corn has three basic forms: on the cob;
as a meal; and, in the ancient form

of grits or hominy, processed in an alkaline medium that removes the hulls of the kernels and beneficially alters the starch within. Grits are a processed form of hominy in which the whole kernels have been mechanically cracked or smashed into tiny fragments that cook quickly. Dried whole-kernel hominy is a popular food in Mexico, where it often appears in a country pork stew called *pozole* or in a stew with tripe called *menudo*. In the United States, whole kernel hominy is sold in cans, moist and ready to eat.

BASIC CORN RECIPES

Corn on the Cob

Fans of sweet corn on the cob make a religion of getting the corn to the pot and then to the table as soon as humanly possible after it is picked. This preserves the sweetness, which degrades rapidly. Or it did. However, in recent years growers have developed a strain of sweet corn that keeps its sweetness. If you are buying this modern corn, the strenuous old way of doing things isn't necessary. But it's not easy to know what you've got underneath the husk, so it can't hurt to continue buying corn from a farm stand at the last minute. It may be unnecessary, but it still is more fun. Buying corn in a supermarket and holding it for two days in the refrigerator is, to me, as perverse as an all-you-can-eat sushi restaurant. Perhaps for sentimental reasons only, this recipe reflects traditional ideas about corn on the cob.

Yields
4 servings

6 quarts water
12 ears corn, unshucked
½ cup salt
8 tablespoons (1 stick) butter, at room
     temperature

1. In a 16-quart stockpot, bring the water to a full rolling boil.

2. While you wait for the water to boil, shuck the corn. Pull off the husks, rub away any remaining silk, and snap off the stalks if any.*

3. Add the salt to the boiling water and put in the ears of corn. Very freshly picked corn—the only kind worth bothering with—will be ready almost as soon as it is heated through. Certainly, as soon as the water returns to the boil, you should pull out an ear with tongs and cut off a kernel or two to test for doneness.

4. Serve immediately. Any delay will degrade the taste of the corn. Serve on a large platter. Pass more salt and the butter.

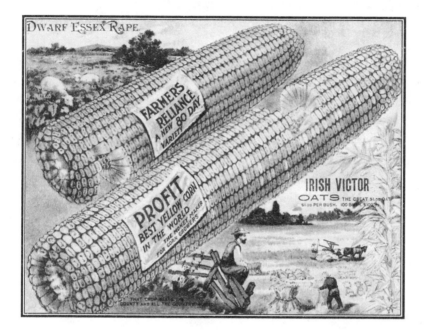

Grits

Grits is what most southern Americans call hominy. Hominy is the modern survival of an Indian word for corn kernels treated with an

---

* The husks can be salvaged if you are cooking fish over an open fire outdoors. Set a layer of husks on top of the grill, then place the fish on top. The moist husks burn slowly and protect the fish from the brunt of the fire. They also impart an attractive sweet, smoky taste to the fish. Eventually the husks burn away, but by this time the fish should be finished (and the problem of disposing of a mountain of corn husks has gone up in smoke).

alkali, originally wood ash and now most often one of various chemical compounds all known as lime. When the corn kernels are alkalized, their seed hulls separate and float to the top of the mixture. When the hulls are strained away along with the liquid, the starchy kernels are ground, usually to a fairly rough consistency—grittier, so to speak, than regular cornmeal. The alkalization of hominy also has a beneficial nutritional effect. It chemically alters the niacin naturally present in corn and makes it available to the human metabolism. Until this was understood, certain Europeans who tried to survive almost entirely on a diet of corn got sick with the classic niacin deficiency disease pellagra.

Grits, then, are a good thing that we have adopted from the Indians. In our cuisine they are served as a kind of thick porridge with eggs at breakfast. If they are left overnight, they thicken and solidify to the point where they can be fried in small muffinlike squares. The zenith of traditional grits cookery is cheese grits, for which cheese is melted into the hot grits to make a sort of down-home version of polenta with Gorgonzola.

In supermarkets grits are generally available in two varieties, normal and instant. Why anyone would want to buy instant (i.e., extraprocessed) grits when normal grits cook in a few minutes (as long as you ignore the illogical recipe printed on the box) is beyond me.

The conventional directions for grits insist that the cook sprinkle the raw grits into five times their volume of boiling salted water. It then takes a very long time, at least 30 minutes, to evaporate enough of the water to produce a properly porridgy consistency. The grits themselves have cooked long before. Obviously, the thing to do is start with less water and pay a little more attention to the pot, stirring as the grits thicken.

Yields	3 cups water
6 servings	1 cup grits
	½ teaspoon salt

1. Bring the water to a full boil.
2. Stir in the grits and salt.
3. Reduce the heat and simmer for 10 to 15 minutes, stirring with increasing frequency as the water evaporates and the mixture thickens.

Fried Grits

Once you have made grits, you can use them to make other dishes. This is the most popular variation. All grits cookery is part of a rural, farmhouse cuisine, but it takes real finesse to fry grits, whence the chilling in step 1. The simple elegance of the result has been attracting some very sophisticated cooks lately. Fried grits can function like their first cousin, polenta (see below), as a bridge between their rustic, finger-lickin'-good origins and the brave new cooking of our time that applies classic principles to ingredients previously considered humble and mixes these peasant foods with foods from other places and much higher social planes. I have been served dainty slices of foie gras on fried-grit triangles with a "red-eye" gravy made with *glace de viande* and the tiniest bit of cayenne pepper. Bill Neal, in his *Southern Cooking* (University of North Carolina, 1989), looks to the East for the inspiration that prompted his stir-fry of shrimp, scallions, and mushrooms over cheese grits.

Yields   1 recipe Grits (see page 49)
6 to 8 servings   Butter, oil, or bacon drippings

1. Pour the hot grits into a 4 by 8-inch loaf pan and chill overnight. The grits will solidify.
2. Heat the butter, oil, or drippings in a medium skillet.
3. Unmold the grits onto a cutting board. Cut into ½-inch squares. Transfer a few with a spatula to the skillet and fry until browned on both sides. Instead of the canonical syrup, you could serve them without sweetening as a side dish with almost any meat course.

Basic Polenta

This is the famous cornmeal mush of northern Italy. It began as the staple of the very poor, who fastened on corn when it came to Europe from Mexico in the sixteenth century because it would grow on land no one had previously bothered to claim for farming. Over the centuries inventive peasant cooks—and later on some very sophisticated ones—

evolved a whole cuisine based on polenta. There is an Italian cookbook entirely devoted to polenta, with more than 170 recipes ranging from braised beef with polenta gnocchi, to polenta with dried cod and cauliflower in the style of Messina, to a sweet torte combining polenta and ricotta cheese. There are traditional quail and polenta pies, polenta with herring, polenta with mushrooms. Other recipes for polenta are distributed throughout this chapter: Polenta Canapés, page 53; Galantina di Polenta, page 59; Polenta with Gorgonzola, page 70; Polenta with Fennel and Tomato-Cheese Sauce, page 71.

Like its American first cousin grits (see pages 49–50)—which is made from hominy—polenta, made from regular cornmeal, is often served after it has cooled and solidified. Then, cut into strips or squares or triangles, it can be grilled or fried.

Yields	8 cups water
6 servings	1 teaspoon salt
	2 cups yellow cornmeal, coarsely ground

1. Bring the water to a full rolling boil.
2. Stir in the salt.
3. Pour in the cornmeal in a slow, steady stream, stirring constantly.
4. Lower the heat to medium and stir, occasionally at first but constantly, as the water is absorbed. The polenta is done when it pulls away from the pot in a smooth mass, about 20 to 25 minutes.
5. Transfer to a shallow serving platter or a bowl.

⌁ FIRST COURSES ⌁

Corn Chowder

In corn season, when you have tired for the moment of corn on the cob, this is the next thing to try. The very simple method of extracting the delicious sweetness from each kernel may take you a few minutes, but the result is instant Americana.

Yields	8 ears corn, shucked
8 servings	8 cups milk
	1 large onion, peeled and finely chopped
	½ cup flour
	Salt and pepper

1. Run a sharp knife point down all the rows of corn kernels. Then press the kernels with the back of the knife and collect their contents, including the corn milk, in a bowl. Discard the cobs.

2. Heat 6 cups of the milk with the onion until the milk begins to foam. Remove from the heat, stir in the corn mush, and simmer for 10 minutes.

3. Meanwhile, stir the flour into the remaining 2 cups of milk. When the soup has finished cooking in step 2, pour a cup or so of the hot soup into the milk-flour slurry and stir well. Then pour the mixture back into the soup. Cook another 5 minutes, stirring, until the soup palpably thickens and there is no trace of flour, either as lumps or from any raw, floury taste. Season with salt and pepper.

Polenta Canapés with Black Olive Paste and Sage

This attractive, savory polenta "pie" can be passed during cocktails or served as a side dish with a hearty main course or roasted fish. Made in advance, it is meant to be reheated at the last minute.

Yields	4 cups water
8 to 12 slices	½ teaspoon salt
	⅔ cup yellow cornmeal
	⅓ cup black olive paste (available in Italian
	import groceries), approximately
	12 fresh sage leaves, soaked in olive oil for
	1 hour and drained (optional)

1. Bring the water to a full rolling boil. Add salt.

2. Add the cornmeal in a steady stream, working it with a whisk while you pour. Lower the heat and continue stirring with a wooden spoon until the mixture forms a thickish mass and pulls away from the pan— about 20–25 minutes. The idea is to cook the cornmeal slowly so that it ends up smooth, not cluttered with little clumps of meal.

3. Scrape the cooked cornmeal into an 8-inch pie tin and let it cool. The polenta will solidify.

4. With a dinner knife, spread olive paste in thin parallel lines over the surface of the polenta, making a checkerboard pattern. You may also distribute the oil-soaked sage leaves inside the lines at regular intervals across the surface of the polenta.

Run the polenta under the broiler briefly, just long enough to heat it through. Cut into pieces like a pie and serve.

Variations

Grilled Polenta

Reheat individual slices over a gentle charcoal fire.

Fried Polenta

Eliminate the olive paste and sage. Cut the basic polenta into slices and fry in olive oil until lightly browned on both sides.

Corn Pakora

Pakoras are the fritters of North India, little spicy balls of crisp chickpea flour filled with all manner of things, from chopped cauliflower to . . . corn. Indians are probably the world's most xenophilic eaters, welcoming ingredients from everywhere and turning them to account with a local flair that Indianizes them completely. Here corn kernels are roughly ground and worked into a chickpea batter. They retain only their flavor and sweetness—the main theme in a symphony of typical Indian flavors and textures. Once you have assembled all the ingredients, corn *pakoras* are a breeze to make. You could call them the Indian answer to U.S. corn fritters (see recipes, pages 68 and 69).

Yields *2 dozen* pakoras	6 tablespoons fresh or frozen corn kernels ¾ cup chickpea flour 2 tablespoons rice flour 1¼ tablespoons sesame seeds 1¼ teaspoons salt 1 tablespoon chopped fresh ginger ½ teaspoon cayenne pepper ¾ teaspoon garam masala (spice mixture available at Indian food outlets) ¼ teaspoon baking soda 2½ tablespoons lemon juice 1¼ teaspoons sugar Oil, for deep-frying

1. Chop the corn coarsely in a processor, using the steel blade. Mix it together with all other ingredients (except the oil for frying) to make a sort of dough.

2. Pour the oil to a depth of 3 inches, preferably in a karhai (the Indian half-spherical skillet) or a wok, or other metal vessel. Heat the oil to approximately 350° F.

3. Roll the dough into small balls the size of large grapes. Carefully slide them into the oil a few at a time. Do not splash. Cook until golden brown. Set aside on paper towels and repeat until all batter is cooked.

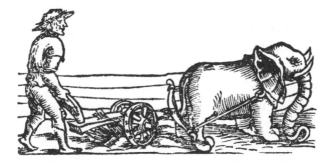

Corn Crêpes à la Michel Guérard

In *La Cuisine Gourmande* (1978) the greatest chef of the late twentieth century described how he dropped canned corn kernels into crêpe batter and made petite pancakes, which he served either as cocktail snacks or as a special accompaniment to poultry and game. In the book he combined the crêpes with elaborately roasted and sauced woodcock (*bécasse*). For various reasons this dish has not caught on with home cooks, perhaps primarily because woodcock is hard to find, and, not least, because the average amateur will not calmly follow Guérard's very stern admonition NOT to remove the innards from the little birds and NOT to truss them but instead to cross the feet and hold the legs close to the body by piercing them in several places with "the long beak attached to the neck." The head is not severed, but Guérard does suggest removing the eyes with a paring knife.

The accompanying crêpes are unintimidating, easy to make, and yours will probably be even better than Guérard's because they will be made with fresh corn.

Yields 6 dozen small pancakes, 12 to 16 large

1¾ cups flour
1 teaspoon salt
2 whole eggs plus 2 yolks, lightly beaten
¼ cup milk
4 tablespoons butter, melted
2 cups fresh corn kernels
Oil

1. In a food processor, combine the flour, salt, eggs, milk, and butter. Turn off and on until the batter is well mixed. Transfer to a bowl and let rest 1 hour.

2. Just before cooking, stir the corn into the batter.

3. Coat the bottom of a skillet with oil. If you want to make tiny Guérardian crêpes, 5 at a time, use a 12-inch skillet. If you want to make larger crêpes, one at a time, use a 7- or 8-inch skillet.

4. Place the skillet over moderate heat. Then, for the tiny crêpes, drop 5 soupspoonfuls of batter in rapid succession into the skillet. The little

pancakes will cook very rapidly. Flip them as soon as the surfaces begin to bubble. Wait 30 seconds, then remove to a warm plate. Repeat until all the batter is used up.

For larger pancakes, pour ½ cup of batter in the skillet, tilting to distribute the batter evenly. For either method, it is necessary to stir the batter from time to time, to redistribute the corn kernels.

Mozzarella in Conestoga

In classic Italian cuisine, slices of snow-white, moist mozzarella cheese are wrapped in bread, dipped in egg, and deep-fried—to create the elegant first course called *mozzarella in carrozza,* "mozzarella in a carriage." In this Americanization the "carriage" is a Conestoga wagon of cornmeal that makes a crisp crust around the melting cheese.

Yields
6 servings

8 ounces mozzarella cheese
3 cups yellow cornmeal
½ cup olive oil
Salt and pepper
1½ cups water, approximately
Oil, for deep-frying

1. Cut the mozzarella into 12 thin slices. (Depending on the shape of the cheese, you may want to do this by cutting 6 slices and then cutting them in half or by cutting 12 thinner, broader slices.)

2. Make a thick dough with the cornmeal, olive oil, salt, pepper, and water. Mix thoroughly, then scoop out about ¼ cup of dough and pat out a thin layer approximately 2 inches by 2 inches on a floured board. Place the mozzarella slices on the dough. Pat the dough over the slices and press the package together so that the cheese is completely enclosed. Continue in this way until all the cheese slices are encased in dough. You should have 12 packages.

3. Heat about 2 inches of oil to around 375° F, or until it begins to smoke.

4. With a slotted spoon, carefully lower a few of the wagons into the oil. Three at a time is probably a maximum. Fry until lightly browned on

both sides. Remove with a slotted spoon and place the wagons on a serving dish. Continue until all 12 are done. Serve immediately.

Variations: Add ½ pound diced country ham or ½ cup chopped black oil-cured olives (pitted) to the cornmeal dough.

Wrap a paper-thin strip of prosciutto around each mozzarella strip before putting it in its wagon. Then proceed as above.

✐ MAIN COURSE DISHES ✐

Corn with Oysters

In the early days of Colonial America, oysters were so prevalent that they got tagged as food for the poor. Corn was everyman's staple grain. Combining the two was obvious, and their taste contrast made the dish a winner for any era.

Yields
4 servings

3 cups (4 ears) fresh corn kernels
1¾ cups soft bread crumbs
1 cup shucked oysters, drained
1 egg, lightly beaten
1¼ teaspoons salt
1 teaspoon whole celery seed
½ teaspoon pepper
4 tablespoons butter

1. Preheat the oven to 350° F. Grease a 1-quart ovenproof casserole.
2. Combine the corn, ¼ cup of the crumbs, the oysters, egg, salt, celery seed, and pepper.
3. Cut half the butter into small pieces and stir together with the corn mixture. Place the mixture into the greased casserole.
4. Melt the remaining butter, mix it with the remaining bread crumbs, and spread the crumbs over the top of the casserole.
5. Bake for 40 minutes, or until the crumbs are browned.

Galantina di Polenta

Normally a galantine is an elaborate salamilike concoction in which a boned chicken is stuffed with other ingredients and tied up into a roll, which is later sliced like a big sausage (whose "casing" is the chicken). Here the outer layer of the galantine is polenta, which is rolled around veal and mushrooms.

Yields
4 to 6 servings

1 recipe Basic Polenta (see page 51)
¼ pound prosciutto, chopped
1 tablespoon parsley, finely chopped
2 tablespoons oil
1 clove garlic, sliced thin
1 pound stewing veal, diced
1 pound mushrooms, chopped
1 large onion, peeled and chopped
Salt and pepper to taste
1 large red bell pepper, cut into rings and
   sautéed until soft

1. When the polenta has finished cooking, stir in the prosciutto and parsley, and then spread in a ½-inch-thick layer on a baking tray to cool. Spread the polenta as neatly as possible, in the shape of a rectangle whose short side is 6 inches long.

2. While the polenta solidifies, heat the oil in a skillet and sauté the garlic until it browns. Remove with a slotted spoon and discard. Add the veal and brown. Lower the heat and add the mushrooms and onion. Continue cooking slowly until the onion has softened and the mushrooms have given up all their water. (The oil will audibly perk up and sizzle at this point, and steaming will have ceased.) Remove the skillet from the heat and season the veal mixture with salt and pepper to taste.

3. Spread a clean dish towel over the polenta. Holding the cloth tightly, invert the pan so that the polenta rests on the dish towel on a countertop. Spread the veal-mushroom mixture on the polenta.

4. Working gently, grasp the free corners of the dish towel closest to you and tip the long edge of the polenta forward so that it rolls up on

itself. Continue until you have a long log of filled polenta. Roll it carefully onto an ovenproof serving platter.

5. When you are ready to serve, brush the surface of the roll with oil and reheat in a 325° F. oven for 10 minutes, or until the center of the galantine is hot. Decorate the margins of the platter with rings of sautéed red bell pepper.

Aiguillettes de Foie de Veau aux Grains de Maïs

There is a classic French way of using leftover duck—cutting the meat into very thin strips, or needles, then reheating with a sauce. Here the same notion is applied to fresh calf's liver, but the basis of the dish is corn: cornmeal for the light dusting of the meat, corn kernels for a clear, clean taste to balance the liver. The sauce is inspired by a similar decoction applied by Michel Guérard to sautéed foie gras.

Yields
6 servings

1½ pounds calf's liver, thinly sliced
Milk
3 cups fresh corn kernels (4 ears sweet corn)
1 cup yellow cornmeal
Salt and pepper
½ cup red wine vinegar
4 tablespoons oil
½ cup walnut or peanut oil
2 tablespoons chopped parsley

1. Trim away all membranes or tendons from the liver and soak in enough milk to cover for several hours in the refrigerator.

2. Blanch the fresh corn kernels for 2 minutes in lightly salted, boiling water, drain, and reserve. (If using frozen corn, cook according to directions on package, drain, and reserve.)

3. Drain and rinse the liver. Pat it dry and cut into ¼-inch strips.

4. Put the cornmeal in a bowl. Season liberally with salt and pepper.

5. Dredge the liver strips in the cornmeal mixture.

6. In a saucepan, bring the vinegar to a boil and reduce by half. Remove from heat and reserve.

7. Heat the oil in a large skillet. When it is very hot, add the liver strips and stir-fry for 2 to 3 minutes, until the strips have browned on the outside but are still pink inside. Add the corn kernels and stir just long enough to heat them through.

8. Transfer the liver and corn to a serving dish.

9. Stir the walnut or peanut oil and parsley into the reduced vinegar. Pour the mixture over the liver and corn and serve immediately.

Variation: Try this with duck instead of liver. Buy the same quantity of boned duck breast *(magret de canard)*, or cut the breasts from 3 raw ducks yourself, reserving the rest of the birds for pâté, or a simple *sauté de canard,* or a cassoulet.

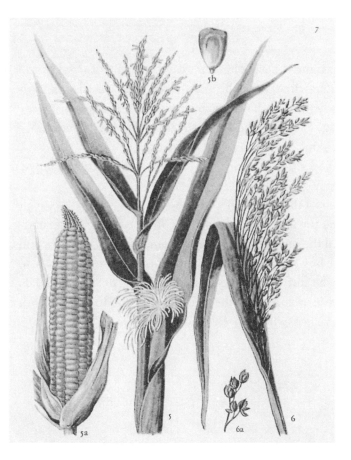

Corn-Stuffed Chiles Poblanos

Chiles poblanos are big, fairly mild green chiles from Puebla, the colonial city near Mexico City. They are perfect for stuffing, and their subtle flavor and heat make them a good foil for corn and sour cream. Chiles poblanos are regularly available in Mexican markets and specialty shops.

Yields
4 servings

4 chiles poblanos
2 tablespoons lard or oil
1 small onion, peeled and chopped
1 clove garlic, minced
3 cups fresh or frozen corn kernels
4 ounces Cheddar cheese, diced
Sour cream

1. Roast the chiles: hold them over the flame of a gas burner, turning from time to time, until the skins char. This can also be done under a broiler if you don't have gas burners. When charred, place them in a plastic bag, close it tight, and let them sweat for 15 minutes. Then peel away the skin.

2. Make a slit in the side of each chile and carefully remove the seeds. Set aside.

3. Preheat the oven to 350° F.

4. Heat the lard or oil in a small skillet. Add the onion and garlic and sauté until the onion is translucent. Combine with the corn and cheese in a separate bowl. Stuff the chiles with enough of this mixture to fill them. Transfer the stuffed chiles to a covered baking dish, spread the remaining corn-cheese mixture over the top, and bake for 40 minutes.

5. Serve hot, with sour cream on the side.

Pozole

This is the great Mexican country stew/soup made from whole-kernel hominy *(pozole)* and various cuts of pork. In Mexico cooks start with dried, or parched, corn kernels; then they hominy-ize them with slaked lime, to remove the seed coats, and cook them slowly with a hog's head and other "rough" cuts of pork. There are many regional variations involving various chiles, avocado, tomatillos, and so forth. Few American cooks are likely to plunge into making a full-bore *pozole,* because the conditions that make it simple for a Mexican cook do not obtain north of the border. But there is a way. For the hog's head, substitute universally available pigs' feet. For the parched corn, substitute canned hominy. For the chiles guajillo, ancho, or cascabel, substitute cayenne pepper. (This last substitution follows the authentic method for producing the purest of *pozoles—pozole blanco,* or "white pozole.") The result is rich, warming, filled with personality—an easy stovetop dish that will serve a crowd of people on a winter day.

Yields	6 quarts cold water
8 to 10	3 quarts canned hominy, drained
servings	3 pigs' feet, split into 6 halves
	1½ pounds boneless pork loin
	1½ pounds pork neck, cut up for stewing
	4 cloves garlic, minced
	Oregano
	Salt and pepper
	Cayenne pepper
	1 small head Savoy cabbage, shredded
	1 bunch radishes, sliced
	2 medium onions, peeled and chopped

1. Fill a large, heavy pot with the cold water and bring to a boil. Add the hominy and the meat. When the water returns to the boil, lower the heat and simmer for about 1 hour, or until the pigs' feet have begun to fall apart and the pork loin can be shredded easily.

2. Remove the meat with a slotted spoon or tongs. Roughly shred the pork loin and return the meat to the pot. Pull the large bones out of the pigs' feet and discard. Cut the remaining pigs' feet parts into serveable pieces and return them to the pot. Cut meat off the neck bones; discard the bones and return the meat to the pot.

3. Add the garlic and other seasonings. Taste as you add. This dish needs quite a bit of salt. The amount of cayenne pepper will depend on your tolerance or appetite for high heat. Start with at least 2 teaspoons. Stir well, let simmer for a minute or two, then taste and consider adding more.

4. Continue simmering until you have only a bit of liquid left above the level of the solid ingredients. This dish can be prepared well ahead of time and reheated. When ready to serve, sprinkle the cabbage on top. Pass the radishes and onions on the side and let guests sprinkle what they want on top of their portion.

↶ SIDE DISHES ↷

Succotash

This very simple combination of corn kernels and lima beans is always said to have been borrowed by East Coast Colonists from the first Americans, whom they found living in New England before it got its name. The etymologies I've come across ascribe the word "succotash" to various tribal languages, but in each of these cases, succotash is translated as corn kernels. The beans, which must have been part of the dish from the beginning even if they get no credit in its name, make an appealing contrast with the corn, and they provide us with what used to be called the complete protein (all the amino acids that are the component chemicals of animal protein, in the same relative quantities that they occur in red meat). The only possible drawback to succotash, if it is made from fresh corn and lima beans, is that it might not be quite as delicious as the same dish made with corn and double-skinned favas.

Shelled favas, or broad beans, are undeniably better-tasting than limas, although they are superficially similar. But they are only at their best if they are double-skinned: first popped out of the big phallic pod (Italians have made so much about this resemblance that it is almost impossible to discuss favas in Italy without provoking reflexive ribaldry), then skinned. Skinning enough favas for 4 to 6 people is hard work, but it is slightly easier if you blanch them for a minute in boiling water (purists may draw the line here; I do not), let them cool for a few minutes, and then pull away the outer skin.

By substituting favas for limas in this dish, you are quite effectively stretching the favas with the corn and halving the labor favas normally would take.

Yields	2 tablespoons olive oil
4 servings	1 cup fresh corn kernels
	1 cup lima or fava beans
	Salt

1. Heat the olive oil in a heavy skillet.
2. Toss the corn and beans in the oil briefly, just long enough to soften the beans and turn them a bright green. Add salt to taste and serve.

Variation: As an alternate, fat-free method, steam the corn and beans over boiling water in a Chinese steamer for as little as 3 minutes, or longer if they are not as fresh.

Corn with Okra and Tomato

Okra came to the New World from its native Africa with slaves, some of whom called it gumbo. They combined it with the native American tomato to create a classic dish of our southern cuisine. Too many people outside the southern/black taste ambit look down on okra as slimy (which it can be if it is cooked overlong); tomato masks this, especially if the okra is stewed with it only long enough just to be softened. By adding corn kernels, we get a third accent—and another bright color—of taste and chewiness. This dish will go nicely with broiled fish, especially a full-flavored one like bluefish or mackerel, or with roasted chicken.

Yields
6 servings

2 tablespoons oil

1 large clove garlic, minced

3 scallions, trimmed and chopped, or 2 medium
    onions, peeled and chopped

10 ounces okra, topped, tailed, and roughly
    chopped

3 cups tomatoes, chopped

2 cups fresh or frozen corn kernels

Salt and pepper

Cayenne pepper, to taste (optional)

1. Heat the oil in a large skillet. Sauté the garlic until it begins to brown, then add the scallions or onions.

2. When the scallions have wilted or the onions are translucent, add the okra and tomatoes. Lower the heat and simmer until the okra has just softened. Stir in the corn kernels and cook briefly to soften the corn.

3. Add salt and pepper to taste and stir in a little cayenne if desired. This dish can be set aside and gently reheated.

CAN YOU PICK OUT ALL THE CORN PRODUCTS SHOWN HERE?

Maisotto con Ventriglio alla Modena
(Corn and Rice Risotto with Gizzard)

The combination of corn and rice occurs spontaneously in Mexico, where one is native and the other an assimilated remnant, among many, of the conquest of Cortés. The cooking method is pure Italian, and the inclusion of gizzard, which the squeamish can simply ignore, is meant to add an extra dimension to an otherwise undramatic but delicious dish—while sneaking an unfairly scorned organ onto the table and into the hearts of unsuspecting millions.

Yields
4 to 6 servings

4 ears corn
2 tablespoons corn oil or lard
1 clove garlic, chopped
3 chicken gizzards, with outer membrane cut
    away, chopped
1 cup Arborio or other risotto rice
Salt
2 cups boiling chicken broth

1. Shuck the corn, cut away all the kernels, and reserve.

2. Heat the corn oil or lard in a heavy saucepan. Sauté the garlic until it begins to brown. Add the gizzards and the rice. Stir until the rice begins to color.

3. Add salt to taste and then begin adding the boiling broth ½ cup at a time, letting each addition be almost completely absorbed into the rice before pouring in the next. Stir constantly. When you add the last ½ cup of broth, stir in the corn kernels, reduce the heat as low as possible, cover, and let stand for 5 minutes.

Deep-Fried Corn Fritters

Fritters are essentially deep-fried pancakes. The batter, which is loose and eggy, firms up in the hot oil. But fritters also often contain other foods—little chunks of vegetables or meat and, most famously, corn kernels.

Yields 6 servings as a side dish, 8 as cocktail canapés

Oil, for deep-frying
2 eggs, separated
½ cup milk
1½ cups flour
2 teaspoons baking powder
1 teaspoon salt
Cayenne pepper
1 cup corn kernels, fresh-cut from the cob
    or frozen and defrosted

1. Heat the oil in a heavy saucepan. The oil should be 3 to 4 inches deep, but the actual quantity will vary, depending on the geometry of the pan. A wok, or the Indian equivalent called a karhai, will enable you to use less oil.

2. Meanwhile, beat together the egg yolks, milk, flour, baking powder, salt, and cayenne.

3. Beat the egg whites until stiff but not dry.

4. Fold the kernels into the egg-yolk–flour mixture, then fold in the egg whites.

5. When the oil has begun producing a haze or when it reaches 375° F. on a deep-frying thermometer, start frying the fritters a few at a time. Drop the batter from a spoon held close to the oil. Avoid splattering the oil, which can burn you badly. Fritters are done when golden brown. Drain them on paper towels and continue deep-frying the batter until there is none left.

Variations: Substitute chopped ham, sausage, salami, or other highly spiced meats for half the corn kernels.

Add 2 chopped, seeded, and pickled jalapeño peppers when you fold in the corn kernels.

Pan-Fried Fritters

Yields 6 break-fast portions, 10 to 12 side-dish portions

5 cups corn kernels
2 egg yolks, lightly beaten
Salt
Cayenne pepper (optional)
2 egg whites, beaten until stiff but not dry
Butter, for frying

1. In a mixing bowl, stir together the corn, egg yolks, salt, and cayenne pepper if you are using it.
2. Fold in the egg whites.
3. Over medium heat, melt enough butter to lightly coat the bottom of a heavy skillet.
4. With a large spoon, pour the batter into the skillet. There is no rule for how much batter equals a fritter. If you want a runny center, pour a larger amount. For a crisper fritter, pour less batter. When the surface begins to bubble, flip the fritters over with a metal spatula. They should be lightly browned on both sides. The second side will brown quite quickly, in a minute or so. Remove the fritters to a serving platter and keep them warm in a low oven while you repeat this step until all the batter is used up.

These fritters can be served as a side dish with meat of all kinds or as pancakes at breakfast with maple syrup. (You will probably want to eliminate the cayenne at breakfast.)

Hush Puppies

These spicy cornmeal nuggets evolved from an African recipe brought across the Atlantic by slaves. The original dish was made from the flour of black-eyed peas. You can still find fritters made this way in northeastern Brazil and in western Africa. Their New World cousins, made with cornmeal or wheat flour, are mixed with all manner of ingredients, from little shrimps to chopped vegetables, and they are favorite dishes in Creole kitchens from Charleston to Salvador da Bahia. In the United States, the local version—the hush puppy—is a southern specialty most often served with fried fish, canonically catfish. Hush puppies can also be served by themselves, as cocktail snacks.

Yields about 2 dozen hush puppies

Oil, for deep-frying
2 cups cornmeal
1 medium onion, chopped
1 teaspoon baking powder
1 teaspoon baking soda
1 teaspoon salt
2 cups buttermilk or whole or skim milk
2 eggs

1. Heat the oil in a heavy saucepan. The oil should be 3 to 4 inches deep, but the actual quantity will vary, depending on the geometry of the pan. A wok or the Indian equivalent called a karhai will enable you to use less oil.

2. Meanwhile, stir together all the remaining ingredients in the order listed. The batter should be of uniform consistency. When you achieve this, stop stirring and wait for the oil to get hot enough to begin giving off a visible vapor, at around 360° F. on a deep-frying thermometer.

3. Drop a few large spoonfuls of batter into the saucepan. Be careful not to spatter hot oil on yourself—it burns. Cook the hush puppies until golden brown. Drain on paper towels. Repeat until all the batter is used up.

Polenta with Gorgonzola

This is a traditional Italian combination of ingredients: boiled cornmeal (polenta) and cheese. The easiest way to effect the mixture of tastes is to "butter" strips of almost solid, but still warm polenta with a small amount of room-temperature cheese. In this equally well known dish, the polenta is mixed directly with butter and cheese, to taste.

A ratio of ¼ pound cheese to 2 cups of cornmeal should work well for most people.

Yields
4 to 6 servings

8 cups (2 quarts) water
1 teaspoon salt
2 cups yellow cornmeal, coarsely ground
¼ pound Gorgonzola cheese, cut into
    1-inch cubes
2 tablespoons butter

1. Bring the water to a full rolling boil.
2. Stir in the salt.
3. Add the cornmeal in a slow, steady stream, stirring constantly.
4. Lower the heat to medium and stir, occasionally at first but constantly as the water is absorbed. The polenta is done when it pulls away from the pot in a smooth mass, about 20 to 25 minutes.
5. Stir in the cheese and butter. Stir until melted together with the polenta. Transfer to a shallow serving platter or a bowl.

Polenta with Fennel and Tomato-Cheese Sauce

Not content with a Gorgonzola cheese flavor in their polenta, some inventive Italians add anise-flavored bulb fennel.

Yields
4 to 6 servings

4 cups milk
4 cups water
2 cups yellow cornmeal
1 teaspoon salt
¼ teaspoon pepper
Oil
3 bulb fennels, trimmed and sliced
1 large onion, peeled and chopped
1 cup chicken stock
3 cups tomato purée
3 cloves garlic, minced
½ cup yogurt
¼ pound Gorgonzola cheese

1. Bring 3 cups of the milk and 3 cups of the water to a boil. Reduce to a simmer.

2. Stir the cornmeal into a mixture of the remaining cup unheated milk and the remaining cup unheated water. Add the salt and pepper. Then pour the cornmeal mixture into the simmering milk-water mixture and cook, stirring, until very thick—about 20–25 minutes. Paint the top with oil to prevent the formation of a skin and reserve the polenta in a warm oven.

3. Sauté the fennel slices in oil until lightly browned. Add the onion and continue sautéing until translucent. Add the chicken stock, tomato purée, and garlic. Return to a simmer and continue cooking for a few more minutes, until the fennel has softened. (You may want to stop sooner, when the fennel still has some crunch left in it.)

4. Off heat, stir in the yogurt and Gorgonzola. When the cheese has melted into the sauce, bring it to the table in a serving dish. Serve the reserved polenta on individual plates and then distribute the fennel-cheese-tomato mixture over it.

Cheese Grits

Here is the Southland's answer to polenta with Gorgonzola. Both are cornmeals mixed with cheese.

Yields
6 servings

2 tablespoons oil
2 medium onions, peeled and chopped
1 recipe freshly cooked Grits (see page 49)
½ cup diced Cheddar cheese
½ teaspoon cayenne pepper
2 egg yolks, lightly beaten
Salt and pepper

1. Preheat the oven to 375° F.

2. Heat the oil in a medium skillet over medium-high and sauté the onions until translucent.

3. While the grits are still hot, stir in the onions and all the other ingredients. Continue stirring until the cheese has completely melted.

4. Pour into a greased 4 by 8-inch loaf pan, or into 6 greased 6-ounce ramekins. Set in oven and bake for 30 minutes, or until the top is lightly browned. Let stand 5 to 10 minutes. Then run a knife around the outside of the "loaf," and if you can, without destroying it, invert the grits onto a cookie sheet and then invert again onto a serving platter so that the browned top will be visible. If using ramekins, serve one to each guest.

Gratin of Chanterelles and Corn

In mid-August, when the sweet corn is at its best and the woods are full of golden chanterelle mushrooms, this will give you an alternative to corn on the cob that doesn't abandon the season or the setting. The sweetness of the whole kernels joins textures and flavors with the mushrooms.

Yields
4 servings

8 ears very fresh sweet corn
2 tablespoons corn oil
2 cloves garlic, minced
1 large onion, peeled and finely chopped
Salt

>2 cups chanterelles or other wild mushrooms
>2 small fresh green chiles (serranos), seeded
>   and chopped
>½ cup heavy cream
>½ cup grated Parmesan cheese

1. Husk the corn. Then cut off all the kernels and set aside.

2. Heat the corn oil in a 6-cup saucepan. Add the garlic and cook over medium heat until it begins to brown. Add onion and sauté until translucent.

3. Preheat the broiler.

4. Stir in a little salt, then the chanterelles and chiles. Toss until the mushrooms are well coated with oil and slightly wilted. Add the corn and heavy cream. Simmer until most of the liquid has evaporated. This will take just long enough to heat the corn through and take the edge off its rawness. Transfer to a shallow, ovenproof pan just large enough to hold the mixture (and presentable enough to serve the gratin from). Sprinkle all the cheese on top.

5. Place under the broiler, a few inches away to avoid scorching but close enough to promote melting and a bit of attractive browning. Leave the oven door ajar and keep looking. When the cheese has run and colored, remove and serve immediately.

∿ *BREADS* ∿

Cornmeal will not produce real bread in the sense of a risen, high loaf. Unlike wheat, it will not transform itself into a smooth, elastic, air-holding dough in the presence of yeast and warm air. But this has not prevented cooks in places that consume corn as a staple from preparing a remarkably varied panoply of corn "breads," some leavened (in company with wheat flour), some flat (but not dense and leaden). Of course, the preeminent corn bread is the tortilla, which is just a flat, thin disk of moistened hominy meal cooked on a hot surface. The corn-bread range extends from there all the way to light, light southern U.S. corn bread and on to sensually chewy Colombian *arepas*.

Corn Muffins

Combining cornmeal and wheat flour makes for a lighter texture than what an all-cornmeal dough would yield. The cornmeal itself will make a significant difference to the result. The market offers a wide variety of milling standards, from coarse to fine, of both yellow and white cornmeals. They are all worth trying, unless you are already committed to one of the fiercely defended regional styles of corn muffin. This same recipe will also produce U.S. basic southern-style corn bread if baked in a loaf pan (see recipe, page 76).

Yields about 10 muffins

4 teaspoons baking powder
½ teaspoon salt
1 cup cornmeal
1 cup flour
1 cup milk
1 egg, lightly beaten
4 tablespoons shortening or melted butter,
    lard, or rendered poultry fat

1. Preheat the oven to 425° F.
2. Grease a 10-cup muffin tin.
3. Stir together the baking powder, salt, cornmeal, and flour. Then stir in the milk, egg, and shortening, butter, lard, or poultry fat, beating just enough to blend the ingredients. Overbeating produces leathery muffins.
4. Fill the containers of the muffin tin two-thirds full. Bake for 20 to 25 minutes, until the muffins begin to pull away from the sides of the tin and are no longer gooey inside.

Variation: Add ½ cup cooked corn kernels along with the dry ingredients in step 3.

Southern Corn Bread

To make the standard corn bread of southern U.S. tradition, follow the previous recipe, but bake the bread in an 8-inch-square pan. When it's done, cool on a rack and then cut into brownie-size squares and serve.

Corn bread is normally served with a meal, but it could easily be converted into a cocktail canapé if cut into slightly smaller pieces, say 2 inches by 2 inches. The basic recipe can be varied almost infinitely and with great ease. Here are a few suggestions. Once you start thinking about the possibilities of expanding humble corn bread into a mini-cuisine, the ideas will keep coming.

1. Beat any of the following into the batter in step 3 of the Corn Muffin recipe (page 75):

Yields
8 servings

- ½ cup chopped pitted oil-cured olives rolled in fennel seed
- 1 tablespoon chopped pickled jalapeño peppers
- 4 chopped oil-packed anchovy fillets
- ½ cup grated Parmesan, or Pecorino Romano cheese
- ½ cup chopped walnuts
- ½ cup crumbled, crisply fried bacon or country ham
- ½ cup ground beef or veal
- ¼ cup green or black olive paste, approximately
- confit of 3 medium onions and 2 minced cloves garlic sauteéd in oil until very soft and lightly browned

2. Pour half the basic batter into the pan. Spread the top with either of the following and then add the rest of the batter before baking as directed in the Corn Muffin recipe:

- ¼ cup chopped sun-dried tomatoes
- 1 tin oil-packed anchovy fillets

Country Corn Bread

Lard is an obsolete ingredient. It is high in cholesterol (although no higher than butter) and high in calories (although no higher than any other cooking fat or oil). Most of all, it has an unchic connection with its source, the hog, and with the farm. It is, in fact, a highly purified substance, long-lasting in the refrigerator, and it imparts a fine taste to other ingredients, as here. Unhydrogenated natural lard, if you can find it at an old-fashioned butcher (or render your own), is now considered by some reliable authorities to be as healthy as olive oil.

Yields
32 pieces

5½ cups water
3 tablespoons lard
1 teaspoon salt
½ teaspoon black pepper
1½ cups yellow cornmeal
Cayenne pepper

1. Bring the water to a boil in a heavy 3 to 4-quart pot.

2. Add the lard, salt, pepper, and cayenne to taste.

3. When the lard melts, begin whisking and swirl in the cornmeal. Continue whisking for 2 to 3 minutes, then lower the heat as far as possible and continue cooking for 20 minutes, uncovered, stirring often, or until the mixture is very thick.

4. Pour into a greased 8- or 9-inch brownie or cake pan. Let cool to room temperature, then chill for several hours so that the bread can be cut.

5. Score into approximately 32 squares. These can be served as is, heated in a microwave (covered with plastic wrap on a nonmetal platter for about 2 minutes at full power) or in a conventional oven at 400° F., or fried in very hot lard in small batches, allowing about 3 minutes per side.

Leavened Corn Bread

By adding plenty of all-purpose white flour, you can make a cornmeal dough rise—not to the heights of a pure wheaten loaf, but far enough, and the bread retains the liveliness of corn.

Yields
1 loaf

1 cup yellow cornmeal
1 package active dry yeast
1½ cups lukewarm water
½ cup lukewarm milk
1 tablespoon butter or oil
1 teaspoon salt
6 cups flour

1. Whisk together ⅓ cup of the cornmeal and the yeast in a bowl. Then whisk in ½ cup of the lukewarm water. Cover with a dish towel and let stand for about 40 minutes, or until doubled in bulk.

2. Beat in the remaining 1 cup lukewarm water, the milk, butter or oil, and salt. Now work in the remaining cornmeal and the flour, a handful at a time, until you have a dough that cleans the bowl. Form into a ball and knead on a well-floured board until springy. Depending on your vigor, this should take from 5 to 10 minutes. Let the dough rise in a lightly oiled bowl covered with a dishcloth for 1 hour, or until doubled in bulk.

3. Turn the dough out and knead again on a well-floured board. Reshape into a ball and let rise once more, until doubled in bulk.

4. Knead the dough a third time, form into a ball, and set it in a lightly oiled cake pan. Sprinkle with cornmeal. Cover and let rise until doubled in bulk, about 50 minutes.

5. Preheat the oven to 450° F. Bake for 15 minutes, then reduce the heat to 400° F. and bake another 15 minutes, or until the loaf is done (when it has browned and sounds hollow when tapped sharply). Let cool completely on a rack.

Spoon Bread

Somewhere between corn bread and a soufflé, spoon bread is the most delicate of all the corn-based quick breads.

Yields
6 servings

1½ cups water
1 cup yellow cornmeal
¾ teaspoon salt
3 tablespoons butter
3 eggs, separated
1¼ cups milk

1. Preheat the oven to 350° F.
2. In a saucepan, bring the water to a boil. Meanwhile, mix the cornmeal and salt in a bowl.
3. Pour the seasoned cornmeal mixture into the boiling water and add the butter. Stir together well.
4. Beat the egg yolks, stir the milk into them, and then beat into the cornmeal mixture.
5. Beat the egg whites until stiff but not dry. Fold into the cornmeal mixture.
6. Turn into a greased 6-cup soufflé dish and bake 40 to 50 minutes, or until browned.

Corn Pone

From Maine to Tierra del Fuego, there are dozens of variations on this obvious idea: cornmeal fry bread. In New England they call them hoecakes or johnnycakes, and people fight about what cornmeal from which side of the neighboring river a serious cook ought to use. This is not, in fact, a silly dispute. The quality of the meal determines the quality of the pone. Variation can be wide, even among hand-milled boutique varieties from places with names like Skunk Holler. Even the same little mill will not always be a reliable source of the very same quality meal at all times of year, or year in year out. It is this unpredictability that supplies a good deal of the interest in cornmeal baking. Still, you can hardly go wrong with any of these traditionalist meals.

Yields about 1 dozen cakes	1 cup water 1 cup white or yellow cornmeal ½ teaspoon salt 1 tablespoon shortening

1. In a saucepan, bring the water to a full rolling boil.

2. In a bowl, mix the cornmeal and salt. Stir in the boiling water.

3. When the water has been absorbed, let the cornmeal cool until you can shape it into balls the size of plums. Flatten with your hand.

4. Heat the shortening in a skillet. Brown the hoecakes on both sides. Serve hot.

∽ DESSERT ∾

Indian Pudding

Perhaps this cornmeal-and-molasses dessert really did begin with the Indians of New England, where it is now a tried-and-true regional specialty. But under any circumstances, it could not have begun as much more than corn gruel, since neither molasses nor milk would have been available in North America before the Colonists brought in sugar from the Colonial plantations in the Caribbean and dairy cattle from Europe. Therefore, the Indian pudding we eat today is more accurately appreciated as a survival from the early days of tremulous contact between the first Americans and the English. I see it as a symbol of a productive encounter that might have prospered further but didn't.

Yields 6 to 8 servings	4 cups milk ½ cup yellow cornmeal ⅔ cup molasses

1 teaspoon salt
Heavy cream or half-and-half

1. Preheat the oven to 325° F.

2. Bring the milk to a boil in a 6-quart pot. When the milk starts to foam, reduce the heat to low, add the cornmeal, and simmer slowly for 15 minutes, stirring occasionally.

3. Stir in the molasses and add the salt. Simmer another 5 minutes.

4. At this point, people in search of a pudding with greater dash than plain old Indian pudding add raisins, egg, cinnamon, nutmeg, ginger, and milk. I hold out for simplicity. Just transfer the pudding batter from step 3 to a lightly greased 6-cup baking pan or soufflé mold and bake for 1½ hours or longer, until the pudding barely trembles when the mold is shaken. Serve while hot; the pudding can easily be kept warm in a turned-off or low oven or reheated in a microwave (but only if it is not in a metal container).

Pass heavy cream or half-and-half separately.

Oats (Avena sativa)

are not glamour food. The most famous thing
ever said about them is Dr. Johnson's
mocking definition in his dictionary of 1755:
"A grain, which in England is generally given
to horses but in Scotland supports the people."
Behind this approximate description
of reality lay a biological fact. Oats prospered
in the wet, inclement climate of the North,
where high-gluten wheat would not grow
dependably. Scottish cooks, therefore, developed
their cuisine around oats, giving the world a host
of fine dishes from flatbreads to haggis to oatmeal. Oatmeal
is laborious to mill and hard to store because of
its high fat content, but it has come into its own
recently: its bran may help to protect us
against heart disease by fighting the accumulation
of cholesterol.

In southern Europe oats do not play an extremely important role as a cultivated grain, but in classical times they were well known and associated with the pastoral life. Shepherds, according to a widespread poetic conceit, made flutes out of oat grass, and the word "oat" was a literary equivalent for a rustic flute.

As a practical matter, most U.S. markets sell oats in a single form—rolled oats for porridge, processed for quick cooking. In the store this product is simply labeled oatmeal, as if there were no other kinds. In fact, the variations available in an oat-centered culture such as Scotland are almost infinite. In the United States, health-food stores and other specialty purveyors sell a much better, but slower-cooking product called steel-cut oatmeal. The texture and the nutty flavor of these oat fragments are much superior to the gluey (rolled-oat) oatmeal we all know from childhood. The very best steel-cut oats normally available here are so-called pinhead oats, which are sold as Irish steel-cut oats. They are worth the effort for porridge, but you cannot substitute them, uncooked, for rolled oats in standard American recipes. This is why many of the recipes that follow call for cooked oatmeal where your previous experience may lead you to expect uncooked oats. Please pay attention to specifications in the ingredients list, especially where oat flour—a completely different product from any oatmeal—is called for.

Oatmeal

How you cook oatmeal (thick or loose, gluey or grainy) depends partly on your taste, but a lot hangs on what kind of oatmeal you buy in the first place. All quick-cooking, or instant, varieties are to be avoided altogether. They have been rolled and steamed and otherwise processed to the point where they have lost a lot of nutrition and all of their character. Even plain rolled oats turn to mush and give oatmeal an undeserved bad name. You should be looking for steel-cut (Scottish or, better still, Irish) oats. Barely processed (some are lightly toasted), these nutty, delicious groat fragments are worth the extra time it takes to cook them. You can reduce the wait by soaking them overnight.

Yields
about 3 cups

3 or 4 cups water
1 teaspoon salt
1 cup steel-cut oats

1. Bring the 3 cups water (4 cups for Irish pinhead oats) to a boil in a heavy saucepan. Stir in the salt, then stir in the oats slowly.

2. Return to the boil and lower the heat right away to a simmer. Cook, uncovered, or until the water has been absorbed and the oats have thickened to a luxurious, bold porridge in which each grain still retains a backbone of its own. This is supposed to take as much as 40 minutes for Irish pinhead oats, but 30 minutes, or even 15, seems to do the job with other steel-cut varieties. Serve with dried fruit, brown sugar, honey, milk, or cream.

Familia

This is the granddaddy of all healthy cold breakfast cereals. Obviously, there is a cost advantage in mixing the ingredients yourself. You also ensure that the individual ingredients will be fresh and of top quality.

Yields
12 servings

3 cups rolled oats
1½ cups raw or toasted wheat germ
8 ounces dried apricots, cut up
1 cup chopped walnuts
3 cups wheat flakes
2 cups raisins

1. Mix all the ingredients together and store in a jar in the refrigerator.
2. Serve with milk and honey.

Variation: Substitute any dried fruits or nuts and any flaked grain, such as rye or bran.

Cream-Crowdie or Crannachan

In the Scottish Highlands, crowdie is an everyday word for food or a meal. Crowdie was originally just gruel—meal plus water. This basic idea, one of the most primitive and fundamental in human life virtually everywhere, has evolved into a group of special gruels, or broses, mixed with whiskey and eaten or drunk during various holidays. The toasted oatmeal referred to below has been cooked, left to cool, and then toasted until fairly dry and browned. Catherine Brown in *Scottish Regional Recipes* (Edinburgh: Chambers, 1981) lists five ways to prepare crowdie.

Stapag Uachair: whipped cream, cooked steel-cut oatmeal, whiskey, and sugar, mixed in any proportion according to the taste of each guest.

Fuarag: 1 cup sour cream, ½ cup toasted cooked steel-cut oatmeal, at room temperature, and sugar, all stirred together and left for several hours until thickening takes place. Then spread on oatcakes (see page 93) or eat with berries and other acid fruit.

Atholl Brose: 1½ cups cooked steel-cut oatmeal mixed with enough water to make a paste, left to infuse for 1 hour, pressed through a fine sieve to extract liquid, which is stirred together with 4 teaspoons dark (heather) honey and then combined in a large bottle with 3 cups whiskey. Shake well before using.

Gromack: Equal parts cooked steel-cut oatmeal, honey, and whiskey mixed with cream, to taste, in a glass and eaten with a spoon, especially by people just rescued from winter emergencies.

Crannachan is the most elaborate:

Yields *4 servings*	½ cup cooked steel-cut oatmeal ⅓ cup malt whiskey 2 tablespoons dark honey 3 tablespoons cream cheese, mashed ½ cup raspberries ⅔ cup heavy cream, beaten to stiff peaks 4 teaspoons light honey

1. Let the oatmeal steep in the whiskey and dark honey overnight.

2. Stir in the cream cheese and raspberries.

3. Put a spoonful of heavy cream in the bottom of a wineglass. Pour in a quarter of the oatmeal-honey mixture. Top with a quarter of the remaining cream. Make a slight well in the cream and pour 1 teaspoon light honey in it. Fill three more glasses in this way. You can serve this any time, but my suggestion is to have it ready when you or people you know will be coming indoors after a cold, wet walk or ski run.

Greens and Meal Soup

The meal helps thicken this egg-drop-and-greens soup, which may remind you of its Italian or Chinese cousins. If you are making it in the early spring, pick nettles (with gloves on to avoid getting stung) for a seasonal treat. After they're cooked, they don't sting and they have a gentler tang than kale or mustard greens.

Yields
6 servings

6 cups chicken or vegetable stock
1 pound greens (spinach, mustard, kale, young nettles)
½ cup barley or fine oat flour
Salt and pepper
6 eggs, lightly beaten (optional)

1. Bring the stock to a boil.

2. Meanwhile, wash the greens very carefully. If you are using nettle leaves, be sure to wear rubber gloves to avoid stinging. (Cooking neutralizes this natural defense.) Drain and add to the stock with the barley or oat flour. Season with salt and pepper.

3. Simmer until the greens have just wilted. Remove from heat and immediately whisk in the eggs, if desired. They will coagulate and produce an attractive contrast to the greens and the meal.

Kibbeh

This is the national dish of Lebanon, where it is eaten in hundreds of variations, from raw to baked to stuffed, but almost always made with bulgur wheat (see Kibbeh recipe on page 160). If, however, oatmeal is substituted for bulgur, the result is unexpected and thoroughly attractive.

Yields 4 servings as a main course, 6 to 8 as an appetizer

¾ pound ground lamb
1 cup cooked steel-cut oatmeal
1 medium onion, peeled and quartered
½ teaspoon ground cinnamon
¼ teaspoon ground allspice
1 tablespoon ground cumin
2 teaspoons salt
A few grindings pepper
Fresh parsley
Raw scallions

1. Put all the ingredients in the jar of a processor fitted with the steel blade. Process for several minutes to produce a homogeneous paste.

2. Form into a single mound or many small balls. Decorate with parsley and serve raw at room temperature, with oatcakes and perhaps raw scallions.

Variations

Baked Kibbeh

Form raw kibbeh into small patties, brush with oil, and bake for 15 minutes at 350° F. Just before serving, run the patties under the broiler and brown on both sides.

Baked Kibbeh Stuffed with Walnuts in Yogurt

Take 1 cup chopped walnuts and grind them in a nut grinder or clean coffee grinder, or pulverize the nuts with a mortar and pestle. Work together with 4 tablespoons butter to make a paste, then work that into the raw kibbeh. Now proceed as for plain baked kibbeh above. After baking, heat with 8 ounces plain yogurt in a saucepan. Do not boil the yogurt.

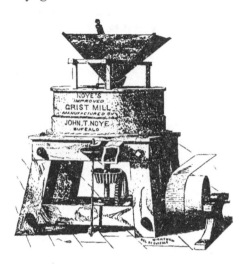

Haggis

Haggis is the notorious national dish of Scotland, a "pudding" of lamb innards (traditionally the heart, liver, and lungs) and oatmeal steamed for hours in a sheep's stomach. By legend, it is served up with plenty of single malt whiskey on such Scottish feast days as Hogmanay (New Year's Eve) and the birthday of Robert Burns. In fact, haggis is available every day in modern Scotland. Its mild, virile taste is not a patch on truly intimidating food such as the French chitterling sausage, *andouillette*. It is the idea of haggis, and the details of traditional preparation, that put people off.*

---

* Catherine Brown recalls: "My first haggis-making exploits were as a student when the whole process took the best part of a day to complete. The raw sheep's pluck, while not a pretty sight, didn't worry me at all but the windpipe hanging over the side of the pot which the whole pluck was cooking in, quietly disgorging the blood and other impurities from the lungs into a jar . . . did not appeal."

In the United States you have to own your own sheep and be willing to slaughter it yourself if you want to make an authentic haggis, since lungs are not legally for sale anywhere. On the other hand, since there is ample Scottish precedent for lungless or "lightless" haggis, I offer this recipe, if for no other reason than to include what is, after all, the most important oatmeal recipe of all.

Yields
6 servings

1 quart water
½ pound lamb's liver
1 lamb's heart
1 large onion, peeled and chopped
1 cup cooked coarse "pinhead" or Irish steel-cut
　　oatmeal
2 ounces suet (beef kidney fat), finely chopped
1 tablespoon salt
1 tablespoon pepper
½ teaspoon ground coriander

1. Bring the water to a boil. Add the liver, heart, and onion. Return to the boil, reduce the heat, and simmer for about 30 minutes, or until the meat is tender.

2. Meanwhile, put the oatmeal in a heavy skillet and stir over low-medium heat until dry but not browned.

3. Drain the meats and chop fine in a food processor. Transfer to a mixing bowl and combine with the oatmeal and suet. Add the salt, pepper, and coriander.

4. Spoon the mixture into a ceramic dish or mold. Cover with aluminum foil, then set in a larger pan with just enough boiling water in it so that the water level comes halfway up the sides of the mold. Adjust heat so that the water barely simmers and cook for 2 hours. Serve with "bashed neeps" (mashed rutabaga).

⤙ SIDE DISH ⤚

Oatmeal "Kugel"

This is an improvisation that builds on the basic similarity between the Scottish oatmeal side dish skirlie and Jewish kugel. Both are very straightforward and old-fashioned starch accompaniments to meat. Skirlie is often used as a stuffing for chicken, so the substitution of chicken fat for mutton suet makes both practical and gastronomic sense. Vegetable oil is also a possible substitution, but it will somewhat reduce the guilty pleasure this insidiously rich but deceptively plain-seeming dish can give.

Yields
4 servings

¼ cup chicken fat
2 medium onions, finely chopped
1½ cups cooked steel-cut oatmeal
Salt and pepper

1. Heat the chicken fat in a skillet. Add the onions and sauté until translucent.

2. Stir in the oatmeal and salt and pepper. Cook for a few minutes until the oatmeal has absorbed the fat. At this point, the dish can be served with meat or poultry, or it can be reserved for use as a stuffing.

⤙ BREADS ⤚

Oatmeal Bread

If you have been looking for a way to use up leftover oatmeal, this is the answer. A better reason for making it is that you like the oat flavor and the smoothness of the loaf enough to make a batch of oatmeal especially to produce it. A significant amount of wheat flour is necessary for the dough. Otherwise the bread would be very dense.

Yields
1 loaf

1 package active dry yeast
¼ cup lukewarm water (approximately 110° F.)
2 tablespoons maple syrup or honey
1 tablespoon oil or lard
1 teaspoon salt
1½ cups leftover cooked steel-cut oatmeal
    (around 110° F.) (If made fresh, let the oatmeal
    cool to the desired temperature;
    otherwise reheat it gently in a double boiler.)
¼ cup uncooked steel-cut oatmeal
2 cups flour (preferably bread flour),
    approximately

1. Dissolve the yeast in the warm water. Then stir in the maple syrup or honey and wait until yeast begins to show some life.

2. In a large mixing bowl, combine the mixture with the oil or lard, salt, and oatmeal. Beat until well blended.

3. Now work in the uncooked oatmeal and the flour, a handful at a time. This ought to produce a stiff dough that will clean the bowl. If not, add more flour until it does.

4. Knead the dough for 10 minutes on a floured board.

5. Let rise in a clean, lightly oiled bowl enclosed in a plastic bag in a warm place for about 1½ hours, or until the dough has doubled in bulk.

6. Punch down the dough, shape into a loaf, place in a lightly oiled loaf pan, enclose in a plastic bag, and let rise again until doubled in bulk, 30 to 45 minutes.

7. Preheat the oven to 375° F. Bake for 35 minutes.

8. Turn the loaf out onto a rack and let cool before slicing.

Oat Flour Rieska

Following a suggestion of Beatrice Ojakangas in *Great Whole Grain Breads* (Dutton, 1984), I decided to use oat flour instead of oatmeal for this traditional Finnish flatbread. I've also omitted any baking soda, figuring that a flatbread might as well be a flatbread.

Yields
2 flat, circular loaves

½ cup milk, approximately
¼ cup lard or oil
1 teaspoon salt
½ cup barley flour
1½ cups oat flour
1 cup flour
Melted butter or honey

1. Preheat the oven to 450° F.

2. Combine all the ingredients in a mixing bowl to make a smooth dough. If the dough seems stiff and floury, add more milk until you can work it easily.

3. Grease 2 baking sheets.

4. Divide the dough in half. Roll each half into the largest circle you can (10 to 12 inches) on a board floured with oat flour.

5. Transfer the dough circles to the baking sheets and pierce the surfaces with a fork to make a stippled pattern and to permit rapid baking.

6. Bake the "loaves" one at a time for 10 minutes, or until nicely browned on top. Traditionally these were served hot, brushed with melted butter. The cholesterol-conscious could happily substitute honey.

Oatcakes

This flatbread takes us back to the earliest days of subsistence cooking in Europe, when oats were everything. The baking soda is a later addition, which adds some lightness to the intractable oat flour. The result

is serious but addicting. After oatcakes have been baked in the primordial manner, on a griddle or in a skillet (the closest most of us can come to an open hearth and a bake stone), they will last almost forever.

Yields	2 teaspoons butter or bacon drippings
4 farls	¼ cup hot water
	1 cup oat flour, approximately
	½ teaspoon salt
	1 teaspoon baking soda

1. Melt the butter or bacon drippings in the hot water.

2. Pour over the oat flour and stir to make a stiff dough, adding the salt and baking soda as you stir.

3. Before the dough cools and becomes difficult to work with, roll or pat it out into an ⅛-inch-thick round on a board dusted with oat flour. Use oat flour liberally to prevent sticking.

4. Cut into farls (quarters) and let dry for 30 minutes. Then cook on a griddle or heavy iron skillet over medium heat until the oatcakes harden and the edges begin to curl, about 30 minutes. Turn and cook for another 5 minutes. Let cool before eating.

⤚ DESSERTS ⤙

Sweet Haggis

Savory haggis is the legendary Scottish national sausage in which sheep innards and oatmeal are cooked in the stomach of a sheep (see page 89). This so-called sweet haggis is an oatmeal pudding in which the dried fruit mimics the look of the chopped liver and lights in regular haggis. For this dish—a dandy steamed pudding—you only need your own stomach.

*Yields
8 to 10
servings*

4 cups uncooked steel-cut oatmeal

1½ cups flour

2 cups (4 sticks) butter, cut into small pieces

¼ cup brown sugar

1 cup chopped dried fruit (raisins, currants,
    or apricots)

1 tablespoon salt

1. Mix all the ingredients. Stir in enough water to make a loose sort of dough, about 4 cups.

2. Grease an 8-cup ovenproof dish. Spoon in the batter, cover tightly, and set in a shallow pan of boiling water. Place over low heat on top of the stove and cook for 3 hours, or until the oatmeal is cooked through. Replenish the boiling water as needed. Serve hot.

Oatmeal and Fig Cookies

Chewy oatmeal cookies are the best justification in the world for rolled instant oatmeal. It makes an inferior porridge, but it can be baked raw and yields a cookie that can be embellished with all manner of dried fruit (see variations below). But for me, chopped dried figs match the earthiness of the oat flavor best of all.

*Yields
4 dozen
cookies*

1 cup dried figs, finely chopped

½ cup honey

½ cup boiling water

8 tablespoons (1 stick) butter, at room
    temperature

½ cup sugar

1½ cups flour

½ teaspoon baking soda

½ teaspoon salt

1½ cups quick-cooking rolled oats

3 tablespoons milk, approximately (optional)

1. Try to buy figs that are not totally dried out. They should be easily bendable. Cut away any stems and discard. Chop fine.

2. Dissolve the honey in the boiling water. Remove from the heat and stir in the chopped figs.

3. With an electric mixer, beat the butter until it is smooth and light. Add the sugar in a stream and continue beating until you have a smooth, creamy paste.

4. Mix together all the remaining ingredients (flour, baking soda, salt, and oats) except the milk in a large bowl. Then, using a wooden spoon or spatula, beat in the fig-honey mixture and, finally, the butter-sugar mixture. The result may be too dense to roll out easily. If so, add milk or water, 1 tablespoon at a time, until you have a pliable dough. Wrap in waxed paper and chill for at least 30 minutes to facilitate rolling out.

5. Preheat the oven to 350° F.

6. Roll out the dough until it is about ⅛ inch thick. Using a 2-inch-round cookie cutter, cut about 4 dozen cookies and cook in batches on an ungreased baking sheet for approximately 12 minutes.

Variations

- Substitute raisins, currants, dried mango, chopped blanched orange peel, chopped pitted dates, or any chopped glazed fruit, for the figs.
- Spread the tops of half the rolled-out rounds with fruit preserves, place the other halves on top of them, and bake for 15, instead of 12,minutes.
- Instead of rolling out the dough, simply drop tablespoonfuls directly onto the baking sheet.
- Cut the rolled-out dough into rings or other shapes with appropriate cookie cutters.

Oaten Chocolate Chip Cookies

Oat taste from oat flour, not meal, smoothly wrapped around chocolate chips.

Yields 4 to 5 dozen cookies, depending on size

4 sticks unsalted butter
2 cups sugar
2 cups dark brown sugar
4 cups wheat flour
5 cups oat flour
1 teaspoon salt
2 teaspoons baking soda
2 teaspoons baking powder
½ pound grated semisweet chocolate
5 eggs, lightly beaten
1 teaspoon vanilla extract
1½ pounds chocolate chips
3 cups chopped walnuts

1. Preheat the oven to 375° F.

2. Cream the butter with the sugar; then add the brown sugar.

3. Sift together wheat flour, oat flour, salt, baking soda, baking powder, and grated semisweet chocolate.

4. Beat the eggs and vanilla into the sugar-butter mixture. Then work in the mixture from step 3.

5. Fold in the chocolate chips and chopped nuts.

6. Drop the batter off a soupspoon onto ungreased cookie sheets. Bake in batches, 7 or 8 minutes a batch, until the tops or edges begin to brown. Cool on a rack.

Rice (Oryza sativa)

is only the second-most popular grain,
after wheat, but it keeps billions alive, and for
our purposes, it is more interesting than wheat
because it usually reaches us as a whole grain, not pulverized
into flour. Even when rice has been converted or pre-
steamed or otherwise processed, it is still basically
the seed of a single plant variety. Wheat flour,
on the other hand, is almost never identifiable as
anything more specific than "wheat." "All-purpose"
tells the consumer almost nothing, but every rice eater
can see that she has bought long-grain or
short-grain rice. Even in the United States, now,
we can choose the aromatic Indian long-grain
basmati rice (some is grown domestically). Whole
cuisines rest on this ability to make rudimentary
biological distinctions about rice seed.
From there to connoisseurship about elite varieties
of basmati is but a short step.

✓ LONG-GRAIN RICE ✓

The Chinese Method

This is the world's most popular way of cooking rice. Compared to the Indian method (see below), cooking long-grain rice (also known as Carolina rice) the Chinese way is more energy-efficient. You boil only the amount of water that will eventually be absorbed into the swelling rice grains. The process occurs over low heat. On the other hand, the resulting rice has a slightly gummy texture. Habitués find this desirable, and it is the authentic result for Chinese and other non–Indian-Asian dishes. The rule of thumb usually given is one part rice to two parts water, by volume. That would mean for every cup of raw rice, add two cups of water. In fact, best results occur with slightly less water.

Yields
3¼ cups
cooked rice

1 cup raw long-grain (Carolina) rice
1 teaspoon salt
1¾ cups cold water

1. Put the rice, salt, and water in a saucepan. Cover and bring to a full rolling boil. Stir once with a wooden spoon, cover again, and reduce the heat to low (or whatever heat will produce a very slow simmer).

2. Cook for 15 minutes, covered. Then let stand until all the water is absorbed, about 10 minutes. The grains will be separate and fluffy.

The Indian Method

The Indian way of cooking rice is also the method practiced in the kitchens of rice plantations in the South Carolina lowlands during the days of slavery. The food historian Karen Hess argues persuasively that plantation cooks were carrying on a tradition brought from Africa on the slave ships and that it had originally come there across the Indian Ocean from India. In any case, the principle is the same: rice is added to a large quantity of boiling water and cooked over high heat for 10 minutes, drained, and then is left to stand, covered, until fully cooked. Typically, each individual grain is separate from every other.

Here is a recipe for Carolina-style rice, transcribed in the words of Goliah, slave of Robert F. W. Allston, as quoted by Hess from Charles Joyner's *Down by the Riverside: A South Carolina Slave Community* (University of Illinois, 1984):

> Fust t'ing yo' roll up yo' sleeve as high as yo' kin, en yo' tak soap en yo' wash yo' hand clean. Den you wash yo' pot clean, fill um wid col' wata en put on de fia. Now w'ile yo' wata de bile, yo' put yo' rice een a piggin [wooden pail] en yo' wash em well, den when yo' dun put salt een yo' pot, en 'e bile high, yo' put yo' rice een, en le' um bile till 'e swell, den yo' pour off de wata, en put yo' pot back o' de stove, for steam.

In modern language this can be expressed as follows:

Yields	1 quart or more water
3¼ cups	1 cup rice
cooked rice	Salt

1. Bring the water to a full rolling boil.
2. Add rice and salt and continue boiling for about 10 minutes, or until the rice is no longer translucent and can be chewed.
3. Drain the rice in a colander, return it to the pot and let stand, covered, over low heat for 10 minutes, or until tender.

Variation: If you are using basmati rice from India, it must be thoroughly rinsed and then soaked in twice its volume of lightly salted water for 30 minutes before cooking.

The Spanish Method
Rice with Pork and Fava Beans

This recipe illustrates the standard Spanish technique, which is best known from recipes for paella. The basic idea is to add rice to a combination of solid ingredients stewing in broth. The rice completely absorbs the broth precisely at the moment that it and the other ingredients are finished cooking.

My version of *arroz con magro de cerdo y habas* is adapted from *The Heritage of Spanish Cooking* by Alicia Rios and Lourdes March (Random House, 1992). It is only one of many possible illustrations of the basic Spanish way of cooking rice. Since all of them involve ingredients in addition to rice, it would make no sense to abstract an artificial "basic" recipe that would seem parallel to the basic methods above.

Yields
4 servings

¼ cup olive oil
½ pound lean pork, diced
13 ounces fresh fava beans, shelled
1 tomato (3½ ounces), peeled and finely
    chopped
1 teaspoon paprika
6 cups chicken or beef broth
Pinch of saffron
Salt
1⅓ cups medium-grain rice

1. Heat the oil in a casserole. Fry the diced pork until browned. Then add the fava beans, tomato, paprika, and the broth.

2. Cook for 15 to 20 minutes, according to the tenderness of the beans. Then add the saffron.

3. Check the seasoning and add salt to taste. Then add the rice and cook, uncovered, over medium heat for 16 to 18 minutes. Taste the rice to check that it is ready. Remove from the heat and serve immediately.

↜ SHORT-GRAIN RICE ↝

The difference between risotto and paella or paellalike dishes such as the one previously given is, perhaps, a small one viewed in a narrow, technical way. In both methods rice absorbs large quantities of broth. But the Spanish way puts an equal emphasis on the rice and the other ingredients. Risotto, as its name implies, puts rice first and usually has much more rice than it does other ingredients. You could say that risotto is more Asian in its quantitative bias toward rice, which turns other solids into a sort of garnish. The short-grain Po River Valley rice (Arborio is the best-known trademark) yields a notably chewy result. Long-grain rice cooked this way would turn to mush.

The Italian Method
Risotto with Celery

This recipe is slightly adapted from *Essentials of Classic Italian Cooking* (Knopf, 1992) by Marcella Hazan.

Yields *6 servings*	5 cups homemade beef broth (see Light Meat Stock recipe, page 129) or 1 cup canned beef broth diluted with 4 cups water 3 tablespoons butter 2 tablespoons vegetable oil ½ cup chopped onion 2 cups celery stalk, very finely diced 1 tablespoon chopped leafy tops of the celery heart Salt 2 cups Arborio or other imported Italian short-grain risotto rice Black pepper, ground fresh from the mill ⅓ cup freshly grated Parmigiano-Reggiano cheese 1 tablespoon chopped parsley

1. Bring the broth to a very slow, steady simmer on a burner near where you'll be cooking the risotto.

2. Put 2 tablespoons of the butter, the vegetable oil, and the chopped onion in a broad, sturdy pot and turn the heat to medium high. Cook and stir the onion until it becomes translucent, then add half the diced celery stalk, all the chopped leaves, and a pinch of salt. Cook for 2 to 3 minutes, stirring frequently to coat the celery well.

3. Add the rice, stirring quickly and thoroughly until the grains are coated well. Add ½ cup of the simmering broth and cook the rice, stirring constantly with a long wooden spoon, wiping the sides and bottom of the pot clean as you stir, until the liquid is gone. You must never stop stirring, and you must be sure to wipe the bottom of the pot completely clean frequently or the rice will stick to it. When there is no more liquid in the pot, add another ½ cup, continuing always to stir as before. Maintain the heat at a lively pace.

4. When the rice has cooked for 10 minutes, add the remaining diced celery and continue to stir, adding more broth, a little at a time.

5. Cook the rice until it is tender but firm to the bite, with barely enough liquid remaining to make the consistency somewhat runny. Off heat, add a few grindings of pepper, the remaining tablespoon of butter, and all the grated Parmigiano-Reggiano, and stir thoroughly until the cheese melts and clings to the rice. Taste and correct for salt. Mix in the chopped parsley. Transfer to a platter and serve promptly.

Sticky Rice

Sticky rice is universally available in Asian markets. It is meant to clump together and is valued for that special texture. On American tables it can provide a novel and appealing change.

Yields   ½ pound (about 1 cup) sticky rice
about 3 cups

1. Soak the rice overnight in enough cold water to cover.
2. Drain and rinse thoroughly.

3. Line the top of a steamer with two layers of cheesecloth. Put the rice on top and steam for 30 minutes. Serve.

∼ *BROWN RICE* ∼

Brown rice has been hulled, but it still has its bran and germ, which give it its color and its chewy, earthy taste. The nutritional reputation of brown rice rests primarily on the medical discovery that it contains B vitamins lost when brown rice is processed into white rice. People who eat only white rice develop a B-vitamin deficiency called beriberi. This is not a risk for anyone eating the diverse diet typical of modern life. Since white rice can now be bought with many of its nutrients reinstated (converted rice), the only reason to eat brown rice is aesthetic, because you like its gutsier taste and texture.

Basic Recipe

Yields
6 servings

1 cup brown rice
1 teaspoon salt
2¼ cups water

1. Mix the rice and salt together with the water in a 3-cup saucepan. Cover and bring to a boil.
2. Reduce the heat to low, cover, and cook at a slow simmer for 40 minutes. Remove from heat and let stand, covered, for 10 minutes. All the water will be absorbed, and the rice will be light, fluffy, and a light brown color.

CONGEE
(Pai Chou)

This is the rice porridge that sustains more than a billion Chinese at breakfast or when they are sick. (Chinese chicken soup!) It is made from so-called sticky, or glutinous, rice. This oval-shaped rice has no gluten, but the name has "stuck." After the rice is cooked, a solid ingredient is often added: a vegetable, fish, or meat.

For non-Chinese, congee may require a certain adjustment of attitude, especially if served as a traditional breakfast. But at other times of the day it offers a change of pace. The smooth, comforting texture ingratiates itself quickly.

Plain Congee

Yields
4 cups

4 quarts water
1½ cups sticky rice
Soy sauce

1. Bring the water to a full boil. Wash the rice several times, add it to the boiling water, lower the heat to medium, and simmer for 40 minutes. Turn the heat to low, cover, and cook for 1 hour and 15 minutes, or until the rice is very soft and the water is thick.

2. Stir in the soy sauce to taste and serve very hot. Congee can be reheated.

Chicken Congee

This is real Chinese chicken soup—comfort food your mother never dreamed of.

Yields
4 servings

4 quarts chicken stock
1½ cups sticky rice
2 to 3 cups trimmed leftover chicken, shredded
    or chopped

1. Bring the stock to a boil and proceed as for plain congee.

2. When the rice is cooked, add the leftover chicken. Heat through and serve very hot.

Congee "Haddie"

Chinese tradition combines congee with fish, so there is nothing outré about this Sino-Scottish hybrid.

Yields
4 servings

1 pound smoked haddock (finnan haddie)
4 cups cooked Plain Congee (see page 106)

1. Add the haddock to the hot congee. Simmer, covered, until the fish flakes and begins to fall apart.

2. Serve very hot.

Ham Congee

If eternity really is best defined as two people and a ham, here is a fine way to pass all that time.

Yields
2 servings

½ pound ham, preferably country ham or
Spanish *jamón serrano,* chopped
2 cups cooked Plain Congee (see page 106)

1. Add the ham to the cooked congee. Simmer briefly, to heat the ham.

2. Serve very hot.

Turkey Congee

For the morning after Thanksgiving.

Yields
4 servings

4 cups chopped leftover turkey
4 cups cooked Plain Congee (see page 106)

1. Add the turkey to the hot congee.

2. Serve very hot.

Risi e Bisi Cinesi
(Italian Rice and Pea Soup, in a Chinese Mood)

Bisi is Venetian dialect for peas, and the original dish behind this mock-Chinese improvisation is traditionally served in Venice on April 25, the feast of the city's patron saint, Mark. Rice is the staple of the Veneto, and sweet spring peas would be just in season then. If you want to taste this soup in its pristine form, substitute a medium onion for the scallions and eliminate the tree-ear mushrooms, the hot pepper oil, and the rice vinegar.

Yields
6 servings
	2 tablespoons oil
	4 scallions, trimmed and chopped
	6 cups water or light meat stock (see recipe,
	    page 129)
	1 cup risotto rice
	1 cup tree-ear mushrooms, soaked for 30 minutes
	    in hot water and trimmed
	3½ cups peas
	Salt and pepper
	Szechuan hot pepper oil
	Chinese rice vinegar

1. Heat the oil in a 4 to 6-quart pot. Add the chopped scallions and stir-fry for a few minutes over medium heat until wilted.

2. Add the water or broth. Bring to a boil, add the rice, lower the heat, cover, and simmer gently for 15 minutes, or until the rice is al dente.

3. Add the tree-ear mushrooms and simmer for 5 minutes, uncovered. Then add the peas and simmer another 5 minutes.

4. Season to taste with salt and pepper. Pass the hot pepper oil and rice vinegar. Let each person adjust the heat of the soup by adding a little oil and then tempering it with the vinegar, as they might with Szechuan hot-and-sour soup.

Stuffed Grape Leaves

Stuffed grape leaves are the tamales of the Levant. An otherwise useless leaf is turned to account as a miniature cooking vessel inside which a staple grain (rice, usually, instead of the cornmeal used to stuff tamales in Mexico) and other ingredients are cooked. The difference is that the grape leaves are edible, whereas the corn husks or banana leaves normally used to wrap tamales are not.

Grape leaves themselves are available canned. These are ready to use once the brine they come in has been rinsed off. Wild or cultivated grape leaves are widely available and should be picked in May or June, when they are tender. If you have a vine at your disposal, it is child's play to pull off two dozen leaves and blanch them briefly in boiling water to soften them. Then snip off the stems and proceed as with the store-bought kind.

Yields
24 stuffed
grape leaves

2 cups chopped onion
¼ cup olive oil
¼ cup pine nuts
½ cup rice
¼ cup currants
¼ teaspoon ground clove
Salt and pepper
2 dozen grape leaves, rinsed if canned or
    blanched if fresh
4 cloves garlic, slivered
1 cup chicken stock or water, approximately

1. Sauté the onion in the olive oil over medium heat until the onion is completely softened. Stir in the pine nuts and cook briefly until lightly browned. Then stir in the rice and coat with the oil. Remove from heat.

2. Stir in the currants, clove, and salt and pepper to taste.

3. Stuff the grape leaves. The classic method is to lay the leaf, smooth side down, on the counter. Put 1 tablespoon of stuffing at the base of the leaf (stem end) and, starting from the base, roll some of the leaf over the stuffing. Now fold the sides over the stuffing and continue rolling from

the base end until the leaf is completely rolled up into a loose package. (The rice will expand in cooking.) Continue in this manner until all the stuffing is used up.

4. In a large saucepan, cover the bottom with flat leaves: this keeps the rolled-up leaves from sticking. Then arrange the rolled-up leaves seam down in alternating layers (one layer north-south, the next east-west), interspersing slivers of garlic as you go. Add enough chicken stock or water to cover. Set a plate on top of the leaves to hold them in place. Bring the stock or water to a boil, reduce the heat, cover, and simmer for 45 minutes to 2 hours, until the leaves are tender.

Variation

Grape Leaves Stuffed with Rice and Lamb

*Yields
24 stuffed
grape leaves*

2 cups chopped scallions
¼ cup olive oil
1 pound ground lamb (or beef or pork)
½ cup rice
¼ teaspoon ground cinnamon
Salt and pepper
2 dozen grape leaves, rinsed if canned or
    blanched if fresh
4 cloves garlic, slivered
1 cup chicken stock or water, approximately

1. Sauté the scallions in the olive oil over medium heat until they are completely softened. Stir in the ground meat and cook until the individual grains of meat have browned. Then stir in the rice and coat with the oil. Remove from heat.

2. Stir in the cinnamon and season to taste with salt and pepper. Then continue as in the recipe above.

Arroz con Costillas de Cerdo, Coliflor y Alubias
(Rice with Pork Chops, Cauliflower, and Beans)

This recipe is adapted from *El Libro de la Paella y de los Arroces* by Lourdes March (Madrid: Allianza, 1985).

Yields
4 servings

¼ pound white beans, soaked overnight
2 quarts water
2 tablespoons olive oil
½ pound pork chops, boned and thinly sliced
2 cloves garlic, peeled
¼ pound tomatoes, peeled and chopped
½ teaspoon black pepper, plus more to taste
Pinch of saffron, plus more to taste
Salt
½ pound cauliflower
1 cup medium-grain rice (DO NOT WASH RICE)

1. Put the beans in a pot with the water, bring to a boil, reduce the heat, and simmer for 30 minutes.

2. While the beans continue to simmer, heat the oil in a skillet and brown the pork slices over medium-high heat. When the pork has taken on an appealing brown color, add the whole garlic cloves and the chopped tomatoes, as well as ½ teaspoon pepper. Simmer for 2 minutes and then stir into the beans.

3. Let the beans cook for another 20 minutes. Then add a pinch of saffron, salt to taste, and cover the pot. Reduce the heat and cook at a slow simmer, covered, until the beans are almost cooked.

4. Correct the seasoning. Then break the cauliflower up into flowerets and add them to the pot. Raise the heat to high. Let the pot come to a boil. Throw in the rice all at once, stir quickly, and cook, uncovered, over

medium heat, for 16 to 18 minutes. There will still be liquid, because this is a *caldoso,* or rice stew.

5. Remove from heat and let rest for a minute or two before serving.

FRIED RICE

Until I went to the Philippines, I always assumed that fried rice was a dish made from scratch, for which white rice was first steamed, then fried in a wok along with hundreds of additional ingredients that dressed up the basic dish and gave it variety. The truth, all over Asia, is that fried rice is an ingenious way of using up leftover rice. Obviously, in rice-eating cultures it was inevitable that something be figured out to do with the tons of rice that weren't consumed immediately after steaming. Resteaming would leave the rice gummy. But frying reseparated the grains and saved the precious food. The genius of millions of cooks took it from there and evolved a multinational minicuisine. Here are a few examples. All of them use leftover cooked rice that has been stored in a covered container to prevent dehydration.

Chinese Fried Rice

This will make a light meal for one person. To make the dish in larger quantities, you will most likely have to steam rice from scratch in advance. (Few of us cook rice in such large quantities that we have several cups left over at any given time.) Then you will want to hold the rice for several hours or overnight to get the optimal texture: separate, barely moist grains.

Yields
1 serving

2 scallions
2 tablespoons oil
1 egg, lightly beaten
2 cups leftover rice
Soy sauce

1. Trim the scallions. Then slice into rounds, dividing them into white and green.

2. Heat the oil in a skillet or wok until it smokes. Toss in the white scallion rounds and stir a few times. Then pour in the egg. As soon as it begins to set, stir in the rice and continue stirring for several minutes until the rice is heated through and any clumps have been broken up.

3. Remove from heat and stir in soy sauce to taste. Transfer the fried rice to a bowl and sprinkle with green scallion rounds before serving.

Variations: In step 2, just after the scallions have wilted, add 1 to 1½ cups of any of the following: ground beef, veal, or pork; diced eggplant; sliced mushrooms. Any of these ingredients can be mixed and, even better, marinated for 1 hour with cayenne pepper to taste, salt, black pepper, 1 tablespoon oil, and 1 teaspoon ground coriander or ground cardamom. Stir-fry with the scallions for 3 minutes, or until the beef or other solid ingredients have cooked sufficiently—as you would eat them. Then pour in the egg and proceed with step 2 above.

Filipino Garlic Rice

This is the standard Filipino breakfast. If you are in the mood, you might want to pep it up even more than the garlic already has with a dash of hot sauce.

Yields	2 tablespoons oil
2 servings	2 cups leftover rice
	3 cloves garlic, peeled and minced

1. Heat the oil in a wok or skillet until it begins to smoke.
2. Add the rice and stir-fry with the garlic until the garlic has browned and the rice grains are heated through and glistening.

Fried Brown Rice with Gizzards and Beets

For my taste, brown rice takes more time than it is worth, either aesthetically or nutritionally—*if* you are substituting it for plain boiled white rice as a side starch for a conventional main dish. The 45 minutes or so of cooking can easily become the main timing obstacle in the orchestration of the various components of the meal. How much better then, since brown rice is worth having and does submit to rough treatment much more graciously than white, to cook it the day before in real quantity, when you are under no pressure whatever, and then reheat it as fried rice. This combination pits the dark and chewy characters of the rice and the carefully trimmed and demembraned gizzards against the bright, soft lightness of the beets. Everything in this recipe can be prepared well ahead of time and reheated in a trice when you are ready to assemble the dish and serve it, as a first "pasta" course or as a main course, perhaps following a mussel soup or raw shellfish or a seafood salad.

Yields	2 tablespoons oil
4 to 6 servings	2 cloves garlic, peeled and minced
	6 chicken gizzards, peeled and thinly sliced
	4 large beets, boiled until tender, peeled and diced
	2 cups leftover brown rice, boiled
	Salt and pepper
	1 dozen beet greens, well washed and blanched
	(optional)

1. Heat the oil in a skillet or wok. Add the garlic and stir until it begins to brown. Then add the gizzard slices. Stir-fry 2 minutes.

2. Add the beets and rice all at once. Stir until well mixed and heated through. Take care to break up any clumps of rice.

3. Season with salt and pepper. Arrange the rice on a bed of well-washed beet greens, if handy, and serve immediately.

Variations: Heat the oil in a skillet and toss 2 cups of roughly chopped smoked salmon or sturgeon for 2 minutes. Then add the rice and stir until heated through. Garnish with chopped scallions or coriander leaves.

Alternatively, stir together all the ingredients in this variation (including the oil and the scallions or coriander) and combine with 2 lightly beaten egg yolks. Transfer to a greased 6-cup soufflé mold or to several smaller baba or custard molds. Bake in a 350° F. oven for 30 minutes.

Fried Glutinous Rice

Yan-kit So, the London food writer, says in her *Classic Chinese Cookbook* (Dorling Kindersley, 1984, 1993): "Glutinous rice is usually steamed or boiled, but because it is very starchy, these methods of cooking can make it into a rather stodgy food. Stir-frying glutinous rice from its raw state until cooked through, however, makes the rice much lighter and more fragrant in taste."

Her technique is a hybrid of stir-frying and risotto: solid, non-rice ingredients are fried in oil in a wok; then the rice is added and allowed to absorb several small additions of water.

This is a cross-cultural response to Yan-kit's basic recipe, which she garnishes with shrimp, Chinese mushrooms, and wind-dried Chinese duck-liver sausage.

Yields	1 pound (2½ cups) glutinous rice
4 servings	4 short ribs or 6 spareribs
	2 tablespoons oil
	2 carrots, scraped and diced
	2 ribs celery, trimmed and diced
	1 tablespoon fennel seeds
	Salt and pepper

1. Rinse the rice in 3 or 4 changes of water. Drain and then soak in several quarts of cold water for several hours.

2. Cut the meat off the bones and reserve. Discard the bones or save for stock or soup.

3. In a wok or skillet, heat the oil until it smokes. Stir-fry the carrots and celery for 2 minutes. Add the meat and fennel seeds and continue stir-frying for another few minutes, just long enough to brown the meat.

4. Lower the heat to medium and add the rice, stirring vigorously to prevent burning. After a minute or so, stir in ¼ cup water. Cover and cook for 2 minutes. Repeat this procedure, allowing the water to be absorbed each time, until the rice is cooked through. Season with salt and pepper and serve.

Khao Pad
(Thai Fried Rice)

A briskly spiced Thai variation on an idea that feeds millions—really billions—every day in Asia.

Yields
2 servings

2 tablespoons oil
2 cloves garlic, peeled and minced
2 teaspoons cayenne pepper
¼ pound chopped chicken or peeled shrimp
    or chopped flesh of 1 pineapple
2 cups leftover rice
1 tablespoon Thai fish sauce
1 tablespoon soy sauce
1 teaspoon sugar
Coriander leaves, for garnish

1. Heat the oil in a wok or skillet until it smokes. Add the garlic and stir-fry until it begins to brown. Add the cayenne pepper along with the selected main ingredient (chicken, shrimp, or pineapple). Stir-fry for a few seconds.

2. Add the rice and stir briefly. Then add the fish sauce, soy sauce, and sugar. Continue stir-frying until the main ingredient has cooked and the rice has reheated. Remove from heat, garnish with coriander leaves, and serve.

Rice Salad Basic Recipe

Here is another ingenious way to use up leftover rice. Or, let's say, that was how rice salad must have originated. But since the idea is so strong and can include so many different other foods, since it suits a summer lunch menu so well and answers to the modern taste for light low-fat dishes so perfectly, many people will make rice from scratch and let it cool, just in order to serve rice salad.

In her wonderful survey, *The Rice Book* (St. Martin's Press, 1994), my friend Sri Owen comes up with six variations on this theme: among them, rice salad with asparagus, with curried eggs, with avocado and smoked salmon, with stuffed squid.

This is a basic recipe, with some other suggested garnishes. In every case, brown rice can be substituted for white rice. It will just take longer to cook (see Basic Brown Rice recipe, page 105).

Yields
3 to 4 servings

3 cups leftover white or brown rice, or 1 cup rice cooked from scratch in a large quantity of lightly salted water (see page 101 for method)
3 sprigs fresh thyme or 1 teaspoon ground
1 tablespoon chopped chives
3 tablespoons olive oil
2 tablespoons red wine vinegar or lemon juice

1. Combine all ingredients in a serving bowl.
2. Serve at room temperature.

Variation

Favas and Ham

Yields
6 servings

6 cups water
1 tablespoon salt
3 pounds favas (or limas)
2 tablespoons olive oil
2 large cloves garlic, peeled and chopped
½ pound country ham or Spanish *jamón serrano,* roughly chopped
3 cups leftover white or brown rice or 1 cup white rice cooked from scratch

1. Bring the water to a full boil with salt. Meanwhile, hull the favas.

2. Blanch the favas in the boiling water for about 1 minute. Drain and let cool for a few minutes; then pull off the outer skins from all the beans. Unless these beans are very young, fresh, and tender, they will be dramatically better without their skins. The work is worth it.

3. Heat the olive oil in a heavy skillet. Sauté the garlic over medium heat until it begins to brown. Discard. Add the ham bits and sauté until heated through. Then stir in the favas and continue stirring regularly until the favas have heated through and lost their starchiness.

4. Let cool to lukewarm and arrange over the rice in a serving bowl. At the table, toss and serve.

Khitchri

This is the Indian equivalent of chicken soup—rice and lentils (usually moong dhal, which will remind you at first of split peas) cooked until soft but not disintegrated: the grains hold their shape. In the classic preparation the dish is finished with milk curds. If you wish, you can make your own curds by stirring a tablespoon of yogurt into a quart of lukewarm (110° F.) milk and letting it stand until the milk separates into a solid portion, or the curds, and a gray liquid, the whey. Pour off the whey or feed it to a pet. Substitute the curds for the milk-and-cream mixture below.

Khitchri makes an excellent breakfast dish and can certainly be offered to a sick friend or family member tired of tea and toast. But it will most likely work for you best, and most frequently, as a light main course or as a side dish with broiled fish or meat. Khitchri was also adopted long ago by Anglo-Indian cooks and transformed into kedgeree, turmeric-colored rice tossed with smoked haddock or kippers, the centerpiece of breakfast in Imperial India.

Yields
6 servings

1 cup basmati rice
1 cup moong dhal or other lentil variety
    (see Note, below)
2 tablespoons salt
2 medium onions, peeled and sliced
½ cup ghee or clarified butter (see box,
    page 121)
¼ teaspoon ground cardamom
1 teaspoon ground cumin
1 cup milk
½ cup heavy cream

1. Put the rice and dhal in a large bowl. Rinse in several changes of cold water. Then soak for 2 hours with 1 tablespoon of the salt in enough cold water to cover the rice and dhal.

2. In a heavy 4-quart saucepan, sauté the onions in the ghee or clari-

fied butter until nicely browned. Remove with a slotted spoon and set aside, leaving the ghee or clarified butter in the saucepan.

3. Preheat the oven to 300° F.

4. Set the saucepan over medium heat. Drain the rice and dhal, put them in the saucepan, stir in the cardamom and cumin, and stir-fry for several minutes until the butter is completely absorbed and the rice glistens. Add 1½ cups water and boil, uncovered, until the water is almost completely absorbed, about 12 minutes.

5. Meanwhile, combine the milk and cream in a saucepan. Set over medium heat. When it foams, reduce the heat and stir into the rice mixture.

6. Cover and place in the oven for 20 minutes, or until the liquid has been absorbed.

Note: If you use ordinary lentils or any other pulse besides moong dhal, cook them separately in a generous amount of boiling water until they have softened enough to be edible. Then mix in with the rice and continue as indicated in step 4. This is necessary because many lentil types (pulses) will take longer to cook than the rice. They can be prepared ahead of time.

To prepare ghee, melt 1 pound of unsalted butter and boil until the milk solids have browned and fallen to the bottom of the now darkened butter. Pour through a fine strainer and reserve.

To prepare clarified butter, melt a pound of unsalted butter, remove from heat, and carefully skim off the white milk solids floating on top of the butter. Then strain through a fine strainer and reserve.

Laab
(Thai Ground Chicken Patty with Browned Ground Rice)

This is a Thai-inspired alternative to the hamburger, low in fat and exotic in taste. Anyone with access to Southeast Asian ingredients should try this NOW. The browned (not brown) rice is not included as a "hamburger helper," but to add complexity to the texture of the dish. If you like this ingredient, you might find it convenient to prepare a larger quantity so as to have some around for the future.

Yields
4 servings

¼ cup long-grain rice
1 pound chicken breast, skinned and boned
½ cup lemon juice
¾ cup chicken stock
½ cup Thai (or Vietnamese) fish sauce
1 teaspoon to 1 tablespoon cayenne pepper, to taste
1 medium onion, finely chopped
2 stalks lemongrass, finely sliced
4 kaffir lime leaves, minced
1 scallion, chopped
Coriander leaves, for garnish

1. Put the rice in a skillet large enough to hold all the grains in a single layer. Set over medium heat, all by itself, and toast until the rice turns a pale brown, shaking the pan periodically to make this happen evenly. Then grind the rice roughly in a clean coffee or spice grinder.

2. Put the chicken through the coarse blade of a manual meat grinder or process with the steel blade of a food processor, using the ON/OFF button to produce a rough grind. Alternatively, you could chop the chicken with a knife.

3. Combine the lemon juice, chicken stock, fish sauce, and cayenne pepper in a large skillet. Bring to a boil. Add the chicken and stir-fry until the meat turns opaque. Add the onion, lemongrass, lime leaves, browned rice, and scallion. Continue stir-frying just long enough to soften the onion. Garnish with coriander leaves and serve immediately.

Basmati Salmon Rice Pulao

Pulao is the most widespread name in India for a rice casserole of global significance. From Delhi to Charleston, pilau/pilaf/perloo cooks stew rice and a galaxy of other solid ingredients with broth or plain water until the water is absorbed, the rice is tender, and the other ingredients are fully cooked. Risotto is an Italian special case in which the liquid is added in small increments to short-grain rice, which is stirred constantly, producing an especially elegant unctuousness. This example of the pulao family is Indian in inspiration and uses superlative Indian long-grain basmati rice. The liquid, as in other pilafs, is added all at once, and the rice in the completed dish is light and separate, grain from grain.

Yields
6 servings

1 cup basmati rice
2 tablespoons butter
6 cloves
1 teaspoon ground cinnamon
1 teaspoon caraway seeds
½ teaspoon turmeric
Salt
2 pounds salmon fillets, skinned and cut into
    1-inch triangles

1. Rinse the basmati rice thoroughly and then leave it to soak in 3 cups cold water for at least 30 minutes.

2. Meanwhile, melt the butter in a large, heavy skillet. Reduce the heat to very low and put in the cloves, cinnamon, caraway seeds, and turmeric. Stir-fry for 2 minutes. Then drain the rice and stir it into the spices along with 1 teaspoon salt. Stir-fry for another minute or two, to coat the rice grains with butter and spices. Pour in 1¾ cups hot water. Mix thoroughly until the water boils. Then reduce the heat to low, cover, and cook for 10 minutes.

3. Distribute the salmon pieces on top of the rice mixture. Cover and continue cooking another 10 minutes, or until the salmon is just cooked through and the water is all absorbed. Remove from heat and test the rice.

If it is not yet tender enough for you, replace the cover and let stand, off heat for another 5 to 10 minutes, testing occasionally.

Variations: Indian practice suggests a vast number of "main" ingredients for pulao. (Of course, rice is really the main ingredient, so perhaps the best word is garnish.) They include everything from raisins to cauliflowerets to diced potatoes, about 1½ cups of each. All three of these are added to the rice at the start of the steaming process.

Lourdes March's Paella Valenciana

This recipe is adapted from one distributed at the 1988 Oxford Food Symposium.

Lourdes March is a native of Valencia, the rice capital of Spain and the birthplace of paella. She is a famous cookbook author in Spain, and although she now lives in Madrid, she remains a paella missionary, preaching the authentic paella gospel to whoever will listen. Her sermon is this: Paella is an outgrowth of the ecology of the Valencian rice fields. Its authentic ingredients include Valencian medium-grain rice, small barnyard animals (chicken and rabbit) that rice farmers raise on the side, and the snails that populate the fields themselves.

On top of everything else, paella is supposed to be cooked outdoors over a constantly replenished, modest fire made of vine cuttings or other small pieces of wood, in a flat circular steel pan—the paella that gives the dish its name.

This all means that restaurant paellas produced on stovetops with a mixture of seafood in them are not real paellas but travesties, no matter how delicious they may turn out. At the very least, they should be sold as something else, zarzuelas for example.

Here, then, is a real paella, in which the slowly simmering broth is absorbed into the rice along with the flavor of the fire and the juices of the meats.

Yields
10 servings

½ pound large dried lima beans, soaked in cold water overnight
1 cup olive oil

One 3 to 3½-pound chicken, cut into serving
  pieces
One 2 to 2½-pound rabbit, cut into serving
  pieces
1¾ pounds green beans, trimmed
½ pound tomatoes, peeled and finely chopped
2 teaspoons paprika
2 sprigs rosemary or 12 snails
Salt
Saffron
5 cups medium-grain rice (available where
  Hispanic ingredients are sold; do not wash)

1. Boil the limas in 1 quart water for 1 hour. Drain, reserving both the limas and their cooking liquid.

2. Meanwhile, pour the olive oil into a paella pan about 18 inches in diameter. Place over the *paellero,* or barbecue, of vine cuttings or other small wood pieces and level it properly. Set the fire and light. When the oil is hot, fry the chicken and rabbit pieces, turning them over frequently. Then sauté the green beans and tomatoes with the paprika for a few minutes. Let the fire die down a bit and immediately afterward pour in 5 quarts water and also the cooking liquid from the limas.

3. Add more wood to bring the mixture to a boil. Then let the fire die back to medium and maintain the fire at this level by adding a little wood as necessary, until the meat and other ingredients are cooked, 45 to 60 minutes, depending on the tenderness of the meat.

4. Add the rosemary or the snails. Taste the stock and add salt if necessary. Add a small amount of saffron.

5. Check the broth level. It should be just at the height of the paella's handle rivets. Remove if there is too much or add boiling water if there is too little. Then increase the intensity of the fire and add the rice. Spread it as evenly as possible. Simmer, uncovered, for 10 minutes; then reduce the heat to medium and cook gently for 8 to 10 minutes more. Toward the end, taste the rice. When it is al dente, slide the paella to one side of the fire and let it stand for 5 minutes so that the rice grains end up loose, unbroken, and done with superb flavor. Now only your fellow diners' praises are required.

Jambalaya

This is the all-purpose rice pilaf of Cajun Louisiana. It is in the same family of dishes as paella—meat and seafood stewed together in broth with rice. But jambalaya is country food, and because it is Cajun, it starts with a roux—flour browned in fat—for color, consistency, and extra flavor. This is hearty food for a crowd.

Yields 12 to 14 servings

6 tablespoons oil
6 pounds chicken, cut up
Salt and pepper
6 tablespoons flour
3 cloves garlic, minced
2 pounds kielbasa or other smoked sausage
    or ham, roughly chopped
4 medium onions, peeled and chopped
2 green bell peppers, trimmed, seeded, and
    chopped
6 cups tomatoes, peeled and chopped
3 sprigs fresh thyme or 1 teaspoon dried
4 cups long-grain rice
6 cups chicken broth
Hot sauce, cayenne pepper, or red pepper
    flakes, to taste, starting with 1 teaspoon
3 pounds shrimp, shelled

1. Heat the oil in a 16-inch heavy skillet or an 8-quart Dutch oven. Sprinkle the chicken pieces generously with salt and pepper and brown a few at a time. Set aside.

2. Make sure the mixture of fat and oil remaining in the skillet has cooled. Then set the pan over low heat and stir in the flour. Continue stirring until the flour turns a dark brown but does NOT burn. This is a brown roux, the basis of Cajun cooking.

3. Immediately, stir in the garlic, kielbasa or smoked sausage or ham, onions, peppers, and tomatoes. Raise the heat to medium and cook, uncovered, stirring from time to time, for about 10 minutes, or until the

peppers have softened. Stir in the thyme, rice, and chicken broth. Bring to a boil, reduce the heat to medium-low, cover, and cook for about 15 minutes.

4. Add the hot sauce, cayenne pepper, or hot pepper flakes until the taste is right. Stir in the shrimp and continue cooking, covered, until the liquid has been completely absorbed and the rice is tender, about 10 minutes.

Pilaf with Giblets and Mushrooms

Every time you roast a chicken, take the giblets (in my urban universe they tend to come neatly packaged in paper or plastic inside the cavity) and freeze them. When you have four packages, you are ready to make the chicken stock that will be the cooking liquid for this pilaf (which is rice cooked in stock instead of water). If you have access to wild mushrooms, chanterelles or porcini are excellent companions for the giblets.

Yields 4 servings as a main course, 8 as a side dish

Giblets (necks, gizzards, hearts, and livers) from 4 chickens
1 large onion, peeled and sliced
2 cloves garlic, finely chopped
4 cups water
2 cups long-grain rice
Salt and pepper
2 cups chopped mushrooms
2 sprigs fresh thyme or ½ teaspoon dried

1. In a large, heavy pan, combine the giblets with the onion slices, garlic, and water. Bring to a boil and simmer very slowly for 1 hour. (Remove livers after 10 minutes and reserve.)

2. Remove the solid ingredients from the stock with a slotted spoon. Discard the necks. Thinly slice the other giblets, including the livers, and return them to the stock. Stir in the remaining ingredients, bring to a boil, reduce to a slow simmer, cover, and cook for 15 minutes, or until the liquid has been completely absorbed.

RISOTTO

Whole books have been devoted to this extremely versatile northern Italian exploitation of the virtues of the rice of the Po River Valley. This medium-to-short-grain variety has the special virtue of being able to absorb large quantities of liquid, a little at a time, without turning to mush. Instead, the kernels cling together while retaining a sticky, chewy quality—the equivalent of al dente in pasta. Much has been made about the need for extreme care and finesse in the preparation of risotto, and these caveats have not been misplaced so much as overdone. Almost anyone can prepare a fine risotto with a little patience and with twenty minutes or so to spare of reasonably undivided attention.

It is essential that you acquire the appropriate rice. (The leading brand is Arborio, but the best is Carnaroli. Other well-known names include Vialone Nano and Maratelli. Spanish medium-grain rice sold for paella is also appropriate.) The other essential ingredient is usually, but by no means always, a light meat stock. The point is to make the rice absorb the flavor and richness of the stock, but not to be overwhelmed by it, since risottos almost invariably include other ingredients, usually cooked with the rice, to provide special flavor accents. The broth is primarily a means of heightening the clinging, sticky texture of the finished rice. It is a servant of the risotto idea, not a sauce or a separate actor meant to be sharply distinguishable on its own.

The most famous risotto comes from Milan, *risotto alla milanese,* in which the basic dish is colored yellow and miraculously flavored with saffron. But this is only the beginning of what can be done. The risotto idea can encompass almost any ingredient, from fennel to squid. Indeed, risotto is a constant invitation to a cook to try something new.

In the variations that follow, I always specify a quantity sufficient for six people, since the concentrated stove time required is too great to make such last-minute cooking worthwhile in our world unless more than just a few mouths are served. (Reheated risotto is baneful.) I am also supposing that these risottos—which all use meat stock—will be main courses except at the most sumptuous meals. Once you get the hang of it, you can easily invent your own risottos.

Light Meat Stock

Yields
3 to 4 quarts

4 pounds beef or veal, including scraps and
    some bones
4 stalks celery, chopped
2 medium onions, peeled and quartered
2 carrots, scraped and cut into rounds

1. Put all the ingredients in a large, heavy pot. Do not brown the meat: this is a light meat stock.

2. Add enough cold water to go 2 inches above the ingredients. Bring to a boil, lower the heat, and simmer very slowly for 3 to 4 hours, making sure the solid ingredients are always covered with water.

3. Strain and discard the solid ingredients, which will no longer have any attraction as food. The broth can be used immediately. But if you have time, cool it to room temperature and refrigerate. Fat will solidify at the top and can be removed. If you store the stock in the refrigerator, reboil every couple of days. Or freeze.

Basic Meat Stock Risotto
(Risotto in Bianco)

This pure dish is topped with slices of white truffle in Italy in the fall. By itself, it goes brilliantly with osso buco or other meat dishes. As a main course, it should be served with a colorful vegetable; for example, sautéed fava beans, braised radicchio, or Corn with Okra and Tomato (see recipe, page 65).

Yields
6 servings

6 cups light meat stock (see recipe, above)
6 tablespoons butter
1 medium onion, peeled and finely chopped
2 cups medium-grain risotto rice (see page 128)
Salt and pepper
1 cup ground or grated Parmesan cheese

1. Bring the stock to a boil, reduce the heat, and let simmer very slowly.

2. In a heavy 4-quart pot, melt all but 1 tablespoon of the butter over medium heat. When the foam subsides, add the onion. Sauté until onion is translucent. Stir in the rice and keep stirring until all the grains are coated.

3. Add 1 cup of simmering stock, raise the heat, and simmer vigorously. Stir constantly to keep the rice from sticking to the pan. When the first cup of stock has all but evaporated, add another. Continue as before, adding more stock until the rice is done: not mushy but clinging and chewy. This will take at least 20 minutes, probably a bit more. If you run out of stock, continue with boiling water.

4. After the risotto has been absorbing stock for 10 to 12 minutes, you should taste the rice and add salt and pepper to taste.

5. When the rice is done, stir in ¾ cup of the Parmesan cheese and the remaining tablespoon of butter. Cover for a minute or so, to let the cheese melt. Stir to make the rice *mantecato* (an untranslatable Italian word meaning "to beat until smooth as whipped butter") and transfer to a serving dish. Pass the remaining Parmesan.

Risotto alla Milanese

Basic risotto with saffron is the signature dish of Milan, especially when served with osso buco. The marrow is an echo of the marrow pulled out of the osso buco bones with a narrow fork. *Risotto alla milanese* can also be served as a first course, or with veal chops.

Yields *6 servings*	6 cups light meat stock (see recipe, page 129) 6 tablespoons butter 1 medium onion, peeled and finely chopped 2 cups medium-grain risotto rice (see previous recipe) ⅔ teaspoon saffron threads 3 ounces beef marrow, chopped (optional) Salt and pepper 1 cup ground Parmesan cheese

1. Proceed as in steps 1 through 3 in the previous recipe.

2. After the process of stock absorption has begun, pulverize the saffron using a mortar and pestle. Dissolve the saffron in a bit of stock and add it to the risotto after the rice has been absorbing stock for 10 to 12 minutes. At this point, you should try the rice, stir in the marrow, if desired, and add salt and pepper to taste.

3. When the risotto is done, stir in ¾ cup of the Parmesan and the remaining butter, as in the previous recipe. Pass the remaining Parmesan.

Risotto with Nettles
(With thanks to Anna del Conte)

Nettles (*Urtica dioica*) are an Old World weed brought to America with colonization. They sting if you touch them; yet when handled carefully, their tender spring shoots boil down like spinach but have a more delicate taste. They impart this flavor and a green tinge to risotto. Cooking completely de-stings them.

Yields	1½ pounds nettle shoots
6 servings	Salt
	6 tablespoons unsalted butter
	3 shallots or 1 medium onion, very finely chopped
	6 cups light meat stock (see recipe, page 129)
	2 cups Arborio rice
	⅓ cup heavy cream
	⅔ cup freshly grated Parmesan cheese

1. Wearing work gloves, pick the leaves and shoots off the nettles and discard the stalks. Wash in 2 or 3 changes of water. (Be sure to wear rubber gloves.) Put the nettles in a saucepan with 1 teaspoon salt and boil over high heat until cooked. You don't need to add any water; as with spinach, the water that comes from the leaves is enough. When completely wilted and softened, drain, reserving the liquid. Set aside, keeping the nettles in a colander set over the bowl containing the nettle water.

2. Melt all but 1 tablespoon of the butter in a heavy 4-quart saucepan. Sauté the shallots or onion in butter very gently until translucent.

3. Bring the stock to a boil, reduce the heat, and simmer.

4. Squeeze all the liquid out of the nettles into the bowl. Chop coarsely and add to the shallots. Sauté for 1 minute, stirring constantly, then add the rice and stir briefly to coat all the grains.

5. Pour 1 cup of the nettle water into the simmering stock. Then proceed as in Basic Meat Stock Risotto (page 129).

6. When the rice is done, remove the pan from the heat, add the cream, the remaining butter, and half the cheese. Leave it to rest for a couple of minutes, covered, and then stir. Transfer the risotto to a heated dish and serve at once, passing the remaining cheese separately.

Risotto with Potatoes
(With thanks to Massimo Alberini)

Starch on starch may strike you initially as overkill, but this hearty combination is in fact a truly ingenious mix of typically chewy risotto rice kernels with velvety potato purée. The broth perfumes the whole dish. The parsley gives it a flash of green.

Yields *6 servings*	4 to 5 large Idaho or other baking potatoes, peeled and diced
	2 tablespoons butter
	2 medium onions, peeled and finely chopped
	2 tablespoons diced pancetta
	2 cups Arborio or other risotto rice

6 cups boiling light meat stock (see recipe,
   page 129)
2 tablespoons chopped parsley
⅔ cup grated Parmesan cheese

1. Rinse the potatoes in a colander and let drain.

2. In a heavy 4-quart pot, melt the butter over medium heat, and when the foam subsides, add the onions and the pancetta. Sauté until the onions are translucent. Then add the potatoes. Cook for 10 minutes, stirring frequently to prevent sticking.

3. Add the rice and stir briefly to coat the grains with the melted butter.

4. Add the boiling stock 1 cup at a time. Stir constantly until the rice has absorbed almost all the liquid. Then add another cup of stock. Proceed in this way until the potatoes have softened into a purée and the rice is al dente. If you run out of stock, continue with boiling water.

5. Stir in the parsley and half the Parmesan cheese. Let the risotto rest for a few minutes before turning it into a serving dish. Serve immediately and pass the remaining Parmesan separately.

✑

Hoppin' John

This is a famous New Year's dish that originated in Charleston, South Carolina. Since black-eyed peas are African natives, it is reasonable to think that the dish originated with slaves brought into America through the Charleston slave market. According to legend, Hoppin' John was popularized by a peg-legged black Charlestonian named John.

Yields
6 to 8 servings

2 cups (1 pound) dried black-eyed peas or cow peas
   or field peas, soaked overnight
½ pound smoked hog jowl, off the bone, or salt
   pork or bacon, diced
Salt and pepper
1 cup long-grain rice

1. Drain the peas and cover generously with cold water in a large, heavy pot. Add the hog jowl or salt pork or bacon, and salt and pepper to taste. Bring to a boil, reduce the heat to low, and simmer until the peas are barely tender, about 20 minutes.

2. Drain, reserving 1¾ cups cooking liquid. Return the reserved liquid and pea mixture to the cooking pot. Stir in the rice. Return to the boil. Reduce heat to low, cover, and continue cooking until the water is entirely absorbed, the rice is al dente, and the peas are tender but not mushy, about 15 minutes.

Variation: Chop 2 medium onions and sauté in lard or bacon fat until translucent. Add the onions to the peas along with rice in step 2. Season to taste with Tabasco or other hot sauce, or crumble 1 small dried red chile pepper, with seeds removed, into the pot in step 1.

Rice Croquettes

This recipe is my adaptation of a traditional South Carolina dish.

Yields
4 servings

Lard, for deep-frying
1½ cups cooked rice (not al dente, but fairly soft)
½ cup flour
½ teaspoon salt
2 eggs, lightly beaten
1 tablespoon butter, softened

1. Heat the lard in a deep-frying kettle until it just begins to smoke.

2. While the lard is heating up, beat together all the remaining ingredients. Form into balls the size of walnuts or a bit larger and set on waxed paper.

3. When the lard is ready, gently slip in 3 or 4 croquettes, using a slotted spoon. Be careful not to splash boiling lard on yourself. Let the croquettes cook a few minutes, until lightly browned, and then remove them to a paper towel with the slotted spoon. Repeat until all the croquettes are cooked.

⤳ BREADS ⤳

Rice Bread

This recipe is based on Bill Neal's recipe in *Biscuits, Spoonbread, and Sweet Potato Pie* (Knopf, 1990).

Rice bread is a southern idea, very refined and almost unknown outside the Carolina lowlands.

Yields
1 large loaf

1½ cups cooked long-grain rice (not al dente, but fairly soft)
1 egg, lightly beaten
2 tablespoons butter, softened
1 tablespoon sugar
1 cup lukewarm water
1 package active dry yeast
4 cups flour, approximately
2 teaspoons salt

1. In a mixing bowl, stir together the rice, egg, butter, sugar, lukewarm water, and yeast. Set aside in a warm place to let the yeast develop, 30 to 40 minutes.

2. Push the mixture through a sieve with a wooden spoon. It will all go through pretty easily. Next beat it together in a bowl with the flour and salt until smooth. The resulting dough will be soft but not wet; in other words, the dough will clean the bowl and hold a shape. Add extra flour if necessary to achieve this. Knead the dough on a floured board to make sure the yeast is well distributed. Then form into a ball and set it to rise in a lightly oiled bowl, covered, until doubled in bulk, about 1 hour.

3. Punch down the dough, knead it again, and form it into a loaf. Place on a lightly oiled baking sheet, cover, and let rise until doubled in bulk, 40 minutes to 1 hour.

4. Preheat the oven to 450° F.

5. Slide the baking sheet with the loaf into the oven. Immediately reduce the heat to 400° F. Bake until light brown, about 40 minutes.

Variation

Brown Rice Bread

The rice must be cooked for even longer than usual, about 1 hour, so it can pass through a sieve. The result is both gentle and gruff—and definitely nutritious.

Hazel Ramsey's Philpy

Surprise your most gastronomically learned friends with this unleavened Carolina rice bread. I learned about it in *Charleston Receipts,* a collection of regional dishes gathered in 1950 by the Junior League of Charleston, capital of America's former rice-growing center.

Yields
4 to 6 servings

½ cup milk
½ cup flour
½ teaspoon salt
¾ cup soft cooked rice
2 teaspoons butter, melted
1 egg, well beaten

1. Preheat the oven to 450° F. Add the milk slowly to the flour and salt, being careful to avoid lumping.

2. Mash the rice with a wooden spoon until fairly smooth. Then beat into the flour-milk mixture. Finally, beat in the melted butter and egg.

3. Spoon into a lightly oiled cake pan and bake for 30 minutes. Serve with extra butter on the side.

↫ DESSERTS ↬

RICE PUDDING

Even experienced cooks who look at a recipe for rice pudding can hardly believe that so little rice can absorb so much milk. The proportion is 16 to 1, milk to rice. You would think that the result must be a milk soup with a little bit of rice discreetly floating around in it. But, of course, this classic comfort food ends up as a solid, if moist, bowl of sweetened, milk-enriched rice.

The main recipe here is the one every American has eaten. This basic preparation goes back to the dawn of British cookery. Indeed, it came to Europe with the Moors, through Spain, in the low Middle Ages. And they were carrying an idea that originated in India; whence the innumerable variations on this theme that can be found today all over Asia. Our dish carries traces of these origins in the basic procedure and in the flavorings, or at least some of them. If you add vanilla, you are closing the geographic circle with an ingredient unknown in Europe until after the conquistadors found it in Mexico in the sixteenth century.

Basic Recipe

Yields
6 servings

¼ cup raw long-grain rice
4 cups milk (skim milk will work and so will heavy cream, or any other concentration of the two along the milk-fat spectrum)
Pinch of salt
¾ cup sugar
½ teaspoon vanilla or almond extract
¾ cup raisins or chopped dates
Grated nutmeg or cinnamon

1. Preheat the oven to 300° F.
2. Stir together the rice, milk, salt, and sugar in a greased 6-cup soufflé (or other ovenproof) dish. Set in the oven and bake for 2 hours,

stirring occasionally to work the "hide" that collects on the top of the pudding back into the rest of the dish.

3. Stir in the vanilla or almond extract and raisins or dates. Return to the oven for 30 minutes. Sprinkle with nutmeg or cinnamon. Serve lukewarm or cold.

Some people pass a custard sauce (crème anglaise), a sabayon (zabaglione), or a fruit sauce (jam diluted with water and/or spirits). I think this is excessive and a distraction from the fundamental interest of the dish, which is the creamy rice.

Indian Rice Pudding
(Kheer)

Like many Indian desserts and sweets, including Indian fudge, kheer is based on a highly reduced rich milk. In India this is invariably the milk of the water buffalo (also the luxurious source of the best mozzarella cheese). Unless you have a milch buffalo, the following mix of whole milk and cream will boil down to a very fine substitute.

Yields
4 servings

5 cups whole milk, or 4 cups whole milk and
   1 cup heavy cream
5 tablespoons raw long-grain rice
1 cup sugar
2 dozen blanched almonds, thinly sliced
1 tablespoon golden raisins
½ teaspoon ground cardamom
1 tablespoon rose water

1. In a large, heavy saucepan (at least 3 quarts, to prevent the milk from foaming over the sides), bring the milk to a boil. Add the rice and stir. Continue boiling slowly over medium heat for 1 hour, stirring regularly, scraping the sides and bottom.

2. Add the sugar, almonds, raisins, and cardamom. Reduce the heat to a simmer and continue cooking for about 15 minutes. At this stage the pudding will have thickened and will begin to turn a light brown.

3. Transfer the pudding to a serving dish. After it has cooled somewhat, but before it sets, stir in the rose water.

Spanish Rice Pudding with Meringue

The aroma of citrus peel gives a special flavor to the rice pudding. Then a thin layer of apricot preserves goes on top, and *then* a meringue goes on top of that. This is a very dressy version of what you may have thought was nursery food.

Yields
4 servings

4 cups milk
Peels of ½ lemon and ½ orange
¾ cup sugar
⅓ cup medium-grain rice
2 eggs, separated
Apricot preserves
5 tablespoons confectioners' sugar
Ground cinnamon

1. Preheat the oven to 300° F.

2. Bring the milk to a boil in a large saucepan (3 quarts or more, to prevent the milk from foaming over the sides) with the citrus peels and the sugar. Stir in the rice. Reduce the heat and simmer for 30 minutes, stirring regularly, until the rice gets creamy. Remove from heat.

3. With a slotted spoon, remove the citrus peels and stir in the egg yolks. Spread the pudding in a 6-cup ovenproof pan. Cover the top of the pudding with the apricot preserves.

4. Beat the egg whites to stiff peaks, gradually beating in the confectioners' sugar as you work, to make a meringue. Spread the meringue over the preserves, making peaks. Set the pan in the oven until the pudding is lightly browned.

Pudding de Riz Joséphine
(Escoffier's Rice Pudding with Strawberries)

The great master of haute cuisine did not hesitate to print numerous recipes for rice pudding of one kind or another. This one embellishes the white pudding with whole and puréed strawberries.

Yields
6 servings

1¾ cups long-grain rice
2½ cups milk
Pinch of salt
2 teaspoons butter
½ teaspoon vanilla extract
Sugar
3 egg yolks
3 tablespoons heavy cream
Kirsch
1 pound strawberries, with stems and cores
    removed
1 cup whipped cream

1. Put the rice in a 6-quart pot. Add enough cold water so that the level comes an inch or so above the rice. Bring to a boil. At the same time, bring the milk to a boil in another pot. Do this gradually, because the milk will foam and overflow the pot as soon as it boils. To prevent this, reduce the heat to a slow simmer immediately.

2. As soon as the rice water boils, drain the rice and put it back in the pot. Pour in the simmering milk. Stir in the salt, butter, and vanilla. Cover the pot and place it over medium heat. As soon as the milk begins to boil, reduce the heat as far as possible and cook, covered, for 12 minutes.

3. Stir in ¾ cup sugar. Continue cooking for 10 minutes, covered, over very low heat, or until the rice has absorbed all the milk. Remove from heat. Beat together the egg yolks and cream and then stir that mixture into the rice. Transfer the pudding to a serving bowl and let it cool to room temperature.

4. Meanwhile, purée ⅓ of the strawberries in a blender or by pressing them through a sieve. Reserve the purée. Put the remaining whole straw-

berries in a bowl and sprinkle lightly with just enough sugar and kirsch to moisten them. Stir and let macerate until you are ready to serve the dish. Since the pudding itself has to cool, this recipe should probably be done several hours before serving, and that will leave plenty of time for the strawberries to macerate properly. The maceration is meant to flavor and "ripen" the strawberries, not to produce a sauce as well.

5. Just before serving, arrange the strawberries in a circle around the edge of the pudding, or make any design you like with them on the surface of the pudding. Place the whipped cream in the center. Pass the strawberry purée separately as a sauce.

⌒∽

Rice Torte

Turning rice pudding into a cake with eggs and nuts and candied fruit is easy—once you've made the pudding base by steeping a small amount of rice in a large amount of milk until the milk is almost completely absorbed. The result is a rich, comforting torte. The original recipe behind this version is Italian, the *torta di riso,* made with risotto rice, blanched almonds, and candied citron. This Americanization, with pecans and prunes, borders on fruitcake, but there is no flour and it's much lighter on the fork. If you can find sun-dried mangoes (I did in a supermarket), they provide an austere alternative to citron or prune.

Yields
6 servings
	2 quarts milk
	1¾ cups sugar
	¾ cup long-grain rice, preferably basmati,
	    well washed
	Grated peel of 2 lemons
	7 eggs
	1 cup chopped pecans
	1 cup chopped prunes, candied citron,
	    or sun-dried mangoes
	Butter
	½ cup bread crumbs or cracker meal,
	    approximately

1. Bring the milk to a boil in a 6-quart pot. When it foams, add the sugar, reduce the heat, and let simmer. Add the rice and lemon peel. Continue simmering until the milk has been almost completely absorbed. Stir from time to time to prevent sticking and lower the heat a bit if necessary. By the end, the rice should be fairly soft.

2. Remove from heat and let cool.

3. Stir in the eggs, one by one, beating vigorously. Then work in the pecans and chopped prunes, candied citron, or sun-dried mangoes.

4. Preheat the oven to 400° F.

5. Grease a Bundt pan or ring mold with butter. Then dust with the bread crumbs or cracker meal. Fill with the rice mixture and bake for 45 minutes to 1 hour. The cake is done when the surface has browned, the sides have pulled away from the pan, and the cake is springy to the touch.

6. Let cool on a rack. Unmold onto a serving dish.

Rice Ring
(Bordure de Riz pour Entremets Froids)

Yields
6 servings

2⅔ cups milk
½ cup long-grain rice, preferably well-washed basmati
⅔ cup sugar
2 tablespoons butter, approximately

Dash of salt
½ teaspoon vanilla extract
3 egg yolks, lightly beaten
½ envelope gelatin
¾ cup heavy cream, whipped until it stands in stiff
    peaks

1. Bring 2 cups of the milk to a boil in a large pot. When the milk foams, reduce the heat to very low, add the rice, ⅓ cup of the sugar, all but a thin slice of the butter, the salt, and the vanilla. Cover and cook, without stirring, until the milk has been almost completely absorbed, at least 35 minutes.

2. Meanwhile, grease a 1-quart ring mold with the remaining butter.

3. Then prepare a thick crème anglaise: first, heat the remaining ⅔ cup milk but do not boil.

4. Whisk together the egg yolks, the remaining ⅓ cup sugar, and the gelatin. The ingredients should all be smoothly blended and the mixture should be a pale yellow.

5. Whisk the yolk mixture into the hot milk. If you haven't done this before, it is crucial that the temperature of the milk not exceed 165° F., or the yolks will scramble. If you aren't sure, use a thermometer. After you add the yolks, keep whisking over medium heat until the mixture palpably thickens. When this happens, set the pan over ice and continue whisking, to stop the cooking process in its tracks. When the crème anglaise is lukewarm, almost room temperature, strain it through a fine strainer (to remove any bits of scrambled yolk) into the rice mixture. Blend well. Then fold in the whipped cream.

6. With a rubber spatula, carefully fill the prepared mold to the top with the rice-cream mixture. Cover with waxed paper and refrigerate for 3 hours.

7. Just before serving, place a serving platter over the mold. Hold both the mold and the platter, invert them, and set on a table. The rice ring should unmold easily. Fill the center with a fresh fruit salad or with a fruit compote. I prefer a compote of stewed prunes and apricots.

Gâteau de Riz au Chocolat
(Chocolate Rice Cake)

Yields
6 servings

2 cups milk
½ cup long-grain rice, preferably well-washed
    basmati
Dash of salt
¼ cup sugar
2 tablespoons butter, approximately
1 teaspoon vanilla extract
3½ ounces semisweet chocolate, grated or finely
    chopped
3 egg yolks, lightly beaten
3 egg whites
Finely ground bread crumbs
½ cup heavy cream, whipped to soft peaks, for
    garnish

1. Bring the milk to a boil in a 6-quart pot with a heavy bottom. Reduce the heat as soon as the milk begins to foam and adjust so that it cooks as fast as possible without foaming and overflowing the pot.

2. Add the rice, along with the salt, sugar, butter, and vanilla. Cook as briskly as possible, until almost all the liquid has disappeared. Count on at least 30 minutes of cooking time, probably more. This depends on many factors, including the state of the rice and the geometry of your pot.

3. Let the rice cool to room temperature, stirring gently with a fork. Meanwhile, prepare a 1-quart charlotte or soufflé mold: grease the mold with butter; then dust with bread crumbs.

4. When the rice has cooled, preheat the oven to 350° F.

5. Melt the chocolate in 3 tablespoons of hot water. Stir the chocolate into the rice mixture. Without waiting, beat the egg yolks into the rice. Now, in a clean bowl, beat the egg whites until they are stiff but not dry. Then gently fold the egg whites into the rice-yolk mixture.

6. With a rubber spatula, gently transfer the rice-egg mixture to the prepared mold. Dust the top with bread crumbs and bake in the oven for 35 minutes.

7. Run a knife around the edge of the cake. Set an inverted serving plate on top of the mold and, holding the plate and the mold, invert them. If the cake does not slide right out as you raise the mold, rap the bottom and try again. Serve with whipped cream.

Mango with Sticky Rice

One area where East and West have not met well is during the dessert course. Here is an attempt at a merger forged with two Asian ingredients—luscious mango, now so easily available in first-rate condition in U.S. markets, and sticky rice, unctuous and comforting, as a backdrop to the mango's strong character. Other fruits can be substituted, of course: peaches, strawberries, or blackberries (about 2 cups), or even fruit preserves or marmalade (to taste), or thin slices of guava paste.

Yields
4 servings

1 cup fresh-extracted or canned Asian coconut milk
2 tablespoons sugar
Salt
1 recipe Sticky Rice (see page 104)
4 ripe mangoes

1. Combine ¾ cup of the coconut milk, the sugar, and a little salt. Stir until the sugar has dissolved. Stir in just-cooked, hot sticky rice. Let the mixture come to room temperature, about 30 minutes.

2. Peel and slice the mangoes. Discard the pits.

3. Arrange the mango slices around the rice. Pour the remaining coconut milk over the rice and serve.

Wheat

True whole-grain

wheat is rarely seen on our tables.
By the time the vast majority of Americans
taste wheat, it has been very thoroughly
processed into white flour. But wheat starts out,
like all grains, as a seed, a rice-size brown
fibrous torpedo-shaped thing whose thin
outer shell is called bran. At one end is a little
package of protein, fat, and genetic information
called the germ; this is the part that reproduces the
wheat plant when sown in fields. By weight and volume,
however, wheat is mostly starch, contained in the
inner seed, or endosperm.
A tiny part of the world's immense wheat crop is sold in
virtually pristine form (minus the hull) in health-food stores.
These so-called wheat berries offer an earthy
alternative to more conventional, quicker-cooking
whole grains. But most wheat is very thoroughly
processed. The fibrous bran and quick-spoiling

germ are removed, and the endosperm is milled into white flour. Commercial millers restore—"enrich"—their denatured product with some of the nutrition they have removed during the processing stage, and they also normally mix different wheats together to create a compromise flour called all-purpose. This is not as sinister as it sounds. All-purpose flour meets most of the needs of home cooks by offering them a practical mix of two quite different forms of wheat that have come down to us from prehistory (see "What Is Grain?," pages 13–15). One is a very high gluten wheat, ideal for making bread because its elasticity captures the carbon dioxide let off in yeast fermentation and therefore "rises." The other, older form of wheat—semolina or durum—is less elastic and more suitable for noodles and flatbreads like pita. Nowadays you can buy either one separately, but all-purpose flours will suit most needs quite nicely.

Not all processed wheat ends up as flour, of course, and in the cosmopolitan world we now inhabit, such semiprocessed wheat products as bulgur and couscous are widely available. So is the proto-wheat (see page 15) known as spelt or, in Italy, *farro* (sometimes referred to erroneously as emmer, an even more primitive form of wheat not, to my knowledge, sold in the United States). It is even possible to find the Turkish specialty wheat called firik, or frik, which is gathered from fields of unripe (green) wheat that have been deliberately set afire to toast the grain.

Bulgur
Basic Recipe

Bulgur, or burghul, is a crudely processed, cracked and steamed form of wheat that is still the basis of traditional cuisine in the Levant. Since it has already been partly cooked by the manufacturer, all you have to do is pour water over it and a few minutes later the particles fluff up and are ready to eat. This can be done very quickly, with boiling water, or more slowly with cold. Steeping time also depends on the coarseness of the bulgur. Most of the bulgur you are likely to stumble on in supermarkets and health-food stores is relatively fine and will soften in a minute or two after being immersed in boiling water. The quantity of the water is not important as long as you don't stint: a ratio of 3 or 4 to 1, water to grain, should be more than ample. After the bulgur is "cooked," just drain it, season, and serve (or use it in one of the many recipes in this chapter).

Wheat Berries
Basic Recipe

Wheat berries are the whole unmilled seed of the wheat plant—the grain itself minus the hull. Much can be said in favor of their nutritional qualities. But at least as compelling is their crunchy, serious flavor. They take a little more effort than rice and other more familiar grains, but the personality and novelty of wheat berries make them worth the trouble.

Yields
2¾ cups

1 cup wheat berries
3 to 4 quarts cold water
1 teaspoon salt

1. Soak the wheat berries overnight in the cold water.
2. Bring the wheat berries to a boil in the same water and add the salt. Cook, uncovered, for 35 to 50 minutes. Taste after 35 minutes, and every 5 minutes thereafter, to determine whether the berries are soft enough for your taste. Eventually the grains will begin to split. Be sure to stop then, or you will get a weird mush. I prefer to stop much earlier, as soon as the grains are pleasantly chewy.
3. If possible, let stand, covered, for 15 to 30 minutes (or if not serving immediately, let stand until the wheat berries have returned to room temperature). Absorption of water will continue to take place.
4. Drain and serve.

Couscous
Basic Recipe

This is the basic Moroccan method for taking the little semolina wheat globules called couscous throughout North Africa (and now the world) and steaming them into fluffy, delicate, little airy balls flavored with whatever the steaming liquid below them is. The variety, even limiting ourselves to classic Moroccan ideas as referred to by Paula Wolfert in *Couscous and Other Good Foods from Morocco* (Harper & Row, 1987), is immense and runs the gamut from vegetables to fish to meat. It helps a lot if you have the special two-part pot called a couscousiere, but you can improvise with a large strainer and a pot it will nest into.

This classic method is essential for North African recipes in which flavors from the broth below permeate the couscous in the upper chamber of the couscousiere while the couscous steams. For that kind of traditional couscous, you must go to Middle Eastern specialty markets, but if you aren't sure which kind you have, the classic method will not damage "instant" couscous. However, for couscous cooked separately and used in nontraditional ways, adequate nonclumping results can be obtained with the couscous normally sold in U.S. markets and health-food stores by steeping the couscous in double its volume of boiling water. Steep until soft. Drain in a strainer, fluff with your fingers, and serve immediately.

Yields	1 cup traditional Middle Eastern couscous
2 servings	3 cups water

1. Combine the couscous with the water in a roasting pan. Swirl the grain in the water briefly and then drain off the water through a sieve, leaving the couscous in the roasting pan in a level layer.

2. Let the couscous stand for 10 minutes. Then work the grains with your fingers to break up any lumps and to aerate them.

3. Seal the join between the top of the couscousiere and the bottom with a piece of moistened cheesecloth dredged in flour. Individual recipes will dictate the steaming liquid in the bottom part of the couscousiere. If you are using the couscous as a stuffing (see recipe for Red Snapper Stuffed with Couscous, page 172), then 2 cups plain water will do. Bring the liquid to a boil.

4. Pour in enough couscous to cover the bottom of the top section of the couscousiere or colander. Steam for 5 minutes, uncovered, then add the remaining couscous. Reduce the heat to medium and steam for another 20 minutes, again, and as always, uncovered.

5. Return the couscous to the roasting pan and spread it out into a level layer. Salt lightly and sprinkle with ½ cup cold water. Stir gently to break up any lumps and to aerate. Let rest for 10 minutes. The couscous can now be held for several hours under a damp towel.

6. Before the final steaming, check to see that the grains are moist and that no lumps have formed. Add a bit more cold water to the now dry couscous and work it with wet fingers to remove any lumps. Then return the couscous to the top of the couscousiere and steam for 20 minutes over broth or water.

↶ BREAKFAST RECIPES ↷

Flapjacks

These are the thick American-style pancakes also known as griddle cakes. They once fed lumberjacks in winter. The traditional emphasis was on bulk and quantity. It is no accident that flapjacks are served in a pile called a short stack. Typically, butter and maple syrup are added. Finesse in cooking them is, nevertheless, possible. And I am not talking about the ability to flip them in the air after one side is cooked and have them land neatly in the skillet on the other side, every time, without letting any fall on the floor. For my taste, at any rate, thinner is better. So is smaller in diameter.

Yields about 16 pancakes

2¼ cups all-purpose flour
1 tablespoon baking powder
1 teaspoon salt
1 tablespoon sugar
2 eggs, lightly beaten
1¼ cups milk
4 tablespoons butter, melted

1. Mix the flour, baking powder, salt, and sugar together in a bowl. Beat in the eggs, milk, and butter. Stop beating as soon as the solid ingredients are thoroughly moistened. Overbeating will activate the flour's gluten and will yield gluey pancakes, unless you wait for an hour or so to let the gluten relax.

2. Lightly grease an 8- or 9-inch skillet by holding a small piece of

butter in a paper towel or saturating a paper towel with oil or using a pastry brush. The goal is a thin film of grease. More will produce greasy pancakes.

3. Pour ½ cup batter into the skillet and cook over medium heat until the surface of the pancake begins to bubble. Turn with a spatula and cook briefly until done. All of the specifics in this step are meant merely as rough indications of how to go. More batter will make a larger pancake, or a thicker one if you are using a small skillet. You can try several pancakes at a time. Personal preferences for doneness vary widely, but the pancakes ought to be browned lightly on both sides and solid but moist right through.

Rømmegrøt

This recipe was inspired by one in *Classic Scandinavian Cooking* by Nika Hazelton (Scribner's, 1965).

Rømmegrøt is the Norwegian national cream porridge. It goes back to the dawn of settled life in the north of Europe and is still eaten at country weddings and feasts. It is an amazingly delicious treat, no matter how weird it may look at first glance. I'm including it here because I love it, but also because I think it really is the most basic dairy-flour dish imaginable, a defining dish. I suggest serving it toward the end of a brunch filled with salty foods like smoked fish and sausages and bacon. Rømmegrøt will come as a blissful contrast. For the hesitant, keep some berries on hand as a garnish.

Yields	1 quart heavy cream (not ultrapasteurized),
8 servings	at room temperature
	¼ cup lemon juice
	2 cups flour
	1 quart hot milk
	Salt

1. Stir the heavy cream together with the lemon juice and let stand for 15 minutes at room temperature. This should be long enough to begin the mild curdling process that produces the separation of the butterfat later

on. In Norway, sour cream will do this without special treatment, but our commercial sour cream has been processed in a way that prevents the separation. Commercial crème fraîche will work, but it seems a waste to use it in this way in this quantity.

2. Bring the cream mixture to a boil, lower the heat, and simmer for 5 minutes.

3. With the pot still on the heat, sprinkle on 1 cup of the flour and beat, using a wooden spoon or whisk, until well mixed. Continue cooking for another 10 minutes over low heat, until the butter leaks to the surface.

4. Skim off the butter until no more oozes out, beating constantly. Then beat in the remaining cup flour.

5. Beat in the hot milk very gradually, stirring constantly until the porridge is thick and smooth. Add salt to taste. Serve hot with butter, brown sugar, cinnamon, and black currant juice.

✢ *FIRST COURSES* ✢

Stuffed Grape Leaves

As Paula Wolfert tells us in *The Cooking of the Eastern Mediterranean* (HarperCollins, 1994) Macedonians sometimes substitute bulgur for rice when stuffing grape leaves. They also add cracked, dried fava beans (instead of pine nuts) and dried figs or, instead of the favas, tiny black lentils or cracked chickpeas. These are delicious combinations, but many others are possible. Here is one that uses two ingredients also plentiful in the eastern Mediterranean.

Yields 24 stuffed grape leaves

½ cup coarse bulgur
1 large onion, finely chopped
5 tablespoons olive oil
⅓ cup shelled unsalted pistachios or walnuts
    or pecans
1½ tablespoons chopped parsley

1½ tablespoons chopped dill
1½ tablespoons chopped mint
¼ cup chopped dried apricots or pitted dates or
    sun-dried mangoes
Salt and pepper
2 dozen grape leaves, rinsed if canned or
    blanched if fresh
1 cup chicken stock or water, approximately

1. Pour boiling water over the bulgur and soak for 15 minutes.

2. Sauté the onion in half the olive oil over medium heat until the onion is completely softened.

3. Drain the bulgur, pressing out excess water. Stir together with the onion, pistachios or walnuts or pecans, parsley, dill, mint, and dried apricots, pitted dates, or sun-dried mangoes. Then add the remaining oil. Season with salt and pepper.

4. Stuff the grape leaves. The classic method is to lay the leaf smooth side down on the counter. Put 1 tablespoon of stuffing at the base of the leaf (stem end) and roll the leaf over the stuffing, starting from the base. Fold the sides over the stuffing and continue rolling from the base end until the leaf is completely rolled up. Continue in this manner until all the stuffing is used up.

5. In a large saucepan, cover the bottom with flat leaves: this keeps the rolled-up leaves from sticking. Then arrange the rolled-up leaves seam down in alternating layers (one layer north-south, the next east-west). Add enough stock or water to cover. Set a plate on top of the leaves to hold them in place. Bring the stock or water to a boil, reduce the heat, cover, and simmer for 45 minutes to 2 hours, until the leaves are tender.

Antique Soup

Every ingredient in this soup would have been available in prehistoric Europe and the Levant. Spelt and barley both predate modern wheat and contribute a rugged, primordial quality, as do the chickpeas so beloved of the ancient Greeks. The puréed chickpea-and-onion mixture provides a thick basic soup. The grains—one white and soft (barley), the other brown and more resistant (spelt)—offer solid contrasts. The result is a hearty, one-dish meal with an old-fashioned Mediterranean flavor.

Yields
6 servings

2 tablespoons lard or oil
2 cloves garlic, peeled and minced
1 large onion, chopped
One 15-ounce can chickpeas
4 cups water or light meat stock (see recipe, page 129)
½ cup spelt (sometimes sold under its Italian name, *farro*)
½ cup barley
Salt and pepper

1. Heat the lard or oil in a 4 to 6-quart pot. Stir in the garlic and onion, and sauté over medium heat until the onion is translucent.

2. Add the chickpeas with the liquid from the can and the water or broth. Bring to a boil, covered. Lower the heat and simmer briefly, until the chickpeas are soft. Pour the soup through a strainer into a bowl. Process the solid ingredients with the steel blade of a processor until you have a smooth mass with no large solid pieces or onion chunks in it. Recombine with the strained cooking liquid in the original pot.

3. Add the spelt and barley. Bring to a boil, lower the heat, and simmer slowly, covered, for at least 45 minutes or even more, depending on the condition of the grain. The desired result is chewable, but not mushy grain. Add the salt and pepper. Stir frequently.

Tabbouleh

In the birthplace of wheat, the eastern Mediterranean, this bulgur salad combines the primitively processed grain with mint and parsley. All this was possible in biblical times. Trade with Asia brought the lemon. Then, after Columbus, the tomato worked its way into the recipe, where it is now standard on tables from Beirut to Berkeley. The authentic dish is, according to Nancy Harmon Jenkins, a former Beirut resident and author of *The Mediterranean Cookbook* (Bantam, 1994), "more green than grain." This recipe alters the proportions a bit to emphasize the grain. If you choose the cilantro option, the tabbouleh becomes a cross-cultural dish with an Asian or Hispanic touch.

Yields
8 servings

1 cup medium bulgur
1 cup mint, finely chopped
Green ends of 6 scallions, chopped
2 cups parsley, finely chopped, or 1 cup parsley
    and 1 cup cilantro
3 medium tomatoes, cored and roughly chopped
Juice of 1 lemon
⅓ cup olive oil, approximately
Salt and pepper
Pita bread

1. Put the bulgur in a large bowl. Add enough cold water to cover it and then some, to allow for absorption. The bulgur will swell and soften. This should take no more than 30 minutes, but it may take longer depending on the state of dehydration of the grain.

2. Drain in a strainer, pressing out as much water as you can with a wooden spoon. If there is any appreciable moisture left, squeeze it out in a clean dish towel.

3. In a serving bowl, toss together the bulgur with the mint, scallions, parsley or parsley and cilantro, tomatoes, and lemon juice. Then add the

olive oil until you get the degree of smoothness you want. Season with salt and pepper. Serve with pita.

Variation: For the tomatoes, substitute one of the following:

- 1 cup canned chickpeas, drained
- ¾ cup walnuts, chopped and sautéed in olive oil for 3 minutes, then cooled
- 1 pound mushrooms, very finely chopped and sautéed in olive oil until all their water has evaporated, then cooled
- 1 pound leftover chicken, with skin and bones removed, cut into julienne strips

Bulgur Ali Baba

As it did for the storied hero, sesame here opens up, as it were, a new window on the possibilities of bulgur. Coarse-grained bulgur, found in health-food stores, has much more character than the fine-grained variety prepackaged for instant tabbouleh. This variation on the basic theme is served hot and can be used to stuff peppers (see Variation, below).

Yields 2 to 4 servings, depending on other dishes	2 cups water Salt 1 cup coarse-grain bulgur Oil 1 green bell pepper, seeded and chopped 1 red bell pepper, seeded and chopped 1 large onion, peeled and chopped 1 to 2 cloves garlic, finely chopped

1 large tomato, roughly chopped
1 to 2 tablespoons Asian sesame oil
Cayenne pepper
Parsley, for garnish
Lemon wedges, for garnish

1. Bring the water to a boil. Add a little salt and sprinkle in the bulgur. Stir once, reduce the heat to a low simmer, and cover for 5 minutes. By now the water should all be absorbed, or nearly so. Remove from heat and leave covered while you proceed with the rest of the recipe.

2. Coat the bottom of a medium skillet with oil. Heat, and then add the chopped green and red peppers. Stir to coat with oil, cover, and cook over medium heat until the peppers have softened a bit. Then stir in the onion and garlic. Sauté until the onion is translucent. Then add the tomato, cover, and simmer for a few minutes to soften the tomato.

3. Combine the pepper mixture with the bulgur. Cook over medium heat until the liquid from the pepper mixture has been absorbed by the bulgur. Then stir in sesame oil and cayenne pepper to taste. Transfer the bulgur to a serving bowl or platter. Decorate with parsley and lemon wedges.

Variation

Stuffed Peppers

Carefully slice the tops off 4 bell peppers. (Try to find 4 of different colors: green, red, "black," and yellow.) Remove the seeds and white matter from the interiors without piercing the walls of the peppers. Stuff with the finished Bulgur Ali Baba. Replace the pepper tops. Steam the stuffed peppers in 1 inch of simmering water, in a pot just large enough to hold all 4 peppers standing up and propped against one another, covered, for 10 to 15 minutes, until the peppers are completely softened. There should be extra Bulgur Ali Baba to serve as seconds.

Salmon Baked with Bulgur

Cracked wheat matches the flavor seriousness of salmon much better than rice. In this preparation the salmon bakes underneath a bed of bulgur, which protects its moistness and helps it cook evenly.

Yields
4 servings

Oil
4 salmon steaks
4 cups prepared bulgur (see Basic Bulgur recipe, page 149)
Four ½-inch-thick tomato slices
Lemon wedges, for garnish

1. Preheat the oven to 325° F.
2. Coat the bottom of an ovenproof dish with oil. Arrange the salmon in the dish, which should be just large enough to contain them in a single layer.
3. Spread the bulgur over the salmon. It should completely cover the fish. Arrange the tomato slices on the bulgur.
4. Set in the oven and bake for 30 minutes.
5. To serve, scoop up the tomato slices and set 1 slice on each plate. Gently scrape away the bulgur from the tops of the salmon steaks. Put 1 steak on each plate, inverting the steaks so that any bulgur adhering to their tops is no longer visible. Spoon a mound of bulgur onto each plate. Add a lemon wedge.

Kibbeh

This mixture of ground lamb and bulgur is the national dish of Lebanon, where it is eaten in hundreds of variations, from raw to baked to stuffed. Different varieties of bulgur are available and further augment the choices for the cook. Kibbeh is such an attractive dish that it has caught on all over the Lebanese diaspora. It can be found, for example, as street food in the Dominican Republic, thinly disguised as *quipe*. Modern equipment such as power meat grinders and food processors eliminate the traditionally punishing hand labor required for kibbeh.

*Yields 4 serv-
ings as a main
course, 6 to 8
as an appetizer* ¾ pound ground lamb
1 cup bulgur, washed in a sieve and kneaded to
    soften and remove excess moisture
1 medium onion, peeled and quartered
½ teaspoon ground cinnamon
¼ teaspoon ground allspice
1 tablespoon ground cumin
2 teaspoons salt
Pepper

1. Put all the ingredients in the jar of a processor fitted with the steel blade. Process for several minutes to produce a homogeneous paste.

2. Form into a single mound or many small balls. Decorate with parsley and serve raw at room temperature, with pita bread and perhaps raw scallions.

Variations

Baked Kibbeh

Form raw kibbeh into small patties, brush with oil, and bake for 15 minutes at 350° F. Just before serving, run the patties under the broiler and brown on both sides.

Baked Kibbeh Stuffed with Walnuts in Yogurt

Take 1 cup chopped walnuts and grind them in a nut grinder or clean coffee grinder, or pulverize the nuts with a mortar and pestle. Work together with 4 tablespoons butter to make a paste, then work the paste into the raw kibbeh. Now proceed as for plain baked kibbeh above. After the patties are baked, quickly heat, but do not boil, 1 cup plain yogurt in a saucepan. Put the patties in a serving dish and pour yogurt over them. Decorate with sprigs of parsley or cilantro.

Wheat Berry Kebabs

All across the Middle East and India, people cook meatballs, usually lamb, in a yogurt sauce. Often the meatballs end up overcooked and sandy in texture. Wheat berries kneaded into the meat retain moisture and richness while adding their own crunchy, appealing texture. One could even say that they dominate the dish and will make the open-minded person ask herself if the meat doesn't function as the binder or helper here, instead of the other way round.

Yields
4 servings

2 medium onions, peeled and chopped
Oil
1½ pounds ground lamb or beef
Salt and pepper
Cayenne pepper
1 tablespoon ground cumin
1½ to 2 cups cooked wheat berries (see Basic
     Wheat Berries recipe, page 150)
1½ cups nonfat yogurt

1. Sauté the onions in enough oil to coat the bottom of a large skillet. When the onions are lightly browned, mix them in with the ground lamb or beef, salt and pepper, cayenne pepper, and cumin.

2. Now gradually mix in the wheat berries until you have the balance between grain and meat that you want. Since you've gone to the trouble of preparing the wheat berries in advance, you might as well use an appreciable amount. I favor at least 1¾ cups.

3. Form the meat-grain mixture into meatballs about the size of limes. (Smaller ones are fine too, but all the meatballs should be the same size so that they will cook uniformly.) You should get around 2 dozen meatballs. (Double that amount if you make small ones half the size of limes.) Arrange them in the same skillet you used for the onions and set over high heat.

4. Turn the meatballs frequently so as to brown all sides. Lower the heat and continue cooking, if necessary, until the meatballs are cooked to

the desired degree of doneness. Remove them from the skillet to a serving dish with a slotted spoon or tongs.

5. Remove the skillet from the heat and let cool for a few minutes. Then whisk the yogurt into the cooking juices and pour the resulting sauce over the meatballs.

Bay Scallops with Eggplant in the Manner of Yildiz Bey

In Turkey the cookery of eggplant and whole-grain wheat reaches its height. This dish is not a traditional Turkish dish, but, instead, an improvisation inspired by memories of that remarkable secular Muslim democracy.

Yields	2 large eggplants
4 servings	Salt and pepper
	Cayenne pepper
	2 tablespoons oil
	Sugar (if necessary to eliminate any excessive bitter taste)
	1 tablespoon ground cumin
	1 Basic Wheat Berries recipe (see page 150)
	2 tablespoons butter
	1 pound bay scallops

1. Roast the eggplants over an open flame until the skins are charred and pulling away from the flesh, which has completely softened. This is a traditional method from Rabat to Tiflis. The idea is to impart a smoky taste to the eggplant flesh. Clearly, it matters what the source of the flame is. You can do quite a good job over a gas stove burner, rotating the eggplant with a long barbecue fork. Better still is a charcoal flame. Best of all is a wood fire, which adds the desirable flavor of wood to the smoke.

2. Cut away and discard the stems and any particularly woody, solid, stringy matter attached to them. Then carefully peel the eggplant as soon

as it is cool enough to touch. Try not to leave any black skin attached to the flesh.

3. Mash the eggplant in a processor. Transfer it to a clean bowl or saucepan. Season boldly, but gradually, tasting as you add salt and pepper and cayenne. Then stir in the oil, sugar, if necessary, and cumin. Taste again and add more of whatever you think might improve the balance of flavors.

4. Now stir the wheat berries into the eggplant. You should have a mixture with dramatic textural contrast between the oily smoothness of the eggplant and the crunch of the wheat berries. Meanwhile, the plain, nutty taste of wheat berries plays off against the suaver, darker, more sophisticated eggplant.

This can be stored in the refrigerator and reheated over moderate heat just before you are ready to serve the dish. Stir regularly. When ready, spread the purée across the bottom of a serving platter.

5. Heat the butter in a skillet. After it foams and the foam subsides, add the scallops and sauté briefly, just long enough to heat them through. Spoon the scallops in a mound on top of the center of the eggplant mixture.

Variation: This eggplant–wheat-berries appareil is so versatile that it can be combined with a wide spectrum of fish and meat, especially lamb (use about 1 pound, cooked). Since it can be reheated without loss of quality, it is an excellent vehicle for giving variety to leftovers.

Peppers Stuffed with Wheat Berries

Here is a once exotic dish from the cuisine of the Ottoman Empire that conquered the world and turned into a banality. But the basic idea is too strong and filled with promise to be abandoned just because bad cooks in school cafeterias have given it a bad name. Bell peppers are perfect edible containers in which to serve almost any grain made special with other ingredients. And now that we have peppers of many colors, the route to take is clear: mix up green and red and yellow and black and orange. And vary the usual rice filling (still a winner in my view) with couscous or kasha or, as here, wheat berries.

Yields
4 servings

1 cup wheat berries, soaked in 4 cups cold water
     overnight
Salt
4 bell peppers, preferably of different colors
Oil
½ pound shiitake or other mushrooms, trimmed
     and roughly chopped
2 tablespoons pine nuts
1 teaspoon black pepper

1. Pour the wheat berries with their soaking water into a heavy 4-quart saucepan. Bring the water to a boil, stir in 1 teaspoon salt, reduce the heat, and simmer slowly, uncovered, for about 40 minutes, or until the wheat berries are softened but not mushy. Drain and let stand in a covered bowl.

2. Carefully slice the tops off the peppers and save them. Make clean cuts parallel to the counter so that the tops will make good lids for the peppers after they are stuffed. Then carefully cut out the seeds and white interior ribs and discard. Arrange the peppers on a baking sheet with a raised edge.

3. Preheat the oven to 375° F.

4. Heat the oil in a skillet and sauté the mushrooms until they give up their water and the oil begins to sizzle. Then add the pine nuts and cook just long enough to toast them. Mix the mushroom mixture with the cooked wheat berries. Add the black pepper and season with salt to taste. Then stuff the mixture into the prepared peppers. Set the lids on carefully and bake for about 30 minutes, or until the peppers have cooked through and can be easily pierced with a knife point.

Variations: Here are three other stuffings you can try.

Ground Meat

Figuring on roughly 1 cup stuffing per pepper, you could double this recipe by preparing 8 peppers and "stretching" the wheat berries or other grain (as mentioned above) with a pound of par-cooked ground beef or veal or pork.

Sauerkraut and Diced Chicken or Turkey

Rinse and drain sauerkraut. Chop roughly, season with cayenne pepper, and mix together with an equal volume of diced leftover roast chicken or turkey. Stuff the peppers and cook as above.

Yogurt with Rice, Walnuts, and Broccoli

Leave yogurt to drain overnight in a strainer lined with cheese-cloth. Beat yogurt together with cooked rice, chopped walnuts, and chopped broccoli flowerets in roughly equal proportion. Season with ground cumin.

Cabbage Stuffed with Wheat Berries and Lamb

Yields	4 tablespoons salt
4 servings	2 cups wheat berries
	1 large cabbage
	1 pound ground lamb or other ground meat
	2 medium onions, peeled and chopped
	2 teaspoons black pepper
	2 tablespoons ground cumin
	1 teaspoon cayenne pepper or 2 teaspoons red pepper flakes
	6 cups beef stock

1. Bring 2 quarts of water to a boil with 1 tablespoon of the salt. Dump in the wheat berries and cook at a fast simmer for about 45 minutes, or until the grains begin to disintegrate and show bits of white. Drain and set the wheat berries aside to cool enough so that you can handle them.

2. Meanwhile, in another pot, bring a large quantity of water to the boil with 2 tablespoons of the salt. There should be enough water to completely cover the cabbage. Lower the heat so that the water simmers.

Then score the cabbage with a small, sharp knife, cutting a ¼-inch-deep circle around the stem. This makes it easy to remove the leaves. Now, holding the cabbage by its stem, plunge it into the simmering water and hold it there for a few seconds in order to help separate the outer leaf from the rest of the cabbage. Remove the leaf and set aside. Dunk the cabbage in the boiling water again and repeat the procedure until you have 12 leaves. Don't worry if they are torn here and there.

3. Blanch each leaf by holding it under boiling water with a wooden spoon for 2 minutes. Drain.

4. In a mixing bowl, mix together the wheat berries, the remaining tablespoon of salt, the ground lamb or other ground meat, chopped onions, black pepper, cumin, and cayenne pepper or red pepper flakes.

5. Form the wheat-berry–lamb mixture into 12 balls the size of walnuts or slightly larger, at which point you should have used up the whole mixture. Then spread out a cabbage leaf, outer side down. Put a wheat-berry ball on the leaf and fold the edges of the leaf over it, making a fairly tight package, with the rib edge on top. Secure either with string or a toothpick. Continue in this way until you have stuffed all 12 leaves.

6. Pour the stock into a pot large enough to hold all the stuffed leaves in two layers. Then put in the stuffed leaves. Place over medium heat and bring the liquid to a boil, lower the heat, cover, and cook at a slow simmer for 45 minutes, or until the ribs have softened and the stock has imbibed the flavors of the cabbage and its stuffing.

7. Serve in shallow, wide soup bowls. Place 3 stuffed cabbage leaves in each bowl and pour the broth over them. There should be enough broth to come about a third of the way up the sides of the stuffed leaves.

CRÊPES

For all north European peoples, pancakes served much the same purpose. They were, as Elizabeth David has written, "a means of using meals and flours such as barley, buckwheat, oatmeal, which were not suitable for bread proper." These primitive pancakes were leavened with yeast and tended to be cooked on griddles or bakestones in houses without ovens. The humble grains people used were not chosen for their taste appeal or their interesting texture, as we would choose them today, but because they would grow in climates inhospitable to wheat. Pancakes, then, were the northerners' home-style bread in the days before modern transportation made wheat almost universally available.

So a pancake starts out as a loose, pourable dough, or batter, that is cooked on a greased flat surface. The batter flows naturally into a flat circle. The cooked pancake is flexible and can be rolled up into a cylinder that can be stuffed with flavorings and solid food (a subgenre that the French call *pannequets* and which we contribute to by wrapping flapjacks around sausages for pigs in a blanket).

Within this basic definition lurk two fundamentally different beasts: the big hearty flapjack and the delicate crêpe. Harold McGee compared their basic recipes in his scientific analysis of the kitchen, *On Food and Cooking*. He quantified common sense by determining that the main difference between regular pancakes and crêpes was the relative dilution of the flour in their batters. Given equal amounts of flour, the ratio of water for pancakes and crêpes was 15 to 23. In other words, crêpes were 1.53 times more dilute than pancakes. This is why crêpe batter spreads so easily across the bottom of a skillet. It also explains, says McGee, why crêpes don't have baking soda added to them and pancakes do. The thicker pancake can hold the air bubbles, but the thin crêpe batter loses any air during cooking that a chemical raising agent might add to it at the batter stage.

Once you have a stack of crêpes, however, the world is your oyster, so to speak. Whole restaurant menus have been concocted with crêpes, sweet or savory, mixed with God knows what. It was not a recipe for the sublime. There are, of course, traditional crêpe recipes of fabulous complexity, in particular some Hungarian crêpe tortes. But the charm of these delicate pancakes is their simplicity and delicacy, their connection with pagan days—springtime sun on your plate.

Crêpes with Caviar

Since classic Russian cuisine never fills or tops crêpes (blini) with caviar and sour cream, and since I can't imagine mixing sturgeon caviar with pancakes, this recipe acknowledges both reality and the appealing taste of crêpes filled with salty salmon-roe caviar tempered with sour cream. Obviously, the determined epicure can substitute beluga or sevruga if she wants.

Yields 12 pancakes or approximately 4 servings

1 scant cup all-purpose flour
3 eggs
1 cup milk
2 tablespoons butter
½ teaspoon salt
6 ounces salmon-roe caviar
8 ounces sour cream
1 cup (½ pound) butter, melted

1. Stir the flour gradually into the eggs.

2. Bring the milk to a boil. As soon as it begins to foam, remove from heat and add the 2 tablespoons of butter. After the butter has melted and been stirred into the milk, pour the mixture little by little into the flour-egg mixture. Stir with a wooden spoon until you have a smooth batter. Stir in the salt. Do not hold this batter more than 15 minutes.

3. Heat an ungreased but well-seasoned 8- or 9-inch cast-iron skillet or a nonstick frying pan over medium heat. The right heat is difficult to judge until you try a crêpe or two. Typically, a beginner will mess up the first one. Overheating will cause the batter to stick. If this happens, remove the skillet from the heat briefly, lower the heat slightly, and try again. Pour ⅓ cup batter into the pan and then turn the pan back and forth to distribute the batter in a thin film across the whole surface of the pan. The crêpe will cook very quickly. As soon as its surface begins to bubble,

either flip it in the air so that it comes down on the other side in the pan or work a small knife or a fingernail under one edge and turn it over by hand. It takes a matter of seconds to brown the second side. Then slip the finished crêpe onto a plate.

4. Continue as above until the batter is all used up. As you finish each crêpe, add it to the pile. Keep warm until ready to serve.

5. Pass the pancakes, caviar, sour cream, and melted butter, allowing guests to make their own combinations.

Variations: After you have poured the batter into the pan, sprinkle it with 1 teaspoon chopped scallion or chopped smoked fish.

Alternatively, after you have cooked the crêpe on one side, remove it from the pan and spread it evenly with 2 tablespoons chopped sautéed bluefish, chopped sautéed calves' brains spiked with a few capers, or picadillo (see page 224). Roll up and brown all the stuffed crêpes at the same time in butter.

Timbale Abruzzese

In classic French cooking a timbale is a small mold in the shape of a truncated cone. The name actually comes from a sort of drum. In the Abruzzi district of Italy, timbale has been applied to this intricate layered dish, in which chicken and meatballs alternate with crêpe and a lasagne-like sauce of tomato and cheese. This is an extraordinary dish in every way. It is a technical feat and the most sophisticated form of "pasta" cookery I know. The individual ingredients retain their identity when you serve the dish, but they function together as a sort of rustic symphony.

Yields
6 to 8 servings

½ cup olive oil
1 whole chicken breast, bone in
½ small onion, peeled and chopped
Salt and pepper
¼ cup dry white wine
One 35-ounce can Italian plum tomatoes with
    liquid, seeds removed, processed with the
    steel blade

1 teaspoon sugar
3 leaves basil
½ pound ground beef, preferably chuck
6 tablespoons grated Parmesan cheese
1 clove garlic, minced
2 eggs
1 slice white bread, softened in water and
    squeezed dry
2½ tablespoons chopped parsley
½ pound ricotta cheese
¼ pound mozzarella cheese, cut into small cubes
22 to 24 crêpes (see recipe, page 169)
2 slices prosciutto, diced

1. Heat ¼ cup of the olive oil in a saucepan until it smokes. Add the chicken and brown.

2. Lower the heat to medium, add the onion, and cook until translucent. Add salt and pepper to taste. Add the wine and reduce to a glaze.

3. Add the puréed tomatoes, sugar, and basil, and simmer slowly for 1½ hours. Remove the chicken, dice, and set aside. Reserve the sauce.

4. Mix together the ground beef, 2 tablespoons of the Parmesan cheese, garlic, salt and pepper to taste, 1 of the eggs, white bread, and ½ tablespoon of the parsley. Form the mixture into small meatballs, the size of grapes.

5. Heat the remaining ¼ cup olive oil and brown the meatballs in it. Add them to the reserved tomato sauce and simmer for 30 minutes.

6. Beat together the ricotta and remaining egg with an electric beater until smooth. Add the mozzarella, the remaining Parmesan, and the remaining parsley.

7. Preheat the oven to 350° F.

8. Spread a thin layer of tomato sauce on the bottom of a 2-quart ovenproof casserole. Line the pan with crêpes, leaving an overhang.

9. Place half the diced chicken on the crêpes. Cover with a thin layer of sauce and a layer of meatballs. Cover with 2½ crêpes.

10. Spread with half the cheese mixture and then a layer of sauce and a layer of meatballs. Cover with 2½ crêpes. Spread with the prosciutto and more sauce.

11. Cover with 2½ crêpes. Add the remaining chicken, more sauce, more crêpes, the remaining cheese mixture, and 3 crêpes to cover. Turn the overhang back into the casserole. Spread any remaining sauce on top.

12. Bake 30 minutes, uncovered.

c o

COUSCOUS

Red Snapper Stuffed with Couscous

An American ingredient is stuffed with Moroccan couscous and baked to perfect tenderness. Leave the scales on the fish as they will add extra flavor.

Yields
4 servings

1 cup couscous (if traditional couscous, it should be parsteamed, as in Basic Couscous recipe, page 150)
Salt
Olive oil
One 1½-pound red snapper, gutted but with scales, head, and tail left on
Lemon wedges, for garnish

1. Preheat the oven to 350° F.

2. The couscous should be spread across the bottom of a roasting pan. (If it is noninstant couscous, it should be at the stage described in step 6 of the Basic Couscous recipe, awaiting its final steaming.) Sprinkle it with salt and stir it together with a small amount of water, approximately ½ cup. Then drizzle lightly with olive oil and stir again, gently.

3. With a spoon, fill the cavity of the snapper with couscous. Set the fish down on the counter and spread the remaining couscous in the roasting pan into a flat layer just slightly larger than the fish. Set the fish on top of the couscous in the pan. Put in the middle level of the oven and bake for about 30 minutes, or until the fish feels firm when pressed. The ex-

posed couscous will have an appealingly delicate crust. The couscous from the cavity will be unbrowned, very moist, and suffused with the flavor of the fish.

Serve from the baking dish, with lemon wedges.

Chicken with Couscous

Couscous stays moist and fluffy inside a roasting chicken.

Yields
4 servings

One 3½ to 4-pound chicken
2 cups couscous (if using traditional couscous, parcook as in Basic Couscous recipe, page 150)
¼ cup golden raisins
¼ cup currants

1. Preheat the oven to 350° F.

2. Stuff the chicken with couscous. Sew up with a utility needle and thread and tie the legs together.

3. Arrange the couscous not used for stuffing the chicken into a

mound in the center of a nonstick roasting pan. The mound should be roughly the same size as the chicken. Press flat and sprinkle with raisins and currants.

4. Set the chicken on top of the couscous mound. Put it in the oven and roast for 1 hour.

Variation: Instead of the raisins and currants, sauté 1 medium onion, chopped, and stir into the couscous after parsteaming, along with 1 tablespoon sesame oil.

Lamb Chops with Couscous

Because couscous absorbs flavor and color so easily, when it is mixed with sautéed red pepper it acquires a subtle red cast and an appealing sweet pepper taste, which provides an attractive counterpoint to the dark rich lamb chops.

Yields	2 cups water
4 servings	1 cup couscous
	Oil
	2 red bell peppers, seeds removed and diced
	1 clove garlic, minced
	Salt and pepper
	8 rib lamb chops

1. Bring the water to a boil in a 6-cup saucepan. Stir in the couscous, reduce the heat to very low, cover, and cook 5 to 10 minutes, until all the water is absorbed.

2. Meanwhile, heat 2 tablespoons oil in a skillet and sauté the red peppers and garlic until the peppers are softened, about 8 minutes. Stir in the couscous. Add salt and pepper to taste.

3. Film the bottom of a large skillet with oil. Set it over high heat and arrange the lamb chops in the skillet. This should be done over high heat because the idea is to brown the chops on both sides, cooking them only long enough to heat them through.

4. Meanwhile, put the couscous mixture over medium heat, stirring

occasionally to remove clumps. Add additional oil, if necessary, to create a smooth mixture.

5. On a serving platter, arrange the lamb chops like fallen dominoes or shingles, one on top of the next. Spread the couscous mixture in a ring around them.

Couscous "Risotto"

In the classic risotto (see page 129), medium-grain rice is simmered in stock until it absorbs the liquid and swells with rich flavor. Couscous can also be cooked in this way, more quickly and with excellent results. The texture is soft, but the grains remain separate and do not turn mushy. If you serve the dish right away, the couscous will not clump.

Yields
3 to 4 servings

3 cups duck or chicken stock (see Note, below)
2 tablespoons oil
3 cups leftover meat, trimmed and cut into
    1-inch squares
1 cup couscous
Salt and pepper

1. Bring the stock to a boil and reduce the heat to produce a very slow simmer.

2. Heat the oil in a medium saucepan and sauté the leftover meat until it is browned all over.

3. Lower the heat under the meat. Then pour in the couscous all at once and stir vigorously until the couscous grains are well coated with oil. Immediately stir in 1 cup hot stock. Simmer until all the liquid is absorbed, stirring. Continue in this way, adding stock ½ cup at a time, until all the stock is absorbed. The total time for absorbing all the stock should be about 20 minutes.

4. Stir in salt and pepper and serve. You may wish to garnish each serving with a spray of cilantro.

Note: The best way to make a quick poultry stock in this amount is to take the raw carcass left after all the meat of a duck or chicken has been cut away for use in a cassoulet or some other dish. Cover the bones and the giblets with cold water, bring to a boil, reduce the heat, and simmer for 1 hour. For extra flavor toss in 1 sliced onion, 1 chopped rib of celery, and 1 carrot, sliced in rounds. Strain, discard the solid ingredients, and reserve the broth.

Leftover veal breast works very well in this dish, but so will lamb or roast beef. You could also use raw shelled shrimp or broccoli flowerets.

⌒๑⌒

◇ BREADS ◇

SOURDOUGH BREAD

Anyone can bake a superior loaf of bread starting with packaged yeast and all-purpose flour and ending in a standard home oven. But the high road to creating a fabulous loaf at home is to re-create the most primitive possible conditions in your late-twentieth-century kitchen. The first step is to dispense with store-bought yeast and let nature take its course: mix a small amount of flour and water together and wait until "wild" yeasts in the air or lying dormant in the flour begin to ferment. Next take this "chef," or starter, and mix it with more flour and water to make a sour dough. Let this dough rise and then bake it in your oven inside a ceramic bell or cloche that simulates the humid microecology of a clay or stone oven of yore. The result is a very tasty loaf with a wonderful crust. The best results come if you buy high-gluten bread flour.

The basic method described here has been abstracted from an essay by John Thorne in his book *Outlaw Cook* (with Matt L. Thorne; Farrar, Straus & Giroux, 1992). You can order a cloche from the Sassafras Company (1-800-537-5491).

The "Chef," or Starter

1. Pour ½ cup unchlorinated water into a bowl. Work in enough all-purpose flour to make a "moist but cohering dough." Practice will make

this stage obvious: when the soupy slurry turns to a solid, puttylike mass that can be massaged (kneaded) into a small, elastic ball. Please note that no commercial yeast has been added. This starter will ferment—if it does ferment—because of the presence, either in the ambient air or in the flour, of naturally occurring yeasts and symbiotic bacteria.

2. Put the starter in a small bowl. Cover with a damp dish towel secured by a rubber band. Leave it on a shelf in a draft-free kitchen for 3 days, remoistening the towel as needed. (The atmosphere in your kitchen may dry out the towel so rapidly that only round-the-clock surveillance will really keep the towel constantly moist. Eternal vigilance is impossible, so do your best. Also please note that no kitchen temperature is specified, since you will probably have to work with what you've got. Unheated kitchens in severe winter weather are obviously not the ideal, but the normal range of temperature in a modern home should work in something like the times specified here and below.)

3. The starter is activated when it looks and smells active. The fermentation produces a noticeable expansion in its size and a slightly "tangy" odor. Then it is ready to use, or it can be stored in the refrigerator for several days.

The Levain, or Sponge

> 1 Starter recipe (see page 176)
> 1¼ cups cold water
> 2½ cups flour
> ½ tablespoon sea salt

1. Put the starter in a bowl with the cold water (cold to slow the fermentation, based on the theory that a long rising at this point improves flavor and because refrigeration relaxes the gluten, making the job of working in the water easier). Work until the starter has completely dissolved.

2. Stir in the flour and the salt to make a loose mass. With floured hands, move it to a lightly oiled bowl. Cover with a damp towel and a piece of plastic wrap. Secure with a rubber band and leave to ripen overnight in a cool place. (Thorne specifies 60° F.)

The Loaf

Yields
1 crusty loaf

1 Sponge recipe (see page 177)
Flour
Cornmeal

1. Put the sponge on a well-floured surface. Begin to work in the new flour. The idea is to knead in as much flour as the sponge will "take," at which point it turns into a silken, nonsticky dough that is a pleasure to work with. No amount of flour is specified. The limiting factor is the 1¼ cups water added at the sponge stage. This kneading stage takes 12 to 15 minutes, during which time the physical work activates the elasticity of the gluten and traps air in the dough so that the yeast can do its work.

2. Dust the dough with flour, put it in a large, lightly oiled bowl, cover with a damp towel, and let rise to double in bulk. This is a faster rise and needs a warm environment, around 80° F. It takes anywhere from 1 to 3 hours, but usually around 2 hours.

3. Flour your hands and gently rework the dough to break up any air bubbles. Pinch off an egg-shaped piece of the dough and reserve it as the starter for subsequent adventures. Jews call this "taking challah."

Drape a generously floured towel in a colander and secure it with a rubber band. Set the dough on the towel, cover it with a damp dish towel, and let it rise almost as far as it did on the first rise.

4. Preheat the oven to 450° F. Heat the base of the bread cloche for 45 minutes.

5. When the dough is ready, sprinkle the cloche base liberally with cornmeal. Then, grasping the towel, pick up the loaf and roll it gently onto the cloche base, so that the round part faces up. Slash the surface in 3 places with a sharp knife or single-edge razor. Place it in the oven, cover with the cloche top, and bake for 15 minutes.

6. Reduce the heat to 400° F. and bake another 30 minutes, removing the cloche top to brown the crust after 20 minutes. The loaf is done if it sounds hollow when tapped on the bottom. Cool on a rack, then store the loaf in a closed paper bag.

Brioche

In classic French baking, brioche is the rich, eggy alternative to what we call French bread. The French call regular bread simply bread, or *pain,* and this is where the confusion arises in the famous story about Marie Antoinette and her starving people. In the standard English version, when the queen is told that the common folk have no bread, she replies, with a shocking lack of compassion, "Let them eat cake." The French original of the anecdote puts her in a slightly better light. Cake, it turns out, was merely a mistranslation of brioche. It is as if, on hearing the people were out of hot dogs, she had suggested they try burgers.

The other important thing to remember about brioche is that it ought to mellow overnight in the refrigerator. The yeast develops slowly, and the dough is easier to handle.

Yields 12 to 14 servings	1 cup milk
	1 package active dry yeast
	3 cups flour, approximately
	1 teaspoon sugar
	½ teaspoon salt
	4 eggs
	1 cup (½ pound) butter, at room temperature, creamed with a whisk

1. Heat the milk until it begins to foam. Let it cool until it is warm (around 110° F.). Pour half of it into a warm bowl and mix vigorously with the yeast until the yeast has dissolved. Then add enough of the flour to make a dough that cleans the bowl. Cover the bowl with a plastic bag and let the dough rise until it doubles in volume. This can take anywhere from 30 minutes to 1 hour or more, depending on the warmth of your kitchen and other atmospheric variables.

2. Meanwhile, in a large mixing bowl, combine the remaining flour with the remaining milk, sugar, and salt. Then add the eggs and finally the butter, a little at a time. Beat vigorously with a wooden spoon.

3. Working the dough with your hand, add the risen yeast sponge. Keep squeezing and stretching the dough until it is a smooth, blended

mass. Leave this batter to rise overnight or for several hours in the refrigerator, in a large, clean bowl inside a plastic bag.

4. The next day grease a Bundt pan. Punch down the brioche dough and transfer it to the Bundt pan with a plastic spatula. Let rise until it almost fills the pan.

5. Preheat the oven to 375° F. Bake the brioche for 25 to 30 minutes, or until a testing needle comes out clean. It should be browned on top and be pulling away from the sides of the mold. Unmold immediately and let cool on a rack. If possible, serve right away. Brioche is much better very fresh, as it goes stale, or at least dries out appreciably, in a few hours.

Dark Bread

The mystique of dark "black" bread is a nostalgia for something gone for good, something no one who had it really wanted. The world switched to white bread as soon as it could. Only much later did the taste elite begin to lament the lost variety of those old breads of poverty, scoured together from crudely milled wheat—or even oats and barley—and filled out with the leavings of the bread drawer.

Never explain how you achieved the rich dark color of this whole-wheat–cornmeal bread. (Coffee is the reason.) Just serve it and smile smugly.

Yields
2 small loaves

2 packages active dry yeast
2½ cups lukewarm coffee
½ cup yellow cornmeal
10 cups whole-wheat flour, approximately
1½ tablespoons salt
Oil
Milk

1. Dissolve the yeast in ½ cup warm water (around 110° F.).

2. When the yeast bubbles, stir in the lukewarm coffee.

3. Put the cornmeal, 9 cups of the whole-wheat flour, and salt in a large, warm bowl. Add the yeast-coffee mixture.

4. Add enough lukewarm water to make a dough that cleans the side of the bowl.

5. Let the dough rest 10 minutes.

6. Flour a clean surface and knead the dough vigorously for 10 minutes, gradually adding more flour until the dough has lost most of its stickiness.

7. Set the dough to rise in a lightly oiled bowl covered with a dish towel dampened in hot water. Leave it in a warm place until the dough has doubled in bulk, up to 1½ hours.

8. Briefly knead the dough again on a floured surface. Let it rise in a covered bowl, as before, until doubled in bulk. This should take much less time.

9. Turn the dough out again on a floured surface. Gently form it into a ball. Cut the dough in half and form each piece into a round.

10. Sprinkle a baking sheet with cornmeal. Set the loaves on the baking sheet. Brush the tops with water and leave to rise for 20 minutes. Meanwhile, preheat the oven to 375° F.

11. Brush the tops of the loaves with milk and bake for 1 hour.

Healthy (?) Fried Bread

Harold Pinter's play *The Birthday Party* introduced me to the idea of fried bread. And it was not a pretty introduction. As the play opens, an elderly couple are discussing breakfast in an aggressively dull and infuriating manner. She asks him if he liked his fried bread. "Was it nice?"

"Yes, very nice."

And so on and on and on.

Never having eaten fried bread, I assumed it was the epitome of bad British food, a corruption of taste consisting of limp white bread dripping rancid bacon fat.

Then one morning, years later, I found myself with a pan of hot bacon grease. (It was so long ago that I routinely fried bacon to go with fried eggs at Saturday breakfast.) And remembering the Pinter play, I thought, Why not try it? Very nice white peasant bread was at hand. I sliced it and dropped a piece in the very hot bacon grease. It was golden brown in a second. Drained on a paper towel, it was a most delicious thing. I made a few more.

These days I rarely try this adventure in high-fat, high-cholesterol dining, but once in a while it can't hurt. If you substitute goose fat or lard for bacon fat, some nutritional experts will tell you you have sidestepped the cardiovascular threat. With olive oil or one of the other non-artery-closing oils, you can be sure you are safe, except for the calorie boost. A good cooking practice—very hot oil—will keep the grease level as low as possible.

Sliced bread
Oil or bacon drippings or goose fat or butter

1. For the best results the first time you do this, fry 1 piece of bread at a time. Use a cast-iron skillet slightly larger than the bread slice. Fill it with oil, bacon drippings, melted fat or butter to a level of at least ¼ inch. This may look repulsive as you begin, but you don't want to be constantly replenishing the oil or fat as you work, especially because reliably hot temperature is the key to crisp success. Unused oil or fat can be reused.

2. Heat the oil or fat until it just begins to smoke. It would be possible to list the smoke points of all the various oils and fats you might decide to use for this recipe, but this would inject a preposterous note of scientific precision into what is, after all, the most primitive sort of cooking, meant to use up old bread and the residue of bacon frying. The really important thing is to WAIT until the oil or fat is very hot, so that it will immediately seize or "surprise" the bread, as the French say, on contact and will not make it soggy. As soon as you detect a vapor or "smoke" rising from the pan, carefully immerse a slice of bread in the oil or fat. Using tongs is the best way to avoid splashing 370° F. fat on yourself.

3. The bread should sizzle loudly and brown almost immediately. Turn it with tongs. Cook for a few seconds more and remove the bread to a paper towel. If the bread burns right away, then the fat is too hot. Lower the heat, wait a couple minutes, and try again. It should not take much trial and error, if any, to get this process going. Continue until you have as many slices of fried bread as you need. As the level of the oil or fat reduces, take special care that the temperature does not rise too high.

Variation: If you fry 2 or 3 cloves garlic in the oil (and remove them when browned) before you start frying the bread, the oil will impart a garlic flavor to the bread. This process is essentially the same as making croutons. Instead of using slices of bread, cut the bread in triangles or dice it, and then fry. Add to soups.

Bran Muffins

If you've never had a homemade bran muffin, you may not realize how delicious these are by comparison to the mass-produced bran muffins consumed by the jillions with dilute coffee in offices from coast to coast every weekday morning.

Yields about	1 tablespoon baking powder
10 muffins	½ teaspoon salt
	1 cup flour
	1 cup wheat bran
	2 tablespoons sugar
	½ cup milk
	1 egg, lightly beaten
	2 tablespoons butter, melted

1. Preheat the oven to 400° F.
2. Grease a 10-cup muffin tin.
3. Stir together the baking powder, salt, flour, bran, and sugar. Then stir in the milk, egg, and butter, beating just enough to blend the ingredients. Overbeating produces leathery muffins.
4. Fill the containers of the muffin tin two-thirds full. Bake for 30 minutes, or until the muffins begin to pull away from the sides of the tin and are no longer gooey inside.

Variation: Add ½ cup raisins, currants, chopped dates, chopped dried figs, or chopped walnuts along with the dry ingredients in step 3.

∽ PASTAS ∾

Basic Noodle Recipe

From Rome to Beijing, the noodle is a classic way of making flour rapidly and easily available for human consumption. While it is untrue that Marco Polo brought noodles from China to Italy—pasta was widespread in ancient times—there is no doubt that these two cultures, as indeed many others, found it remarkably convenient to boil noodles in ten minutes maximum. Those noodles were for them not only a form of quick bread but also a versatile medium with which myriad sauces and other foods could be combined, and this very simple and technologically uncomplicated idea has continued to attract cooks and diners in our day.

When I think of noodles historically, I think of felt. Felt is the oldest fabric, made from bits of fur compacted together. Felt was technologically possible even before thread had been invented. Indeed, it might be defined as a threadless fabric. Similarly, noodles are yeastless bread (one of many types: dumplings, matzoh, crackers), conceived in those early days before high-gluten bread wheat had been hybridized, before airy, fluffy loaves were possible (see "What Is Grain?," pages 13–15). So noodles really should be made with semolina flour, but our all-purpose flour—a compromise between lower- and higher-gluten flours—will more than suffice.

The essential is to get the feel of noodlemaking by doing it with your own hands. Even if you can buy fresh-made pasta, or own a pasta machine, you should try this process for yourself, by hand. Doing so will not only link you with cooks immemorial, it will also produce very fine noodles with simple tools. Just mix flour and water, roll and cut. Adding an egg will make the noodles even nicer.

Yields
1 pound
noodles

1¼ cups semolina or all-purpose flour
1 teaspoon salt
2 teaspoons olive oil
1 egg, lightly beaten (optional)

1. In a mixing bowl, stir together all the ingredients (including the egg, if used) and then add water, 1 tablespoon at a time, until the flour masses together to make a dough. This point is often referred to as cleaning the bowl. Go slowly. Too much water will give you a sticky slush ball. It would be nice to be able to specify an exact quantity of water, but atmospheric conditions vary, as do flours.

2. Form the dough into a ball and knead vigorously on a well-floured board for 10 minutes. Let stand, covered. Since this is not a yeast-rising dough, room temperature is not crucial. You are just letting the gluten relax so that it will be easier to roll the dough very thin without having it jump back elastically to the thickness it was when you started.

3. Flour a board or counter or tabletop. Take a long rolling pin (any length will work, but the long, thin ones are best for this job). Tap the dough smartly to flatten it. Then begin to roll, leaning into the job, stretching the dough as you roll. Add flour as needed, to prevent sticking. This means sprinkling flour underneath the dough as well as on top. You should be able to roll the dough around the pin and pick it off the table easily. Your goal is to roll out the dough until it is translucent—so thin, proverbially, that you can read a newspaper through it. I recommend *The Wall Street Journal* for this test, because of its nonsmearing ink.

4. Hang the dough over the back of a chair or on a clothesline to dry for about 30 minutes, no longer. It has to be moist enough to roll up again in a long coil.

5. After rolling the dough up, lay it down on a floured cutting board. Slice it into rounds, moving from one end of the coil to the other. These rounds uncoil into noodles. The thinner or thicker the rounds, the thinner or thicker the noodles. My preference is for ¼-inch-thick noodles.

6. Cook like other pasta in salted, vigorously boiling water, but for a much shorter time, as little as 2 or 3 minutes. Homemade noodles usually cook more quickly than fully dried, store-bought noodles. Watch and taste.

Obviously, these noodles can be prepared and garnished just as you would prepare and garnish manufactured pasta. But because you have made them and will want to emphasize their purity, their noodlehood, you may very well wish to limit the other ingredients to relatively nonassertive items. For example, a tablespoon of butter, just enough to make the noodles glisten, and freshly grated Parmesan cheese.

Orzo with Chicken Breasts and Red Peppers

Here is another dormant pun on barley (see page 23). And if you look at these small "noodles" shaped almost exactly like barley groats or rice grains, you will immediately see why Italians long ago named them after a grain they were more familiar with then than now. Orzo is the modern Italian reflex of the Latin *hordeum*-barley. For Italians, as for Jews, who have their own version of this barley "noodle," orzo is primarily a starch that goes in soup, one of many small pasta forms often lumped together as pastina and most commonly seen on menus as *pastina in brodo,* "little pasta in broth." In our supermarkets orzo may also appear as soup barley, barley shape, or farfel. The difference is small, and you can always substitute farfel for orzo (but not matzoh farfel).

This recipe was inspired by a lunch I had on the patio at the Hotel Bel-Air in Bel-Air, California. It is an elegant and refined example of the eclectic cooking sometimes lumped together as California cuisine.

Yields
4 servings

MARINADE

¾ cup oil
¼ cup red wine vinegar
1½ teaspoons salt
½ teaspoon black pepper
¼ teaspoon cayenne pepper
1 bay leaf
Several sprigs fresh chervil or marjoram, or
    ½ teaspoon dried marjoram or tarragon

4 boned chicken breasts
6 quarts water, lightly salted
2 tablespoons oil
2 large red bell peppers, trimmed and seeded, white
    membranes removed, cut into strips
½ pound orzo
Turmeric (optional)

1. Mix together thoroughly the marinade ingredients and marinate the chicken breasts for 6 hours in the refrigerator, stirring occasionally to recoat the chicken.

2. An hour before you intend to serve this dish, start a hardwood fire for cooking or a charcoal barbecue fire; or preheat your broiler 15 minutes ahead of time. Then bring the water to a rolling boil.

3. Heat the oil in a skillet and sauté the bell pepper strips slowly, until they are completely softened. (Do not use green bell peppers or other colors. Only the red will give the sweet, unctuous taste and the color contrast that is appropriate for this dish. If you can't find red bell peppers, cook something else.) When the pepper strips are done, remove them from the heat, cover, and reserve.

4. Drain the chicken breasts (straining and reserving the marinade) and place them over the fire or under the broiler. Don't do this until the water from step 2 is boiling and the red pepper strips are done or almost done. The chicken breasts will cook in a few minutes. Adjust their distance from the fire so as to brown them lightly, but do not char. As soon as the thickest part of the breasts are white and opaque all the way through, they are done. Cut into strips.

5. As soon as you put the chicken breasts on the fire, pour the orzo into the boiling water. Cook at a rolling boil until pleasantly tender but still chewy, al dente. Times will vary, so start tasting 5 minutes after the boiling resumes.

6. Drain the orzo and put it in a mixing bowl. Stir in the reserved marinade, 1 spoonful at a time, until you have a rich but not soupy consistency. The idea is to coat the orzo grains and keep them separate, as well as to flavor them. If you want to take the "grain" concept one step further, stir in a teaspoon or so of turmeric to color the orzo yellow and imitate the appearance of a Milanese risotto, whose rice has been colored with saffron. Spoon the orzo into a mound in the center of a serving platter.

7. Remove the pepper strips from the skillet with tongs and arrange them in a geometric pattern over the orzo. After you have a pattern that pleases you, arrange any extra strips around the perimeter of the orzo. Alternate them with the chicken strips. The idea is to have a red-and-white band encircling the orzo mound.

Serve immediately.

Basic Farfel

Like the Italian orzo, farfel is a pasta shaped like barley. Made from an egg-noodle dough, it is often sold under the names barley shape or egg barley, either plain or toasted. The toasted variety is much tastier. (Plain farfel can be toasted in 15 minutes in a 350° F. oven on a cookie sheet.)

Yields
4 servings

6 cups water
1 cup toasted farfel
Salt
1 large onion, peeled and chopped
2 tablespoons oil
Paprika

1. Bring the water to a full boil. Add the farfel and salt and return to a boil. Continue cooking at full boil for 10 minutes, or until farfel is al dente.

2. Meanwhile, sauté the onion in the oil until it is translucent.

3. Drain the farfel and stir it into the onion. Season with salt and paprika.

Traditional Matzoh Farfel

These matzoh flakes are pasta for Pesach, the Jewish feast of the Passover that occurs at roughly the same time of year as Easter. Indeed, the Last Supper was a ritual Passover meal, a seder, at which the apostles and Jesus consumed wine and matzoh, unleavened bread symbolizing the hasty flight from Egypt when there was no time to wait for bread to rise. Today matzoh farfel is mostly used for stuffing, but it can also be served on its own, as a farinaceous side dish.

Yields
4 servings

2 cups matzoh farfel
2 eggs, lightly beaten
½ teaspoon salt

1. Preheat the oven to 350° F.

2. Stir all the ingredients together so as to completely coat the farfel flakes with the egg. Transfer to a shallow greased baking dish. Smooth into an even, thin layer and bake for 20 minutes, or until browning begins.

New Age Matzoh Farfel

If the classic recipe for matzoh farfel seems unnecessarily high in cholesterol, try this invention, which satisfies both the Jewish and the modern medical dietary guidelines.

Yields
4 servings

¼ cup olive oil
2 cloves garlic, minced
1 medium onion, peeled and chopped
2 cups matzoh farfel
Salt
Cayenne pepper
1 cup skim milk
1 tablespoon sesame oil

1. Preheat the oven to 350° F.

2. Heat the olive oil in a skillet. Add the garlic and sauté until browning begins. Add the onion and sauté until transparent. Stir in the farfel and continue stirring until lightly browned all over.

3. Season to taste with salt and cayenne pepper. Stir in the milk and transfer the mixture to a shallow ovenproof dish. Bake for 20 minutes, stirring once, after 10 minutes.

4. Remove from the oven. Stir in the sesame oil and serve immediately.

~ DESSERTS ~

Crêpes

The ultimate pancake, thin and light, a vehicle for every known flavoring and liqueur, this is wheat flour stretched to the limit of possible refinement.

Yields
12 crêpes

1 scant cup all-purpose flour
3 eggs
1 cup milk
2 tablespoons butter
2 teaspoons rum
½ teaspoon salt

1. In a mixing bowl, stir the flour gradually into the eggs.

2. Bring the milk to a boil in a large saucepan. As soon as it begins to foam, remove from heat and add the butter. After the butter has melted and been stirred into the milk, pour the mixture little by little into the flour-egg mixture. Stir with a wooden spoon until you have a smooth batter. Add the remaining ingredients. Do not hold this batter more than 15 minutes.

3. Heat an ungreased but well-seasoned 8- or 9-inch cast-iron skillet (or a nonstick frying pan) over medium heat. The right heat is difficult to judge until you try a crêpe or two. Typically, a beginner will mess up the first one. Overheating will cause the batter to stick. If this happens, remove the skillet from the heat briefly, lower the heat slightly, and try again. Pour ⅓ cup batter into the pan and then turn the pan back and forth to distribute the batter in a thin film across the whole surface of the pan. The crêpe will cook very quickly. As soon as its surface begins to bubble, either flip it in the air so that it comes down on the other side in the pan or work a small knife or a fingernail under one edge and turn it over by hand. It takes a matter of seconds to brown the second side. Then slip the finished crêpe onto a plate.

4. Continue as above until the batter is all used up. As you finish each crêpe, add it to the pile.

5. Keep them warm until ready to serve. The classic garnish is a simple sprinkling of confectioners' sugar, but you can also pass apricot or other preserves, chopped walnuts, or chocolate sauce. If you spread the preserves on the crêpes, add chopped nuts and roll them up—this is what Hungarians call *palaczinta*. Cover with chocolate sauce or sour cream, heat, and serve.

For crêpes suzette, smear the crêpes with butter, fold in fours, sprinkle with confectioners' sugar, and flambé with curaçao.

Kugelhopf

This is a traditional cake of Alsace that has worked its way into the classic French repertory. Like savarin, kugelhopf is basically a sweet brioche, but whereas the savarin is baked in a ring mold and then soaked in a rum-based syrup, the kugelhopf is mixed with rum-soaked raisins and baked in a metal Bundt pan or a similarly creased and chimneyed terra-cotta mold. Should you happen to come across one of these authentic Alsatian molds, be warned that new ones do not work well; the cake will stick in them unless they have been tempered through use so that the glaze has worn and crazed a bit. Also, baking takes longer, about 1 hour at 350° F. instead of about 30 minutes at 375° F. in the Bundt pan. At least one authority insists that the old-fashioned mold, once broken in, does a superior job. In fact, the Bundt pan works quite nicely, and if you don't mind waiting for the batter to mature overnight, this is a very easy and impressive dessert, with a yeasty personality.

Yields 12 to 14 servings

1 cup milk
1½ packages active dry yeast
3½ cups flour, approximately
6 tablespoons sugar
½ teaspoon salt
5 eggs
1 cup (½ pound) butter, at room temperature, creamed with a whisk
½ cup raisins, soaked overnight or for several hours in 3 tablespoons dark rum
Whole blanched almonds
Butter, for the mold
Confectioners' sugar

1. Heat the milk until it begins to foam. Let it cool until it is warm (around 110° F.). Pour half of it into a warm bowl and mix vigorously with the yeast until the yeast has dissolved. Then add enough of the flour to make a dough that cleans the bowl. Cover the bowl with a plastic bag and let the dough rise until it doubles in volume. This can take anywhere from 30 minutes to 1 hour or more, depending on the warmth of your kitchen and other atmospheric variables.

2. Meanwhile, in a large mixing bowl, combine the remaining flour with the remaining milk, sugar, and salt. Then add the eggs, beating them in one by one, and finally the butter, a little at a time. Beat vigorously with a wooden spoon.

3. Working the dough with your hand, add the risen yeast sponge. Keep squeezing and stretching the dough until it is a smooth, blended mass. Work in the raisins and any remaining rum. Leave this batter to rise overnight, or for several hours in the refrigerator, in a large, clean bowl inside a plastic bag.

4. The next day grease a Bundt pan. Press an almond into each crease in the mold, alternating them high and low to make a pattern in the outside of the finished cake.

5. Punch down the brioche dough and transfer it to the Bundt pan with a plastic spatula. Let it rise, covered, until it almost fills the pan.

6. Preheat the oven to 375° F. Bake for 25 to 30 minutes, or until a testing needle comes out clean. The cake should be browned on top and be pulling away from the sides of the mold. Unmold immediately and let the cake cool on a rack. If possible, serve right away, sprinkled with confectioners' sugar. Brioche is much better very fresh, and it goes stale—or at least dries out appreciably—in a few hours.

Kutia

This is a traditional Polish Christmas Eve dessert. Even if it does not actually predate the arrival of Christianity in Poland, its lusty texture contrast of wheat berries and poppy seeds has a pagan vitality.

Yields
4 servings

1½ cups wheat berries, soaked overnight in 6 cups water in a heavy, non-aluminum pot
2 cups poppy seeds
¼ cup heavy cream
Honey

1. Set the wheat berries and their soaking water over high heat, covered, and bring to a boil. Lower the heat and simmer until tender, at least 35 minutes. Drain if necessary and let cool.

2. Beat the poppy seeds and cream into the wheat berries. Sweeten with honey. Serve as a cold dessert.

Mrs. Beeton's Baked Bread-and-Butter Pudding

Isabella Beeton's immense *Book of Household Management* (1861) is the great culinary landmark of the Victorian Age in Britain. Here is her characteristically self-assured recipe, slightly adapted to our day and this format.

Yields
6 servings

9 thin slices bread, buttered
⅔ cup raisins or dried currants
3 cups milk or heavy cream
¼ cup sugar
Grated peel of 1 lemon
4 eggs
½ teaspoon vanilla extract

1. Preheat the oven to 350° F.

2. Take a pie dish and layer the bread slices with the raisins or currants, ending with a sprinkling of raisins or currants on top (use more raisins or currants if you like).

3. Heat the milk or cream with the sugar and lemon peel until the milk begins to foam. Remove from heat, whisk in the eggs and the vanilla. Strain through a *chinois* or other fine strainer onto the bread slices.

4. Bake for 1 hour or longer, until the pudding is almost solid. Remove from the oven and let rest for at least 2 hours. Do not unmold.

Bread Crumb Pudding

This is really an old-fashioned steamed pudding that exploits bread crumbs—an example of French thriftiness at its most lavish.

Yields
8 servings

2¼ cups dry bread crumbs or cracker crumbs or matzoh meal, plus more for dusting
2 cups milk
1 teaspoon vanilla extract
10 tablespoons sugar
2 whole eggs, plus 2 egg whites
3 egg yolks, lightly beaten

1. Butter the inside of a 4-cup soufflé mold or charlotte mold. Dust the inside with bread crumbs and set aside.

2. Bring the milk to a boil in a large saucepan with the vanilla and the sugar. Stir to dissolve the sugar. Remove from heat as soon as the milk begins to foam up.

3. Stir 2 cups of the bread crumbs, cracker crumbs, or matzoh meal into the milk mixture. Let them soak briefly. Then push the mixture through a *chinois* or other fine strainer.

4. Stir the whole eggs and the egg yolks into the milk–bread-crumb mixture.

5. Beat the egg whites until stiff. Fold them into the pudding mixture.

6. Pour the pudding into the mold. Set the mold into a pan of simmering water deep enough to come halfway up the side of the mold, and set the pan over medium heat. Adjust the heat so that the water barely shakes. Keep up the water level as necessary with additions of boiling water. Continue steaming until the pudding has barely set. This process should take about 3½ hours.

7. Remove the pan from the hot water and set it on a rack. Let the pudding cool to room temperature. Run a knife around the edge of the pudding. Place a serving platter upside down on top of the mold. With one hand on the bottom of the mold and the other on the bottom of the serving platter, briskly invert this sandwich of platter and mold. Set it on a counter. Raise the mold an inch or two off the platter. The pudding

should slide easily out of the mold onto the platter. If it doesn't, set the mold back on the platter and rap the bottom of the mold sharply. Try again. Eventually, the most resistant of puddings do slide out onto the platter. Sometimes, the top (former bottom) will emerge a bit ragged. Disguise this with fruit (see variations below).

Variations: Fruit sauces are always a possibility. Heat 2 cups preserves, sieve, dilute with hot water to desired consistency, and either pour the fruit sauce over the pudding when you serve it or pass it separately. Combine, if you wish, with sliced strawberries or raspberries or very ripe, sliced peaches.

Dark Bread Pudding

This is a bluff American bread pudding: sturdy bread and country apple hooch.

Yields	8 thin slices (about ½ pound) dark bread
8 servings	1½ cups applejack
	3 cups heavy cream
	1 cup sugar
	1 teaspoon vanilla extract
	8 ounces semisweet chocolate, grated
	½ cup apricot preserves

1. Toast the bread lightly to dry.
2. In a bowl, pour the applejack over the bread and break the bread into small pieces with a fork.
3. Whip the cream to soft peaks. Continue beating and work in the sugar gradually. Then add the vanilla and beat until the cream is stiff.
4. In a serving dish, spread a layer of the whipped cream and sprinkle it with chocolate. Top with a layer of bread mixture and drop apricot preserves at random in small amounts. Repeat this sequence until you run out of ingredients. The depth of the layers is a matter of taste.
5. Chill overnight or for several hours before serving.

Apricot Dumplings

Czechs dote on this late summer treat. For me, these are the greatest of all dumplings: a pure, light dough encloses a melting red-orange fruit.

Yields
12 dumplings

1 package active dry yeast
2 eggs, lightly beaten
1 teaspoon salt
4 tablespoons sugar, approximately
2 cups flour, approximately
12 ripe apricots or plums
6 quarts water, lightly salted

1. Stir the yeast into 1 cup warm (110° F.) water. Let stand 5 minutes.

2. Stir in the eggs, salt, 1 teaspoon of the sugar, and the flour. Blend well. Add additional flour, if necessary, to make a stiff dough that cleans the sides of the bowl.

3. Let stand 15 minutes. Then knead until smooth and elastic. Place the dough in an oiled bowl, cover with a damp dish towel or enclose in a plastic bag, and let rise in a warm place until doubled in bulk. The rising may take as much as 2 hours.

4. Pit and peel the fruit. Fill the centers with sugar.

5. Turn out the dough on a floured board and roll into a sheet ½ inch thick.

6. Cut into squares large enough to wrap around the apricots or plums. Set the prepared fruit on the center of each square. Pull up the dough and seal it so as to completely encase the fruit. To seal, moisten your fingers and pinch the dough together. Leave the completed dumplings to rise for at least 30 minutes, covered with a damp dish towel, in a warm place. (The dough should visibly rise.)

7. Bring the lightly salted water to a rolling boil. Add the dumplings with a slotted spoon and cook, covered, for 15 to 20 minutes, until

the dough is cooked through but still light and spongy. Overcooking will produce a leaden dumpling. Remove with a slotted spoon. Serve immediately.

Semolina Pudding

Semolina is a confusing term. It can refer to the comparatively low-gluten flour meant for pasta (see pages 148–49) or to a by-product of the milling process that produces pasta flour from durum wheat. After the final sifting, the particles left over are most often sold as farina. This universally available product is normally used to make a quick-cooking breakfast cereal also called Cream of Wheat, but it is the ingredient used in the following recipe when farina is called for. It is possible to buy untreated semolina "pasta" flour (also sold as farina), but there is really no advantage in the final result if you are making the dessert recipes below.

Classic French cuisine approaches semolina for desserts in much the same way that it does rice for desserts. It elevates the basic cooked starch into pudding, a molded ring filled with fresh or cooked fruit, or cake.

Yields
6 servings

2 cups milk
⅓ cup sugar
1 cup instant farina (Cream of Wheat),
    approximately
Dash of salt
½ teaspoon vanilla extract
2 tablespoons butter
3 egg yolks, lightly beaten
6 prunes (about 1 cup), pitted and chopped
2 egg whites
Stewed prunes or defrosted frozen strawberries
    in syrup

1. Bring the milk to a boil in a heavy 6-cup pot. When the milk foams, reduce the heat and stir in the sugar. Then sprinkle in the farina, gradu-

ally, while whisking to prevent the formation of lumps. Continue stirring and add the salt, vanilla, and butter.

2. Reduce the heat as low as possible, cover, and cook, without stirring, for 2 to 3 minutes. During this time the farina should swell and puff but never spatter or show signs of frank boiling. It is finished cooking when the milk has been absorbed. Set aside.

3. Meanwhile, take a 1-quart charlotte mold or a ring mold and set it in a pot large enough to hold it. Then determine how much water it takes to fill the pot so that the water level comes within an inch of the top of the charlotte mold. Pour that water into a kettle. Then prepare the charlotte mold: grease the inside surfaces with butter and then dust them with uncooked farina. Set aside. Preheat the oven to 300° F.

4. Let the cooked farina cool for a few minutes, uncovered. Bring the water in the kettle to a boil.

5. Fluff the farina with a fork. Beat in the egg yolks, then add the pitted and chopped prunes. In a separate bowl, whisk the whites until they are stiff but not dry. Fold them into the farina mixture. Spoon the mixture into the mold, leaving ½ inch of space at the top for expansion. Tap the mold against the counter lightly and spread the surface to make it even.

6. Set the mold in the larger pot. Pour the boiling water into the pot. Cover and put the pot into the oven. Steam for approximately 35 minutes, during which time it is advisable to check the water to make sure it isn't boiling. If it is or threatens to, remove a few spoonfuls of water and replace them with cold water. The goal here is very even cooking: the water should just tremble. The pudding is done when the surface is firm but elastic to the touch.

7. Remove the mold from the water and cool on a rack. Run a knife around the side of the mold. Invert a serving platter over the top of the mold. Holding both the platter and the mold, turn them over and set on the counter. The mold should lift off, leaving the unmolded pudding or ring on the platter.

8. Serve with stewed prunes or defrosted frozen strawberries in syrup. If you are using a ring mold, fill the center with the fruit. Or for an even richer presentation, first fill the center with whipped cream and then add the fruit.

Date, Prune, and Apricot Dessert Couscous

Yields
6 servings

3¼ cups (1 pound) couscous
3 tablespoons butter, approximately
Salt
½ cup chopped pitted prunes
½ cup chopped pitted dates
½ cup chopped dried apricots
2 tablespoons sugar mixed with 2 teaspoons
cinnamon

1. Combine the couscous with 9 cups water in a large, shallow pan. Swirl the grain in the water briefly and then drain off the water through a sieve, leaving the couscous in the roasting pan in a level layer.

2. Let the couscous stand for 10 minutes. Then work the grains with your fingers to break up any lumps and to aerate them.

3. Put 3 quarts of water in the bottom of the couscousiere. Seal the join between the top of the couscousiere and the bottom with a piece of moistened cheesecloth dredged in flour. Bring the water to a boil.

4. Pour in enough couscous to cover the bottom of the top section of the couscousiere or colander. Steam for 5 minutes, uncovered, then add the remaining couscous. Reduce the heat to medium and steam for another 20 minutes. Here, as always, the couscous steams uncovered.

5. Return the couscous to the shallow pan and spread it out into a level layer. Salt lightly and sprinkle with 1½ cups cold water. Stir gently to break up any lumps and to aerate. Let the couscous rest for 10 minutes.

6. Check to see that the grains are moist and that no lumps have formed. Add a bit more cold water to the dry couscous and work it with wet fingers to remove any lumps. Then butter the inside of the top of the couscousiere. Add the prepared couscous and steam for 30 minutes.

7. Return the couscous to the shallow pan and let it dry again, as in step 5, except toss it with 2 tablespoons of the butter after drying is complete. Return the couscous to the couscousiere and steam for 20 minutes.

Return once again to the shallow pan and gradually work 1 cup water into the couscous with your hands. Cover the couscous with a towel.

8. Put the prunes, dates, and apricots in the top of the couscousiere. Steam for 15 minutes, uncovered. Remove and set aside.

9. Return the couscous to the couscousiere and steam it for 10 minutes. Combine the couscous with the steamed fruit, remaining butter, and the sugar-cinnamon mixture. Transfer to a serving bowl.

Minor Grains

By minor grains,

I mean statistically minor, judged by
a global standard. Wheat is a major grain
because it leads the world in production.
Amaranth is a minor grain because so much
less of it is grown than wheat or the other
world staples. Some of these "minor" crops are
actually major on their home ground:
tef is of overwhelming importance in Ethiopia;
millet in some parts of sub-Saharan Africa.
In the developed world all the minor grains are
exotic and marginal commodities, but they are ever
more available in health-food stores and provide
novelty in taste and in cooking qualities.

ᜫ AMARANTH ᜣ

Perhaps you have not yet heard of amaranth, a broad-leafed plant that once provided the Aztecs and Incas with high-protein "cereal" seeds and greens. Apparently, because of its association with Aztec rituals of human sacrifice, amaranth was suppressed by the Spanish conquistadors. But it spread around the world and established small footholds in the Himalayas and elsewhere. Today amaranth is the object of intensive research, and it has much to recommend it.

Three species of *Amaranthus* produce tiny edible seeds about the size of mustard seeds. Colorful seed heads, sometimes well over a foot in length, can yield more than 50,000 seeds with a protein content of 16 percent. This surpasses the protein content of wheat (12 to 14 percent), rice (7 to 10 percent), and corn (9 to 10 percent). What is more, the amino acid balance of amaranth seeds is heavy on lysine and can therefore be used to balance the lysine deficiency in other grain sources of protein. Like other grains, amaranth can be parched, boiled into porridge, and ground into flour. It is, however, essentially without gluten and won't rise in a yeast dough, unless wheat is added. But it does lend itself to flatbreads, and in India it is popped like corn and mixed with honey to make a sort of candy. The greens are also an excellent protein source, as long as they are boiled to remove the large quantity of nitrates and oxalic acid.

Amaranth is also a good plant for marginal growing areas. Grain amaranths thrive in virtual deserts. Vegetable amaranths survive Africa's rainy seasons. They grow like weeds. In fact, one species, *A. retroflexus*, or pigweed, is one of the world's worst weeds. Pigweed sends down a long taproot; its seeds can be stored without losing their capacity to germinate for at least forty years. The cultivated species are not so feisty, but there is reason to worry about amaranths turning into pest plants.

I am confident that agronomists will guard the world against an invasion of weed amaranths. I also believe that their research will, if continued, produce uniform plants that can be harvested by machine and that will yield amounts of seed per acre competitive with wheat and corn. But will amaranth's brilliant seed heads flutter over large portions of the world's arable land? Will people accustomed to surviving on rice or corn or millet, accustomed to the special taste, feel, and handling of those grains, switch, without political duress or even with it, to an exotic grain that even the Aztecs abandoned without much fuss?

Nutritional jawboning will not sway most farmers or consumers. Amaranth will have to make it in the marketplace, competing with established grains in price, ease of production, and perhaps most important, in aesthetic appeal. Establishing a market for a new staple is an enormous and lengthy undertaking. But peanuts and soybeans are proof that such revolutions of taste and production are possible. Peanuts were once dismissed as pig food; now they are a major crop in the world. Soybeans, an even bigger crop, were very recently introduced in this country. But once tasted, peanuts are incontestably delicious, gobbled up everywhere from Beijing to Dakar. Soybeans, on the other hand, have sneaked their way to success in the form of a usually anonymous oil. Soy, as such, has not won new friends among non-Asians except marginally, as a "foreign" food or a health food.

At this point, with only a handful of American farmers producing amaranth, too little is known about its potential uses to say how it will fare in the real world, if and when it can be grown economically. There is no reason to believe that it will outperform soybeans as a source of edible oil. Its greens appear to duplicate, more or less, the virtues of other potherbs such as spinach. It does appear, though, even now, that if amaranth is to seize more than a small geographical niche in places ideally suited to its growth, it will have to displace other grains. And this will happen only if people want to eat it.

Certainly in the American market, amaranth is an extreme long shot as a crop. The stigma of its relation to pigweed will hurt its acceptance in some quarters. More important, cheap protein sources abound. And there are plenty of worthwhile grains and greens we already know how to grow and already like. The problem in this country is to keep minor traditional grains in production: buckwheat, for example. (It doesn't pack the protein wallop of amaranth, but it makes terrific kasha.)

On the other hand, the nutritional promise of amaranth is so great that if research turns up viable varieties, it just might make a useful animal feed, possibly lowering the price of steak.

Amaranth Basic Recipe

Yields approximately 2 cups

5 cups water
1 cup grain amaranth

1. Bring the water to a rolling boil. Stir in the amaranth, reduce the heat, and simmer, uncovered, until the grains are al dente, about 20 minutes.
2. Drain and serve immediately, as a side-dish starch. Or you might want to try it as a breakfast cereal, with milk and your favorite sweetener.

⌁ FIRST COURSES ⌁

Stuffed Grape Leaves

Amaranth steamed inside grape leaves is a delicate alternative to the standard dish from the eastern Mediterranean made with rice and pine nuts.

Yields 24 stuffed grape leaves

2 cups chopped scallions
¼ cup olive oil
1 pound chicken or turkey breast, skinned, boned, and diced
1 cup grain amaranth
¼ teaspoon ground cinnamon

Salt and pepper
Cayenne pepper
2 dozen grape leaves, rinsed if canned or
    blanched if fresh
4 cloves garlic, slivered
1 cup chicken stock or water, approximately

1. Sauté the scallions in the olive oil over medium heat until the onion is completely softened. Stir in the chicken or turkey breast and cook until lightly browned. Then stir in the amaranth and coat with oil. Remove from heat.

2. Stir in the cinnamon, salt and pepper, and cayenne to taste.

3. Stuff the grape leaves. The classic method is to lay the leaf smooth side down on the counter. Put 1 tablespoon of stuffing at the base of the leaf (stem end) and roll the leaf over the stuffing, starting from the base. Fold the sides over the stuffing and continue rolling from the base end until the leaf is completely rolled up into a loose package. (The amaranth will expand in cooking.) Continue in this manner until all the stuffing is used up.

4. In a large saucepan, cover the bottom with flat leaves: this keeps the rolled-up leaves from sticking. Then arrange the rolled-up leaves, seam down, in alternating layers (one layer north-south, the next east-west), interspersing slivers of garlic as you go. Add enough chicken stock or water to cover. Set a plate on top of the leaves to hold them in place. Bring the stock or water to a boil, reduce the heat, cover, and simmer for 45 minutes to 2 hours, until the leaves are tender.

Gâteau d'Amaranthe

If you let boiled amaranth stand, it gets glutinous. This is why standard directions advise serving it immediately. But sticky amaranth can be a good thing. This savory cake, for instance, capitalizes on the thickening quality of the grain and treats it like a dough. Since amaranth has a naturally peppery flavor, it suits savory dishes of all kinds, like this one.

Yields	3 cups water
8 servings	1 cup grain amaranth
	One 3-ounce can anchovy fillets, chopped
	¼ cup capers
	4 eggs
	Salt

1. Bring the water to a boil. Add the amaranth and simmer for 25 minutes, covered. Let stand, covered, until the grain returns to room temperature.

2. Preheat the oven to 350° F.

3. Beat in the anchovies, capers, and eggs. Add salt to taste. Pour the mixture into a shallow cake pan and bake for about 50 minutes. Let cool almost to room temperature. Then cut into squares and serve with sautéed whiting or trout or other mild white fish.

❧ BUCKWHEAT ❧

Buckwheat (*Fagopyrum esculentum*) is the nutty brown "grain" best known as the main ingredient in primitive pancakes from the age before wheat was common in northern Europe (see page 168). It is really not, in the technical botanical sense, a grain at all. The buckwheat plant is not a grass, and its "seeds" are tiny one-seeded fruits, or achenes, of the type found on the surface of strawberries.

Buckwheat may have come to Europe with the Moors, since the French call it *sarrasin,* or Saracen. Similarly, Italians call it *grano saraceno,* and they make both a "black" polenta and a pasta called *pizzocheri*. In Spain, presumably the passageway for buckwheat to the north in medieval times, it is called Saracen wheat (*trigo sarraceno*) but more commonly goes by a name derived from Arabic, *alforfón*. And a buckwheat bread is said to survive as a regional dish in some parts of Spain. Russia continues to be the world's largest producer and consumer of buckwheat, but the Japanese dote on buckwheat noodles (soba) and have built an entire sub-cuisine around them.

These noodles are now routinely available in neighborhood Korean markets in U.S. cities, but the most common use for buckwheat in America is in its primal form, as barely processed, roasted groats—the eastern European dish called kasha.

Kasha

Only coarse whole groats will produce traditional, "grainy" kasha. Fine buckwheat yields a sort of kasha purée.

Yields
6 servings

1 egg
1 cup coarse (whole) buckwheat groats
2 cups boiling chicken soup or water
1 teaspoon salt

1. In a medium skillet or saucepan, beat the egg vigorously with a fork or whisk until the white and yolk are well mixed. Stir in the buckwheat groats and coat them with the egg. Set over low heat and stir for 2 to 3 minutes. This will cause the egg to set and the groats to separate from one another.

2. Add the soup or water and the salt. Stir well, cover, and cook over low heat for 15 minutes. If all the soup or water is not absorbed, drain well. Overcooked kasha turns to porridge, so if you are particularly interested in an al dente texture, begin testing the kasha after 10 minutes to see if it suits you.

Kasha Varnishkes

Grain with pasta may sound like starch overkill, but generations of Jewish mothers have proved this isn't so.

Yields
6 servings

1 cup chopped onions
2 tablespoons chicken fat, oil, or butter
Salt
1 egg
1 cup coarse (whole) buckwheat groats
2 cups boiling chicken soup or water
1 cup (4 ounces) egg bow tie noodles
    (varnishkes), also known as farfalle

1. Sauté the onions in the chicken fat, oil, or butter until very soft and dark.

2. Meanwhile, set a large quantity of lightly salted water over high heat and bring to a full rolling boil.

3. In a medium skillet or saucepan, beat the egg vigorously with a fork or whisk until the white and yolk are well mixed. Stir in the buckwheat groats and coat them with the egg. Set over low heat and stir for 2 to 3 minutes. This will cause the egg to set and the groats to separate from one another.

4. Add the boiling soup or water and 1 teaspoon salt. Stir well, cover, and cook over low heat for 15 minutes. If all the water is not absorbed, drain well. Overcooked kasha turns to porridge, so if you are particularly interested in an al dente texture, begin testing the kasha after 10 minutes to see if it suits you.

5. Meanwhile, boil the bow tie noodles in the salted water for 10 minutes. Drain.

6. Combine the noodles with the onions and kasha. Add more salt if necessary. Serve.

Buckwheat Blueberry Pancakes

Here is the only buckwheat dish that has entered the American mainstream cuisine. You can even find ready-mix products in supermarkets. This way is better—and cheaper.

Yields 18 to 24
thin pancakes

2 cups buckwheat flour
½ teaspoon baking powder
1 teaspoon baking soda
½ teaspoon salt
1 tablespoon honey
3 cups skim milk
3 tablespoons butter, melted
½ cup blueberries
Maple syrup or honey

1. In a mixing bowl, stir together the buckwheat flour, baking powder, baking soda, and salt.

2. In another bowl, combine the honey and milk with the melted butter. Beat in the dry ingredients so as to make a homogeneous, lump-free batter. Then work in the blueberries.

3. Lightly grease a griddle or heavy skillet and set it over medium heat. With a ladle, pour the batter in 3-inch circles. Cook until bubbles appear on the surface of the pancakes. Flip with a metal spatula and cook for another minute, or just long enough to brown the underside lightly. Continue in this manner until all the batter is used up. Serve with maple syrup or honey.

Stuffed Grape Leaves

Buckwheat, a favorite staple of dark, cold climates, was not historically available in wine-growing countries. This is the main reason why no culinary tradition evolved a dolma, or stuffed grape leaf, dish in which the basic starch was buckwheat. Today, when both main ingredients are easily available even in places where neither is indigenous, no reasonable barrier stands in the way of logical invention. Furthermore, the appealing lemony sourness of the grape leaves makes a nice gutsy match with the earthy, nutlike flavor of kasha.

Yields 24 stuffed grape leaves

1 onion, finely chopped
2 tablespoons oil or chicken fat
1 egg
1 cup coarse (whole) buckwheat groats
Salt and pepper
2 dozen grape leaves, rinsed if canned or
    blanched if fresh
4 cloves garlic, slivered
1 cup chicken stock or water, approximately

1. Sauté the onion in the oil or chicken fat over medium heat until the onion is completely softened.

2. Meanwhile, beat the egg vigorously with a fork or whisk until the white and yolk are well mixed. Stir in the buckwheat groats and coat them with the egg. Set over low heat in a heavy, medium-sized skillet and stir for 2 to 3 minutes. This will cause the egg to set and the groats to separate from one another.

3. Stir in the sautéed onion and add salt and pepper to taste.

4. Stuff the grape leaves. The classic method is to lay the leaf smooth side down on the counter. Put 1 tablespoon of stuffing at the base of the leaf (stem end) and roll the leaf over the stuffing, starting from the base. Fold the sides over the stuffing and continue rolling from the base end

until the leaf is completely rolled up into a loose package. (The groats will expand during cooking.) Continue in this manner until all the stuffing is used up.

5. In a large saucepan, cover the bottom with flat leaves: this keeps the rolled-up leaves from sticking. Then arrange the rolled-up leaves, seam down, in alternating layers (one layer north-south, the next east-west), interspersing slivers of garlic as you go. Add enough chicken stock or water to cover. Set a plate on top of the leaves to hold them in place. Bring the chicken stock or water to a boil, reduce the heat, cover, and simmer for 45 minutes to 2 hours, until the leaves are tender.

Variation: At step 3, gently stir in ½ cup salmon roe or other caviar. Serve with sour cream.

Soba
(Japanese Buckwheat Noodles)

In Japan, soba is everywhere and has inspired a minicuisine. It is possible to experience this at its best in a New York branch of one of the great Tokyo soba restaurants, Honmura An, where a chef makes the delicate brown noodles in full view of the dining room. Elsewhere in America, Korean grocers and other purveyors of Asian specialties routinely sell soba. Some are pure buckwheat; others include an admixture of wheat flour. You must decide for yourself, but the choice is not a simple one between the unadulterated and the crass pretender. Buckwheat/wheat soba is entirely authentic, and many knowledgeable people prefer it. In any case, the mixed-flour noodle cooks in about half the time it takes to boil the pure buckwheat variety. Cold soba is the norm, a refreshing change of pace.

Yields	6 quarts water
2 servings	2 scallions, trimmed and chopped
	2 tablespoons oil
	One 7-ounce package Japanese soba
	1 to 2 tablespoons sesame oil

1. Bring the water to a boil.

2. Meanwhile, sauté the scallions in the oil. Drain off any excess oil and set aside to cool.

3. Immerse the soba in the boiling water. Continue stirring, for 4 minutes if these are buckwheat/wheat noodles, or for 10 minutes if they are pure buckwheat. Drain in a colander and immerse in cold water. Drain again and transfer the noodles to a serving bowl.

4. Toss with the scallions and the sesame oil.

✑ *MAIN COURSE DISHES* ✑

Grano Turco con Funghi Selvatici e Noci
(*Buckwheat with Wild Mushrooms and Walnuts*)

With thanks to Giovanna Falconetti

The dark mystery of the forest comes to the table with this innovative mixture of woodland and field. The color is earthy, and the texture runs the spectrum of crunchiness, from the still grainy buckwheat to the brittle walnut shards, with the chewy chanterelles somewhere in between. All three stand out, but they also work together as something new and strange and serious.

Yields *4 servings*	1 egg, lightly beaten 1 cup coarse (whole) buckwheat groats 2 cups chicken stock or water ¼ teaspoon salt 2 tablespoons olive oil ½ cup chanterelles or other wild mushrooms ½ cup walnuts, roughly chopped

1. Stir together the egg and buckwheat in a heavy skillet. Set over medium heat and keep stirring until the egg has coated all the grains and

any moisture has evaporated. Add the chicken stock or water immediately. Stir in the salt, bring to a boil, reduce the heat, and simmer, covered, for 15 minutes, or until the groats are just al dente. Pour off any residual liquid.

2. While the buckwheat is cooking, heat the olive oil in another skillet. Sauté the mushrooms until they wilt. Then add the walnut pieces and toss so that they are coated with oil and get heated through.

3. Stir together the buckwheat and the mushroom-walnut mixture.

Soba with Pork and Oysters

This combination was inspired by a Korean dish that combines raw oysters, cold pork belly, and very hot, raw green chiles. The idea is to wrap the gray pork belly in a leaf of iceberg lettuce with a slice of chile, eat it, then do the same thing with an oyster. My problem, as you have guessed, was with the anemic-looking pork belly; whence the substitution here of cooked pork tenderloin. The soba noodles knit an otherwise stark dish together, adding a steadying flavor and texture to several more flamboyant ingredients.

Yields
4 servings

6 quarts water
One 7-ounce package all-buckwheat soba
    noodles
2 tablespoons oil, approximately
1 dozen oysters, shucked
¼ pound leftover roast pork tenderloin, sliced
2 long, hot green chiles, trimmed, seeded, and
    sliced into rounds
1 red bell pepper, trimmed, seeded, and diced

1. Bring the water to a boil. Add the soba noodles and stir for 10 minutes. Drain in a colander and immerse in cold water. Then drain again and transfer the noodles to a serving bowl.

2. Toss the noodles with the oil, coating all the strands.

3. It only remains to array the other ingredients on the noodles. This

can be done either in the serving bowl or on individual plates, but either way, the oysters (3 per person) should alternate with the brown and green and red of the pork, the chile, and the red bell pepper.

⌁ *DESSERT* ⌁

Buckwheat Pudding

We head north again for dark grain goodness. Here is an ideal use for fine kasha, which would be too wimpy to use for the savory kind. But in this pudding, delicacy is the way to go.

Yields	2 cups fine buckwheat groats (kasha)
4 servings	1 egg yolk
	1 cup milk
	2 tablespoons butter
	Pinch of salt
	½ cup sugar
	1¼ cups heavy cream
	½ teaspoon vanilla extract
	Bread crumbs

1. Preheat the oven to 375° F.

2. Stir the groats together with the egg yolk and cook over low heat in a skillet, stirring constantly, for a few minutes, until the yolk solidifies and keeps the groats separate.

3. In a large saucepan, bring the milk to a boil with the butter and salt. Add the groats, bring to a boil again, cover, and place in the oven for 30 minutes.

4. Stir the sugar, cream, and vanilla into the groat mixture. Grease a shallow ovenproof dish and coat the bottom with bread crumbs. Fill the dish with the groat mixture. Return the groats to the oven and cook for 1 hour.

5. Remove from the oven and cover until there is no steam. Serve hot with fruit preserves.

ᛜᄀ MILLET ᚦᚢ

Millet *(Panicum miliaceum)* is an ancient grain that continues to be a staple in hot, dry parts of Africa and Asia. It preceded rice as a staple for human beings in China, but there and everywhere else that larger, more desirable grains have proved practical, millet has disappeared, despite its high (16 to 22 percent) protein content. In most Western countries it is sold primarily as birdseed. Still, it is easy to find in health-food stores, and with its mild flavor and crunchy texture, it makes a nice change from more familiar grains.

Basic Recipe

Yields
about 4 cups

1 tablespoon oil
1 cup millet
2½ cups boiling water
1 tablespoon salt

1. Heat the oil in a heavy 2-quart saucepan over medium heat. Stir in the millet and keep stirring until it darkens slightly in color and begins to give off a pleasant toasted smell.

2. Pour in the boiling water, add the salt, increase the heat to maximum, cover, and let the mixture return to a boil. Immediately reduce the heat to low and continue cooking, covered, for 25 minutes, or until softened. Let stand another 10 minutes, covered, off the heat, until the water has been completely absorbed. The individual grains should be separate, relatively dry, and not chewy.

Porridge

This method will produce a luxuriously smooth breakfast cereal on the order of Cream of Rice, but with a bit more grain feeling to it. Add the usual breakfast cereal flavorings: milk, sugar, syrup, brown sugar, jam, or honey.

Yields
about 4 cups

2½ cups water
1 tablespoon salt
1 cup millet

1. Bring the water to a full rolling boil in a heavy 2-quart saucepan. Add the salt.

2. Stir in the millet, return to the boil, lower the heat, cover, and simmer for 25 minutes or until soft. Let stand 10 minutes off the heat, covered, until the water has been completely absorbed.

⌁ SIDE DISHES ⌁

Millet Soufflé

Yields
4 servings

½ cup millet
1 cup water
1¼ teaspoons salt
Pepper
3 eggs, separated
⅔ cup milk
½ cup grated Parmesan cheese

1. A day before you want to serve this dish, set the millet to soak in the water.

2. The next day, put the millet with its soaking water into the top of a

double boiler and stir in ¾ teaspoon of the salt. Steam over boiling water for 20 minutes.

3. Preheat the oven to 375° F.

4. Mix the cooked millet with the remaining salt, the pepper to taste, egg yolks, milk, and ¼ cup of the grated cheese.

5. Beat the egg whites until stiff but not dry and fold them into the millet mixture.

6. Pour the mixture into a greased 6-cup soufflé dish or charlotte mold. Sprinkle with the remaining cheese, set in a pan of hot water, and bake 30 minutes, or until browned and set.

Millet with Lemongrass and Shrimp

Yields
4 servings

1 tablespoon oil
1 cup millet
2½ cups boiling water
1 tablespoon salt
1 stalk lemongrass, lightly pounded and cut into
    strips
2 scallions, trimmed and chopped
1 to 3 dried red chiles, according to taste,
    crumbled
1 pound small shrimp, shelled

1. Heat the oil in a heavy 2-quart saucepan over medium heat. Stir in the millet and keep stirring until it darkens slightly in color and begins to give off a pleasant toasted smell.

2. Pour in the boiling water, add the salt, lemongrass, scallions, and chiles, increase the heat to maximum, cover, and let return to a boil. Immediately reduce the heat to low and continue cooking, covered, for 25 minutes or until softened. Remove the lemongrass and discard.

3. Stir in the shrimp. Remove the saucepan from the heat and let the millet stand another 10 minutes, covered, off the heat, until the water has been completely absorbed. The individual grains should be separate, relatively dry, and not chewy.

⤙ DESSERT ⤚

Millet Kugel

This is an adaptation of a traditional East European Jewish pudding originally made with rice. Millet gives it a completely different, more comforting texture and an attractively nutty flavor.

Yields
8 servings

3 tablespoons oil, plus a little more for greasing the mold
1 cup millet
2½ cups boiling water
1 tablespoon salt
6 eggs
½ cup brown sugar
2 cups tart apples, peeled and minced

1. Preheat the oven to 350° F. Brush the inside of a 2-quart charlotte mold with oil. Set aside.

2. Heat 2 tablespoons of the oil in a heavy 2-quart saucepan over medium heat. Stir in the millet and keep stirring until it darkens slightly in color and begins to give off a pleasant toasted smell.

3. Pour in the boiling water, add the salt, increase the heat to maximum, cover, and let the mixture return to a boil. Immediately reduce the heat to low and continue cooking, covered, for 25 minutes, or until the millet is softened. Let stand another 10 minutes, covered, off the heat, until the water has been completely absorbed. The individual grains should be separate, relatively dry, and not chewy.

4. With an electric mixer, beat the eggs with the brown sugar until light tan in color and greatly expanded in volume. This will take 4 or 5 minutes. Stir in the millet and apples and the remaining oil. Transfer the mixture to the oiled mold. Spread evenly and bake for 25 minutes, or until the kugel is nicely browned on top and firm below. Let cool to room temperature.

✑ QUINOA ❧

Chenopodium quinoa is an annual, broad-leaved, dicotyledonous herb of the Andes, usually standing about one to two meters high. Leafy flower clusters (panicles) rise mostly from the top of the plant. The dry seedlike fruit is about two millimeters in diameter and is enclosed in a hard, shiny four-layered fruit wall (pericarp) containing bitter saponin. Quinoa seeds are usually flat and pale yellow, and they can be steamed, ground into flour, or fermented to make a mildly intoxicating beverage. Quinoa leaves are highly edible and are often used for livestock feed.

You will easily find quinoa grain in health-food stores in the United States. Quinoa has attracted the interest of the nutritionally conscious vegetarian because its protein component has an amino-acid profile that very closely parallels the ideal protein standard sanctified by the Food and Agricultural Organization of the United Nations. Quinoa's protein is high in the essential amino acids lysine, methionine, and cystine, making it complementary to other grains that are notably deficient in lysine, and to legumes such as beans that are deficient in methionine and cystine.

Yes, but how does it taste? Following the directions on the box, I cooked it "like rice," steaming it in twice its volume of water for about 15 minutes. The grains fluffed up nicely, turned translucent, and the "germ ring" was visible, as advertised. The taste was mild—all the bitter saponin on the surface of the grains must have been washed away by the manufacturer. And the texture was delicate and appealing.

Basic Recipe

Yields
4 cups

4 cups water
1 cup quinoa

1. To remove the sticky, bitter soapy saponin that may still be present on the surface of quinoa, put the quinoa in a blender or processor with 2 cups of the water. Turn the motor on and off briefly a couple of times. If

the water turns cloudy, drain through a fine-mesh strainer and repeat until the water remains clear. This can also be accomplished manually, by rubbing the grains in a bowlful of water.

2. Bring the remaining 2 cups of water to a boil in a medium saucepan. Add quinoa and cook over medium heat, covered, for about 12 minutes, or until all the water has been absorbed. Alternatively, combine quinoa with the water and bring to a boil. Let cook 2 minutes; then let stand, covered, for 30 minutes, or until the water has been absorbed.

⌁ MAIN COURSE DISHES ⌁

Ch'aqe de Quinua
(Thick Quinoa Vegetable Stew)

This recipe has been adapted from Nelly de Jordan's *Nuestras Comidas* (Cochabamba, Bolivia, 1962). It approximates the country stew of the high Andes in Mrs. de Jordan's indispensable book. For ch'aqe, she recommends a roughly processed form of quinoa not available here. The imilla potato, with its many eyes and gritty *(harinoso)* texture, is also not a practical choice. The specification for the lamb is an interpretation of the Spanish "8 *nudos*," meaning 8 knuckles' width of lamb. This is apparently the way Bolivian butchers sell meat. Perhaps a single piece of lamb is meant. Perhaps it would also make better culinary sense, given the cooking qualities of our favas and peas, to add them when the potatoes are almost done. In any case, I present this recipe for its "flavor" more than as a strict set of directions for reproducing the dish as one might find it in a Bolivian home.

Yields	8 cups meat stock
8 servings	1 pound stewing lamb, cut into 1-inch cubes
	½ cup onion, finely chopped
	½ teaspoon ground cumin
	½ teaspoon ground oregano
	½ teaspoon freshly ground black pepper
	1 tablespoon cayenne pepper
	1½ cups quinoa, thoroughly rinsed
	½ cup fava beans, peeled and skinned
	½ cup peas
	8 small potatoes (as a substitute for the variety called imilla in Bolivia, which holds its shape during cooking, use Yukon golds)
	1 tablespoon salt, or to taste
	1 tablespoon parsley, finely chopped

1. Bring the stock to the boil with the lamb. Add the onion, cumin, oregano, black pepper, and cayenne. Reduce the heat and simmer 15 minutes.

2. Stir in the quinoa and simmer until it swells and softens (about 12 minutes).

3. Add the favas, peas, potatoes, and salt. Cook 20 minutes more, or until the potatoes are soft, stirring from time to time to prevent burning.

4. Sprinkle with the parsley and serve.

Picadillo

In its original home, Mexico, this chopped meat extravaganza is done with beef and rice. My Sumatran friend Sri Owen adapted the dish for *The Rice Book* by adding ginger, chopped pickles, and chopped hard-boiled eggs to a recipe she found in her (and my) friend Elisabeth Lambert Ortiz's *The Complete Book of Mexican Cooking* (M. Evans, 1980). I am taking this process one step further by substituting quinoa for rice, thereby gaining a certain earthiness. I was tempted to pay further tribute to my learned predecessors in *picadillismo* by suggesting ground water buffalo meat (typically Sumatran) or llama (a nod to Ortiz's interest in Peru), but I got cold feet. Nothing prevents you from doing this, should you find yourself in Ollantaytambo.

Yields
4 servings

3 tablespoons oil
1 large onion, peeled and chopped
3 cloves garlic, peeled and chopped
1 teaspoon fresh ginger, finely chopped
2 to 3 jalapeño peppers, trimmed, seeded, and
    finely chopped
4 quarts water, lightly salted
2 cups quinoa, well washed
1 pound ground beef
1 green bell pepper, trimmed, seeded, and
    diced
One 14-ounce can tomatoes, chopped
Salt and pepper
⅓ cup raisins
2 tablespoons chopped cilantro, for garnish

1. Heat the oil in a skillet. Stir-fry the onion, garlic, ginger, and jalapeño peppers for 3 minutes. Meanwhile, start the lightly salted water to boil for the quinoa in a large pot.

2. Add the ground beef and continue stir-frying for another 3 minutes. Then add the bell pepper and tomatoes (with their juices), mix all the ingredients nicely together, and then simmer slowly for 15 minutes.

3. After the final simmering in the previous step has been going on for 5 minutes, begin cooking the quinoa in the large pot of boiling water. Cook over medium heat, covered, for about 12 minutes or until al dente.

4. When the quinoa is finished, drain and transfer it to a serving bowl. Then, straightaway, add salt and pepper to taste, and then the raisins, to the picadillo in the skillet. Continue cooking for another minute or two, just long enough to heat the raisins through. Toss the picadillo with the quinoa. Garnish with the cilantro and serve.

Maria Baez Kijac teaches the cooking of her native Andes in Illinois, but she also experiments with new ideas. The Quinoa Pilaf on page 227 might be called an Italo-Bolivian invention: New World quinoa made to absorb lots of chicken stock before going to the table.

Quinoa Fritters

This could be called an example of very southern cooking. To a North American, it may suggest the Dixie kitchen or Creole New Orleans after a successful Inca invasion. Serve with a roast or game.

Yields 24 to
30 fritters

4 quarts water, lightly salted
1 cup quinoa, well washed
¼ cup honey
½ cup rye flour
1 tablespoon baking powder
½ teaspoon mace
4 eggs
Oil, for deep-frying

1. Bring the lightly salted water to a boil. Add the quinoa, cover, and cook over medium heat for 12 minutes or until al dente. Drain, stir the quinoa together with the honey in a bowl, and let cool.

2. Beat the rye flour, baking powder, and mace into the cold quinoa. Transfer the mixture to the jar of a blender. Add the eggs and purée into a thick batter. Scrape the batter into a bowl and let rest, covered, for 30 minutes.

3. Heat 2 inches oil to 320° F in a deep-fry kettle. Take 2 soupspoons and use them to drop nuggets of batter, a half dozen per batch, into the hot oil. (Actually, don't drop, but slide the batter in. The risk of injury from splashing oil is serious.) Cook for a few minutes, until nicely browned, turning the fritters once or twice with a wok shovel or other long-handled device. Drain on a paper towel and continue with another batch until all the batter is used up. Serve hot.

Quinoa Pilaf

This recipe was inspired by one in Maria Baez Kijac's *The Art of Cooking with Quinoa* (PM Publishing, 1991).

Yields
4 cups

2 tablespoons vegetable oil
1 to 3 cloves garlic, minced
1 medium onion, chopped
1 cup quinoa, thoroughly rinsed
2 cups chicken stock or water

1. Heat the oil in a medium saucepan. Then sauté the garlic and onion for 2 minutes.

2. Add the quinoa and continue sautéing for another 5 minutes, stirring.

3. Add the chicken stock or water and bring to a boil, cover, reduce the heat, and simmer slowly for 12 minutes, or until all the water has been absorbed. Let stand, covered, for 5 minutes before serving.

↬ DESSERT ↫

Quinoa Pudding

Yields
4 to 6 servings

¼ cup raw quinoa, well rinsed
4 cups milk (skim milk will work and so will heavy cream, or any other concentration of the two along the milk-fat spectrum)
Pinch of salt
¾ cup sugar
½ teaspoon vanilla or almond extract
¾ cup raisins or chopped dates
Grated nutmeg or cinnamon

1. Preheat the oven to 300° F.

2. Stir together the quinoa, milk, salt, and sugar in a greased 6-cup soufflé (or other ovenproof) dish. Set in the oven and bake for 2 hours, stirring occasionally to work the "hide" that collects on the top of the pudding back into the rest of the dish.

3. Stir in the vanilla or almond extract and raisins or dates. Return to the oven for 30 minutes. Sprinkle with nutmeg or cinnamon. Serve lukewarm or cold.

❧ RYE ❧

Rye (*Secale cereale*) in modern life is almost exclusively used as a flour, in combination with other flours, for bread baking. It does contain gluten, but not enough and not the right kind to produce light risen loaves that could compete with wheaten loaves. So-called rye breads, even pumpernickel, normally contain mixtures of rye and wheat. All-rye breads are dense and flat. Ry-Krisp is a familiar example. Scandinavia, Germany, and eastern Europe still favor rye's flavor and color in their breads, which reflects the time when rye was a staple grain in these areas. It thrives in cool, wet climates.

Historically, rye moved westward from Central Asia as a weed in wheat fields. After it was cultivated, in ancient times, the Asian association continued: its flour was mixed with wheat flour to make maslin. In America a large part of the rye crop is converted to whiskey. Ergot, the fungus that grows on the plant's seeds, is toxic, but it contains medically useful alkaloids, as well as lysergic acid diethylamide (LSD).

In the kitchen whole-grain rye is a curiosity. But it does offer a darkly interesting alternative to other grains and potatoes, as a side starch with meat or fish main courses.

Rye Berries

Yields
2 cups

6 cups water
1 cup rye berries (whole-grain rye with the
　　hull removed)
1½ teaspoons salt

1. Bring the water to a rolling boil.

2. Add the rye berries and salt, lower the heat, cover, and simmer until the grains are softened but al dente, about 1 hour.

3. Drain and serve, or let cool to room temperature and serve in a salad.

Karen Karp's Banana Bread

Three flours combine to give this perfect tea cake its serious flavor, but rye stands out and makes it an especially gutsy banana bread. Ms. Karp, who developed this variation on a very popular theme, is a restaurant consultant in New York. She recommends substituting six small finger bananas for the three regular ones whenever possible. Remember that finger bananas must be very ripe, almost mushy in the hand; otherwise they will be fibrous and unappealing.

Yields
1 loaf

½ cup (¼ pound) unsalted butter, at room
    temperature
¼ cup sugar
2 large eggs
3 ripe bananas or 6 finger bananas
1 tablespoon milk
½ cup chopped nuts
1 cup all-purpose flour
½ cup rye flour
½ cup whole-wheat flour
1 teaspoon salt
1 teaspoon baking soda
1 teaspoon baking powder
Sesame seeds

1. Preheat the oven to 325° F. Grease a 9 by 5 by 3-inch loaf pan and set aside.

2. Use a whisk or a hand mixer to cream the butter and sugar in a large mixing bowl until light and fluffy. Beat in the eggs one at a time and continue beating until the color of the mixture is pale lemon.

3. In a small bowl, mash the bananas with a fork. Then mix in the milk and chopped nuts.

4. In another bowl, mix together the all-purpose flour, the rye flour, and the whole-wheat flour, the salt, baking soda, and baking powder.

5. Add the banana mixture to the butter-sugar-egg mixture and stir until well mixed. Add the dry ingredients from step 4 and continue stirring until the flour disappears.

6. Pour the batter into the prepared loaf pan. Smooth and level the top. Sprinkle with sesame seeds and bake for 1 hour, or until a toothpick inserted in the center comes out clean. Set aside to cool on a rack for 15 minutes. Then slide a knife around the edges of the banana bread to make sure it doesn't stick to the pan.

7. Place a platter over the open side of the pan, invert, and unmold. Invert the bread onto a rack (so the top—the convex side that was exposed in the oven—is up) and let cool completely before slicing.

∽ FIRST COURSES ∾

Cabbage Stuffed with Rye Berries and Lamb

Yields
4 servings

4 tablespoons salt
2 cups rye berries
1 large cabbage
1 pound ground lamb or other ground meat
2 medium onions, peeled and chopped
2 teaspoons black pepper
2 tablespoons ground cumin
1 teaspoon cayenne pepper or 2 teaspoons
    red pepper flakes
6 cups beef stock

1. Bring 2 quarts of water to a boil with 1 tablespoon of the salt. Dump in the rye berries and cook at a fast simmer for about 1 hour, or

until the grains begin to disintegrate and show bits of white. Drain and set aside to cool enough so that you can handle them.

2. Meanwhile, in another pot, bring a large quantity of water to the boil with 2 tablespoons of the salt—enough water to completely cover the cabbage. Lower the heat so that the water simmers. Then score the cabbage with a small, sharp knife, cutting a ¼-inch-deep circle around the stem, which will make it easy to remove the leaves. Now, holding the cabbage by its stem, plunge the head into the simmering water and hold it there for a few seconds. This will help separate the outer leaf from the rest of the cabbage. Remove the leaf and set aside. Continue this way until you have 12 leaves. Don't worry if they are torn here and there.

3. Blanch each leaf by holding it under the simmering water with a wooden spoon for 2 minutes. Drain.

4. In a mixing bowl, combine the rye berries, the remaining tablespoon of salt, the ground lamb, chopped onions, black pepper, cumin, and the cayenne pepper or hot pepper flakes.

5. Form the rye-berry–lamb mixture into 12 balls the size of walnuts or slightly larger, which should use up the whole mixture. Then spread out a cabbage leaf, outer side down. Put a rye-berry ball on the leaf and fold the edges of the leaf over it, making a fairly tight package, with the rib edge on top. Secure either with string or a toothpick. Continue in this way until you have stuffed all 12 leaves.

6. Pour the beef stock into a pot large enough to hold all the stuffed leaves in two layers. Then put in the stuffed leaves. Place over medium heat and bring the liquid to a boil, lower the heat, cover, and cook at a slow simmer for 45 minutes, or until the ribs have softened and the stock has imbibed the flavors of the cabbage and its stuffing.

7. Serve in shallow, wide soup bowls. Place 3 stuffed cabbage leaves in each bowl and pour the broth over them. There should be enough broth to come about a third of the way up the sides of the stuffed leaves.

Rye Focaccia
Basic Dough

This is made of a rye dough, yeast-raised, with enough rye flour to give it a tang and a nice dark color, but enough wheat flour to give it some loft. Since focaccia and its first cousin, pizza, are essentially flatbreads improved with yeast, the gluten-defect of rye flour is not so much a liability here as it is a fundamental problem to be wrestled with in conventional rye bread. This recipe shows how the same dough can be turned into a focaccialike bread that is ideal as a finger food with drinks or as a base for pizza.

> 1 package active dry yeast
> ½ teaspoon honey
> 2 cups rye flour
> 1¾ cups wheat flour
> 2 teaspoons salt
> 7 tablespoons olive oil, chicken fat, or lard

1. Whisk together the yeast, honey, and ⅓ cup of warm (110° F.) water. Let the mixture stand in a warm place for 5 minutes, until it bubbles.

2. In a warm bowl, stir together the yeast mixture with the rye and wheat flours, the salt, the olive oil or other fat, and 1 cup warm water, or more if necessary, so as to make a dough that forms a ball easily. Knead for 5 minutes on a floured board until smooth and uniform. Leave the dough to rise in a lightly oiled bowl covered with plastic wrap for 2 hours, or until it doubles in bulk.

3. Turn out of bowl and use in the recipes that follow.

Focaccia

Yields
8 round breads

1 recipe Rye Focaccia Basic Dough (see page 232)
¼ cup caraway seeds
Olive oil
Salt

1. The quantity listed here will make roughly 8 "loaves." You will probably want to divide the dough and freeze some of it for future use, dividing the amount of caraway seeds proportionately. A quarter of the dough will yield two 8- or 9-inch rounds. Once you have decided on quantity, knead in the caraway seeds and let the dough rest, covered in plastic wrap, in the refrigerator for 1 hour.

2. On a floured board, roll out ⅛ of the original recipe into a thin 8-inch circle. Pick it up at one edge and move the dough to a lightly oiled baking sheet. Let it rise, covered with a damp towel, for 30 minutes.

3. Dimple the dough with your fingertips, leaving little basins to collect oil and salt. Cover and let rise another 2 hours, or until doubled in bulk.

4. Preheat the oven to 400° F.

5. Brush the surface of the dough with olive oil. Sprinkle with salt. Bake for 20 to 25 minutes. During the first 10 minutes, sprinkle with a little water every 3 minutes. Serve immediately.

Variation

Rye Pizza

Proceed as above, but when you are ready to bake the dough, spread ¼ pound of any of the following toppings onto the "pie" surface: smoked salmon, pastrami, prosciutto, drained pickled herring.

❧ DESSERT ❧

Rye Cookies

Rye gives these simple triangles a certain strength of character. Rose water or orange flower water will add an ethereal aspect.

Yields about 2 dozen cookies

1 cup (½ pound) butter, at room temperature
¾ cup sugar
1 cup rye flour
1 ¼ cups wheat flour
2 tablespoons rose water or orange flower water

1. Use an electric mixer to cream the butter and sugar. Then beat in the rye flour and wheat flour to make a uniform dough. Beat in rose or orange flower water. Cover and chill for 1 hour.

2. Preheat the oven to 350° F. Butter and flour a cookie sheet.

3. Cut off ¼ of the dough and roll it out as thin as possible between 2 sheets of waxed paper. Cut into small triangles and move them to the cookie sheet with a metal spatula. Prick all over with a fork and bake for 8 to 10 minutes, or until nicely browned.

Repeat until all the dough is used up.

❧ TEF ❧

At the height of the cruel Mengistu regime in Ethiopia in 1985, I made a modest proposal for exerting indirect pressure on the government that might persuade it to treat its starving people with greater compassion. My plan did not involve an expeditionary force of American soldiers such as recently went to Ethiopia's neighbor Somalia. In fact, all I wanted was to divert some of the immense capacity of U.S. agriculture to the cultivation of Ethiopia's staple grain, *Eragrostis abyssinica*.

In the classical language of Ethiopia, Amharic, *E. abyssinica* is just called tef. It yields a tiny seed, about 150th the size of wheat grains, but that smallest of all cultivated grains is the heart of Ethiopian traditional cookery. Tef flour turns into the spongy, pleasantly sour pancakelike bread known as injera, which literally underlies every Ethiopian meal. To set an Ethiopian table, one lays down a circular injera on top of which the other food is arrayed, directly, without the intermediary of any plate. Other injeras are served on the side and torn into pieces to be used as grabbers for the food on the "tablecloth" injera. Eventually, after the meal is finished, you eat the tablecloth, a delicious repository of the juices from the food that has been resting on it.

This method of eating is certainly worlds away from my own traditions, but it has had an immediate appeal for me and for everyone I know who has tried it. And a large part of that appeal has been the opportunity to share in the refinement and wholeness of a very old and independent culture's foodways, right down to the table manners. But back in 1985 in Ethiopia, this idyllic injera-centered cuisine was in dire trouble on its home ground. During the catastrophic famine years under Mengistu, tef production had declined abruptly and people were reportedly consuming the seed stock. Upon hearing this, my first assumption was that enlightened efforts at food relief could bring tef from the outside into Ethiopia. But tef did not really exist as a crop anywhere else. So it began to look as if traditional Ethiopian cuisine was doomed.

Of course, the Ethiopians could survive on other grains. They could even make perfectly traditional types of injera from sorghum, wheat, millet, rice, corn, and barley. And that is precisely what they were doing in the restaurants they established in exile in New York, Washington, and other American cities. Nevertheless, it seemed tragic that tef should drop from view and, with it, one of the most defining features of an ancient way of life.

Fortunately, there was a way of saving tef, nonviolently, through a strategy of agronomic bootstrapping that might even help liberate Ethiopia. It turned out that there was a modest seed stock for tef in the United States. My friend Patti Hagan, a writer on gardening, located a supplier in Nevada selling tef seed to American gardeners who wanted to plant tef as an ornamental grass. (The company's delightful name and address—Garden Magic of Zephyr Cove, Nevada—was in pastoral harmony with tef's vernacular English name, "love grass," a direct translation of its Greek-derived genus name.)

My idea was for the U.S. Department of Agriculture to use these seeds to begin a crash program for a commercial crop of tef. In short order, I argued, there would be a large enough supply of the grain to blackmail Mengistu into concessions on human rights. He could have our tef if he cleaned up his act—or risk the anger of his people when they heard he had rejected a gift of their favorite food.

Ronald Reagan's USDA paid no attention to me. But Mengistu fell anyway. Meanwhile, at least one American grower went ahead and raised tef in serious quantity as a cash crop: Wayne Carlson of Maskal Forages (1318 Willow Street, Caldwell, ID 83605; tel.: 208-454-3330). You can find his tef for sale today in many health-food stores.

Nutrition-minded Americans have turned to tef as a source of calcium, fiber, and protein. It is also an alternative grain for people allergic to the gluten in wheat. It has an appealing, sweet molasseslike flavor.

Whole-Grain Tef

Yields
3 cups

3 cups water
1 tablespoon salt
1 cup tef

1. Bring the water to a rolling boil. Stir in the salt.
2. Add the tef, lower the heat, and simmer, uncovered, until chewy, about 15 minutes. The grains will be separate. Serve this as a side starch with meat or fish main courses.

∿ BREADS ∿

INJERA

Now that tef is readily available in the United States, exiled Ethiopians can at last make their spongy, flat sourdough injera here. Indeed, the largest Ethiopian community in America, in the Washington, D.C., metropolitan area, has its own injera bakery as well as Ethiopian groceries that sell authentic tef injera in plastic packages.

This is an obvious boon for Ethiopian immigrants, who have also found ways of providing themselves with other crucial elements of their unique cuisine, from honey beer to something known in English as false banana *(Ensete edule)*. But for non-Ethiopian cooks, one of the unforeseen advantages of a ready supply of tef is that it offers an alternative route for the investigation of one of the leading mysteries of the kitchen: sourdough baking.

Injera is, among other things, a first cousin of the sourdough breads that have made specialty bakers in San Francisco, Paris, and, lately, New York famous and even revered. In the food press much ink has been spilled over the essential mystery of sourdough—how to start it, how to feed it, how to keep it from getting too sour or from losing its fermentational oomph.

I am in no position to make sophisticated distinctions between naturally fermented tef batters and those made with commercial American yeasts, but it does seem obvious that the no-yeast recipe collected by Steve Raichlen and published in the Washington *Post,* which I have adapted below, must reflect traditional practice in the ancient kingdom of the Queen of Sheba before her descendants learned new tricks in our midst.

Basic Recipe

Yields 10 to 12 injeras

¾ cup tef, finely ground in a flour mill (or in a blender after being moistened in 3½ cups water)

Salt

Sunflower or other vegetable oil

1. Mix the mill-ground tef with 3½ cups water (or moisten whole tef in the water and grind in a blender) and let stand in a bowl covered with a dish towel, at room temperature, until it bubbles and has turned sour. This may take as long as 3 days. The fermenting mixture should be the consistency of pancake batter (which is exactly what it is).

2. Stir in salt, a little at a time, until you can just detect the taste.

3. Lightly oil an 8- or 9-inch skillet (or a larger one if you like). Place over medium heat. Then proceed as you would with a normal pancake or crêpe. Pour in enough batter to cover the bottom of the skillet. If you use a teacup as a dipper, a little more than half its capacity of batter (about ¼ cup) will make a thin pancake covering the surface of an 8-inch skillet. Spread the batter around immediately after pouring it in, by turning and rotating the skillet in the air. This is the classic French method for very thin crêpes. Injera is not supposed to be paper-thin, so you should use a bit more batter than you would for a crêpe but less than you would for a flapjack.

4. Cook briefly, until holes form in the injera and the edges lift from the pan. Turn and cook the other side. Remove and let cool. Repeat with the remaining batter.

Yesuff Fitfit
(Sunflower Water Mixed with Injera)

This recipe is adapted from *Exotic Ethiopian Cooking* by Daniel J. Mesfin (Ethiopian Cookbook Enterprises of Falls Church, Virginia, 3800 Powell Lane, Suite 404, Falls Church, VA 22041).

Yields	2 cups sunflower seeds
4 to 6 servings	10 cups water
	2 cups green (raw) jalapeño chiles, seeded and chopped
	½ teaspoon chopped onion
	¼ teaspoon chopped ginger
	¼ teaspoon chopped garlic
	Salt, to taste
	4 to 6 slices injera (see recipe, page 237)

1. Boil the sunflower seeds in 6 cups of the water for 15 minutes. Remove from heat and drain off the liquid.

2. Grind the seeds in a blender until they turn to a paste.

3. Put the paste in a bowl and add the remaining 4 cups water.

4. Mix thoroughly and then strain the liquid into a bowl. Discard the paste.

5. Stir in the jalapeños, onion, ginger, garlic, and salt to the strained liquid.

6. Break the injera into small pieces and combine it with the liquid mixture. Refrigerate and serve cold in a bowl.

❧ WILD RICE ☙

Zizania aquatica is not rice, but a North American native aquatic grass with an appealingly smoky, chewy nature. Until quite recently it had remained a wild, uncultivated plant that Indians would harvest in northern lakes from their canoes. Now that nonshattering varieties have been hybridized and grown in paddies in California, some of the romance may have gone out of wild rice. But the price has fallen and the quality has not. Among aficionados, there is a debate about how far processors should go in polishing away the bran of wild rice. The Ojibways I met in Minnesota, who jigged their rice (polished it by dancing on it in moccasins), prized grains that had been thoroughly polished, almost to ricelike whiteness. Those of us accustomed to brown-black grains and their funkier taste may be deluding ourselves with visions of pre-Columbian authenticity, but lightly processed wild rice does go very nicely with game or other red meat, not to mention poultry and seafood. I love wild rice, the only exclusively North American grain.

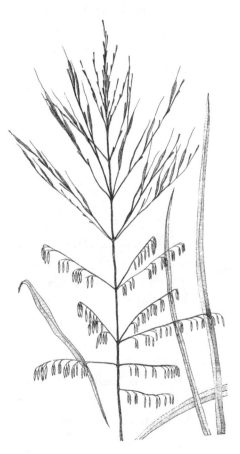

Basic Recipe

Yields
6 servings

1 cup wild rice
1 teaspoon salt
3 cups cold water

1. Put the rice and salt in a 6-cup saucepan with the cold water.

2. Bring to a boil, reduce the heat, and simmer, covered, for anywhere from 30 minutes to 1 hour. Cooking times will vary widely according to the age and degree of processing of the grain. As with true rice, overcooking produces porridge. So until you are familiar with the product you are using, it is excellent practice to start inspecting the pot periodically after 20 minutes or so, to catch the wild rice at the moment when the grains begin to split, become grateful to the tongue, but still retain a slightly "wild" crunch and a nutty flavor. Do not be discouraged if it takes nearly an hour to reach this stage with very dark-looking, lightly processed rice. This is not what will probably happen with machine-harvested and mass-processed rice.

⌁ FIRST COURSE ⌁

Judith Jones's Wild Rice Pancakes

This is a savory pancake not meant for breakfast with maple syrup, but ideal for a first course or a light lunch when you have extra cooked wild rice left from an earlier adventure with this remarkable and now affordable grain. Egg holds the rice grains together and gives the pancakes a nice crunch. The pepper and scallion fragments give them the colors of the Italian flag but will remind you of Chinese or Korean scallion pancakes if you know them. The wild rice offers its own special chewiness and earthiness. These will go very nicely with drinks.

Yields about 1 egg
10 pancakes 2½ cups cooked wild rice
2 tablespoons flour
¼ cup red bell pepper, finely diced
2 scallions, finely chopped
Salt and pepper, to taste
Oil, for frying

1. Beat the egg into the wild rice. Then mix in the flour, red bell pepper, and scallions, and season with salt and pepper.

2. Heat about ⅛ inch of oil in a large skillet. When hot, drop in ¼ cupfuls of the wild rice mixture, flattening the cakes with a spatula to spread them out, and continue at intervals around the pan without letting the pancakes touch. Cook for about 2 minutes over medium heat until the bottoms are lightly browned and the batter is holding together; then turn the pancakes and cook on the other side for a minute or so. Serve hot.

Variation: Use about half the amount specified above for each pancake, about 2 tablespoons or what will fill a serving spoon. This will produce smaller, crisper pancakes that can be drained on paper towels and served as cocktail hors d'oeuvres.

✌ MAIN COURSE DISHES ✌

Brisket with Wild Rice and Apricots

Jewish mothers and their children will recognize everything here— the well-browned and slowly cooked brisket, the onions, and the apricots. Even the red wine might have appeared in some households. But wild rice was never—I can state this with utter confidence—available in Pinsk or Minsk. Only in America.

Yields
8 servings

2 cloves garlic, peeled and pushed through a
    garlic press
Salt and pepper
5 pounds brisket of beef
1 bottle red wine
2 large onions, peeled and sliced
2 cups wild rice
1 pound dried apricots

1. Preheat the oven to 500° F.

2. Make a paste with the garlic and salt and pepper. Rub the paste all over the meat and put it in a roasting pan, fat side up. Put the meat in the oven, uncovered, and cook for 15 minutes, or until it is very brown but not burned.

3. Lower the heat to 350° F. Remove the roasting pan from the oven. Take the meat out and set it on a plate. Put the roasting pan over medium heat and pour in the wine. Bring to a boil and deglaze the pan with a metal spatula. Remove from heat, spread the onions over the bottom of the pan, and set the meat on top of them. Cover the meat with aluminum foil and roast in the oven for 2 hours.

4. Add the wild rice and dried apricots. Cover and continue cooking in the oven until the wild rice is cooked through and tender to your taste, at least 30 minutes, possibly 1 hour.

5. Remove the meat, discard the foil, and slice the brisket in the kitchen. Place slices in a serving dish in an overlapping line. Arrange the wild rice and apricots, mixed together in a ring, around the meat.

Cabbage Stuffed with Wild Rice and Lamb

Many cultures meet in this variation on traditional stuffed cabbage: central Europe (home of the stuffed cabbage), the Middle East (lamb with cumin), the United States (wild rice), and Asia (the ample broth that accompanies the stuffed cabbage packets, which will remind aficionados of a complicated Korean casserole/soup).

Yields
4 servings

4 tablespoons salt

2 cups wild rice

1 large cabbage

1 pound ground lamb or other ground meat

2 medium onions, peeled and chopped

2 teaspoons black pepper

2 tablespoons ground cumin

1 teaspoon cayenne pepper or 2 teaspoons red
      pepper flakes

6 cups beef stock

1. Bring 2 quarts of water to a boil with 1 tablespoon of the salt. Dump in the wild rice and cook at a fast simmer for about 50 minutes. Drain and set aside to cool enough so that you can handle the grains.

2. Meanwhile, in another pot, bring a large quantity of water to the boil with 2 tablespoons of the salt—enough water to completely cover the cabbage. Lower the heat so that the water simmers. Then score the cabbage with a small, sharp knife, cutting a ¼-inch-deep circle around the stem, which makes it easy to remove the leaves. Now, holding the cabbage by its stem, plunge the head into the simmering water and hold it there for a few seconds. This will help separate the outer leaf from the rest of the cabbage. Remove the leaf and set aside. Continue this way until you have 12 leaves. Don't worry if they are torn here and there.

3. Blanch each leaf by holding it under the simmering water with a wooden spoon for 2 minutes. Drain.

4. In a mixing bowl, mix together the wild rice, the remaining tablespoon of salt, the ground lamb, chopped onions, black pepper, cumin, and the cayenne pepper or hot pepper flakes.

5. Form the wild rice–lamb mixture into 12 balls the size of walnuts or slightly larger, which should use up the whole mixture. Then spread out a cabbage leaf, outer side down. Put a wild rice ball on the leaf and fold the edges of the leaf over it, making a fairly tight package, with the rib edge on top. Secure either with string or a toothpick. Continue in this way until you have stuffed all 12 leaves.

6. Pour the stock into a pot large enough to hold all the stuffed leaves in two layers. Then put in the stuffed leaves. Place over medium heat and bring the liquid to a boil, lower the heat, cover, and cook at a slow sim-

mer for 45 minutes, or until the ribs have softened and the stock has imbibed the flavors of the cabbage and its stuffing.

7. Serve in shallow, wide soup bowls. Place 3 stuffed cabbage leaves in each bowl and pour the broth over them. There should be enough broth to come about ⅓ of the way up the sides of the stuffed leaves.

⤙ SIDE DISHES ⤚

Wild Rice Salad

This is a truly native American side dish if you take the trouble to find black walnuts. The nuts have an unmistakable flavor that declares itself even in the throaty presence of wild rice. I do not recommend, however, that you take the trouble to shell these indigenous members of the walnut family. Let professionals take care of this arduous, messy task.

Yields
6 servings

2 tablespoons butter
½ cup raisins, soaked in water for 20 minutes
    and drained

½ cup chopped black or regular walnuts
1 Basic Wild Rice recipe (see page 240)
½ teaspoon ground cinnamon

1. Melt the butter in a medium skillet. Stir in the raisins and chopped walnuts, coating them with butter. Then stir in the wild rice and continue cooking until the rice is heated through and coated with butter.

2. Sprinkle with the ground cinnamon. Serve hot, as an accompaniment to roasted meat or chicken or game; or let cool and serve as part of a buffet or a light lunch with cold meats.

"Dirty" Wild Rice

In New Orleans white rice and chicken livers are a famous specialty called dirty rice, because the chicken livers give a dark cast to the rice. Wild rice is, of course, already dark, but its flavor is a more equal match to the livers, and its virile texture makes a nice contrast with their softness.

Yields
6 to 8 servings

1 tablespoon butter
2 medium onions, peeled and chopped
1 Basic Wild Rice recipe (see page 240)
8 chicken livers, chopped coarsely
1 teaspoon salt
½ teaspoon pepper

1. Melt the butter in a medium skillet. Stir in the chopped onions and sauté until translucent. Then stir in the wild rice.

2. Stir in the chicken livers and stir-fry over high heat very briefly, just until the flesh has firmed up a bit. Stir in the salt and pepper and serve immediately.

DESSERT

Wild Rice Blueberry Muffins

A quick and easy way to bring together two of America's greatest original foods and two regions, with wild rice from the northern lakes and blueberries from down-east Maine.

Yields
1 dozen
muffins

1 cup cooked wild rice
2 eggs, lightly beaten
5 tablespoons oil
1 cup milk
1¼ cups flour
1 tablespoon baking powder
½ teaspoon salt
¼ cup sugar
1 cup blueberries

1. Preheat the oven to 425° F. Grease a 12-cup muffin tin.

2. Beat together the wild rice, eggs, oil, and milk.

3. In another bowl, stir together the flour, baking powder, salt, and sugar.

4. Stir both mixtures together. Then fold in the blueberries.

5. Fill the muffin cups about ⅔ full with batter. Bake 15 to 18 minutes, until lightly browned.

Drinks

In the modern world,
where industrially manufactured flours
and pastas are commonplace and
cheap, the drier end of the moistened
grain spectrum predominates. The
dry products store far better,
and we can consume more grain
more efficiently if it is boiled in barely
the amount of water necessary to cook it
(steamed rice, oatmeal), drained completely
(pasta), or barely moistened (bread, cake).
We no longer need to thin out our
grain allotment with water; so the grain
drinks that once invigorated Europe
have either disappeared or changed their
nature almost completely, leaving behind
a few ghost names, most of them whispering
barley to those who care to listen.

I am not talking here about the myriad beers made from every fermentable grain in the universe in every country. I am not referring to Turkish boza fermented from bulgur wheat, nor premasticated corn-based chicha from the forests of South America, nor African millet beer, nor any of the thousands and thousands of barley-based manufactured brews from Korean Obi to Jamaican Red Stripe. I mean plain old boiled grain decoctions such as Mexican/Aztec corn *atoles* and chocolate-flavored corn-based *champurrados*.

In North America today, the only important survival among the various grain teas of yore is an oat-based powder-form beverage principally consumed by Spanish speakers. In Spain itself, the most venerable of all grain drinks, barley tea or barley water, survives only as the name of a popular beverage called *horchata*. The word derives from the Latin barley word *hordeum*, as do its Italian, French, and English equivalents (respectively, *orzata*, *orgeat*, and *ozyat*).

There is no longer any barley water tradition in the English-speaking world, but there was once, and as C. Anne Wilson explains it in *Food and Drink in Britain* (Academy, 1973), this heritage exemplifies the history of the drink all over early modern Europe:

> It had a long history as an invalid beverage. In the sixth century A.D. Anthimus had recommended a thin drink made of barley with pure warm water as beneficial for fever patients. The later medieval version in France had the name tisane [from the Greek *ptisana* for barley water], was sweetened with sugar and seasoned with licorice and sometimes also figs. Adapted for English use it more often comprised barley boiled in water with licorice, herbs and raisins. It was still a licorice-flavored drink

in the first part of the seventeenth century, but soon afterwards was brought up to date by the substitution of lemon juice for licorice.

Another variant of barley water in France, called *orgemonde,* was flavored with ground almonds. This too reached England during the seventeenth century, its name softening to "orgeat" or "ozyat." Subsequently, the barley dropped out and English ozyat was made from ground almonds and sugar with orangeflower water or the juice of citrus fruits boiled with spring water. It was a cold drink similar to lemonade. Milk ozyat was boiled, spiced milk, cooled and mixed with ground almonds; and special ozyat glasses with handles were designed to serve it in.

Today Italian *orʒata* and French *orgeat* are also almond-flavored sweet drinks, with barley only an etymological feature of their names. Spanish *horchata* is a more complicated case. In one form, rice has supplanted barley. In another one, the most popular, it includes ground chufa, or tiger nut. Penelope Casas states unequivocally in *Foods and Wines of Spain* (Knopf, 1982) that this chufa *horchata* is of Arabic origin. This makes sense (as does an Arab origin for the rice *horchata,* since the Moors also introduced rice to Spain—and Europe) because the tiger "nut" *(Cyperus esculentus)* is the underground tuber, or corm, of the plant's root, the form prized in the ancient Near East. Remains of *C. esculentus* (a.k.a. earth almond, earth nut, rush nut, and Zulu nut) have been found in Egyptian tombs of the third millennium B.C., and Theophrastus mentioned them as something Egyptians harvested and cooked in barley juice.

Nowadays the chufa is grown commercially around Valencia, but it seems likely that it traveled from an ancestral center in Egypt to Spain, where it now provides pleasure to millions. But did the import of chufa, with its ancient connection with barley, start Europe's craze for barley water? Or did chufa, arriving in the low Middle Ages, meet an already entrenched custom of consuming thinned-out barley purée? The second scenario strikes me as more likely and leaves open a more logical route for the substitution of imported rice for homegrown barley in *horchata.*

Those oldtime barley waters have by now all been superseded by zippier potations. In any self-respecting French café, a *tisane* is an herbal tea. In New York's Little Italy almond *orzata* is a staple—and domestically produced. In Mexico City everyone knows that *horchata* is made, as in Spain, from rice—except when it is prepared with melon seeds.

Here, then, are a few of these antique grain beverages that still hold their own on native ground.

✑ *BARLEY* ✑

Poricha
(Korean Barley Tea)

This recipe is adapted from *Flavours of Korea*, by Marc and Kim Millon (London: André Deutsch, 1991).

Here is the way to make this mild and pleasant drink from scratch. Most people, and probably most Koreans, now make *poricha* from a dry, tealike packaged product available in Korean markets. Follow the directions on the package. It stores very well under refrigeration: the grain lover's answer to Evian.

Yields
8 servings

4 tablespoons roasted barley (available from
    Korean grocers)
6 cups water

1. Soak the barley in the water for 30 minutes.
2. Bring the mixture to a boil and simmer slowly for 1 hour.
3. Pour through a sieve into a teapot. Serve hot or warm or, in summer, chilled with honey.

↜ CORN ↝

Atole

This is the original American soft drink, a pre-Columbian corn-and-milk beverage still found in markets and in Mexican homes. Flavored with chocolate, it is called *champurrado*. Puréed fruits of every kind can be added for infinite variations.

Atole can be pleasant at any hour, but it is ideal at breakfast, with pastry.

Yields
4 servings

1¼ cups hominy (whole-kernel dried corn,
    called *pozole* in Mexico)
2 quarts milk
1 cinnamon stick
¾ cup brown sugar

1. Grind the hominy with 2 tablespoons of the milk in a processor with the steel blade. You could also use store-bought *masa* (cornmeal made from hominy), but the texture wouldn't be as "homemade."

2. Bring the remaining milk to a boil. As soon as it foams, remove from heat, stir briefly, and add the cinnamon stick and sugar. Simmer very slowly, for 40 minutes, to reduce the milk by about half.

3. Whisk in the ground hominy in a slow, steady stream. Keep whisking until the mixture thickens. Serve hot.

Variations

Fruit Atole

Add a minimum of 1 cup puréed fruit per quart *atole,* after the basic drink is done.

Champurrado

Whisk in 3 ounces sweet chocolate (preferably Mexican breakfast chocolate), after the basic drink is done.

❧ RICE ❧

Agua de Arroz
(Spanish Rice Tea)

This recipe is adapted from Lourdes March's *El Libro de la Paella y de los Arroces* (Madrid: Allianza, 1985).

Spain's love of rice is proverbial. Think of paella. Here are two healing drinks you may have missed on your visit to Madrid. Look again the next time, or make these at home in warm weather.

Yields
4 servings

½ cup medium-grain rice (available in
    Hispanic markets)
1 quart water
peel of 1 lemon cut in a spiral or 1 teaspoon
    aniseeds
1 cup sugar

1. Boil the rice with the water, over low heat, for 30 to 40 minutes, until the mixture thickens slightly.
2. Strain and discard the rice. To the strained rice water add the lemon peel or aniseeds and the sugar. Stir until the sugar dissolves.
3. Chill. Strain again and serve.

Horchata de Arroz
(Spanish Rice Drink)

This recipe is adapted from Lourdes March's *El Libro de la Paella y de los Arroces*.

Yields
4 servings

1 cup medium-grain rice
Peel from 1 lemon
5½ cups cold water
1¼ cups sugar

1. Soak the rice with the lemon peel in 4 cups of the cold water for 24 hours. (This should be enough to cover the rice.)

2. Remove the lemon peel and purée the rice/water mixture in a food mill or blender to produce a smooth mixture. Strain, adding the remaining 1½ cups water, little by little, as you push the mixture through the sieve. Stir in the sugar until it dissolves, and chill.

❧ WHEAT ☙

Boza
(Bulgur Wheat and Rice Drink)

The Turkish food historian Nevin Halici has brought her English-speaking friends many treasures of her native cuisine. This recipe is a most unusual mix of rice and wheat that is subjected to a yeast fermentation and then drunk like beer. In my adaptation, I have substituted raspberry preserves for the traditional cinnamon and chickpeas, inspired by the raspberry-laced German wheat beer, Berliner Weisse.

Yields
8 servings

6 ounces bulgur
2 tablespoons rice
3 quarts water
1½ cups sugar
½ teaspoon active dry yeast
½ cup raspberry preserves

1. Combine the bulgur and rice with the water. Bring to a boil, reduce the heat, and simmer, covered, for about 1½ hours, until the mixture thickens.

2. Sieve and put the purée back in the pot. Stir in the sugar. Bring to a boil and stir for 2 minutes to dissolve the sugar. Let cool until lukewarm.

3. Activate the yeast by stirring it together with a little of the cooked purée. When it begins to bubble, stir it into the *boza* mixture and leave it to ferment in a warm place, covered, for about 8 hours—until the *boza* has bubbles on the surface. The taste will be bittersweet.

4. Pour into large glasses and stir a tablespoon of raspberry preserves into each glass.

Index

emmer, 13, 149
endosperm, 4, 148
English Bread and Yeast Cookery
    (David), 6
Equador, 24, 27
Essentials of Classic Italian Cooking
    (Hazan), 103
Ethiopia, 13, 203, 234–6
Exotic Ethiopian Cooking (Mesfin),
    238

familia, 85
Fannie Farmer Cookbook, The, 30
farfel, 18
    basic recipe, 188
    matzoh, new age, 189
    matzoh, traditional, 188
farro (spelt), 149
fat(s), xi, 17, 18, 19, 20, 182
fava beans:
    rice salad with ham and, 118
    rice with pork and, 102
    in succotash, 64
fennel, polenta and tomato-cheese
    sauce with, 71
fiber, xi, 19, 20
figs, in oatmeal cookies, 96
Filipino Garlic Rice, 114
firik, 149
fish:
    haddock congee, 107
    red snapper stuffed with cous-
        cous, 172
    see also salmon; salmon roe
flapjacks, 152, 168
flatbreads, 1
    barley, 40
    oatcakes, 93

oat flour rieska, 93
Flavours of Korea (Millon; Millon),
    250
flours, about, 5–7, 148, 184
focaccia:
    basic dough, 232
    rye, 232–3
Food and Agricultural Organiza-
    tion, United Nations, 222
Food and Drink in Britain (Wilson),
    248
food groups, 17
food guide pyramid (USDA),
    16–18
Foods and Wines of Spain (Casas),
    249
France, 208
fritters:
    corn, deep-fried, 68
    corn, pan-fried, 69
    quinoa, 226
fruit sauces, 196

Galantina di Polenta, 59
Gâteau d'Amaranthe, 207
Gâteau de Riz au Chocolate, 144
germ, 4, 5
ghee, 121
giblets, pilaf with mushrooms and,
    127
gizzards, chicken:
    corn and rice risotto with, 67
    fried brown rice and beets with,
        114
Glasse, Hannah, 30, 46
gluten, 5, 13
gorgonzola:
    polenta with, 70

quinoa, 222–8
  basic recipe, 222
  fritters, 226
  pilaf, 227
  pudding, 227
  vegetable stew (Ch'aqe de
    Quinua), 223

rabbit, in paella Valenciana, 124
red snapper, stuffed with couscous,
  172
rice, 4, 11, 24, 99–145
  basic, Chinese method, 100
  basic, Indian method, 101
  basic, Italian method, 103
  basic, Spanish method, 102
  bran, 5
  bread, 135
  bread, brown, 136
  bread, Hazel Ramsey's Philpy,
    136
  brown, basic recipe, 105
  cake, chocolate, 144
  cakes, 5, 6
  croquettes, 134
  flour, 5, 6
  grape leaves stuffed with, 110
  grape leaves stuffed with lamb
    and, 111
  ground, browned, with Thai
    chicken patty, 122
  Hoppin' John, 133
  jambalaya, 126
  khitchri, 120
  long-grain, 100–1
  medium-grain, 102
  paella Valenciana, Lourdes
    March's, 124

peppers stuffed with yogurt,
    walnuts, broccoli, and, 166
  pilaf with giblets and mush-
    rooms, 127
  with pork and fava beans, Span-
    ish method, 102
  with pork chops, cauliflower,
    and beans, 112
  protein content of, 204
  pudding, basic, 137
  pudding, Indian, 138
  pudding, Spanish, with
    meringue, 139
  pudding with strawberries, 140
  pulao, basmati salmon, 123
  ring (dessert), 142
  salad, basic, 117
  salad with favas and ham, 118
  short-grain, 103–5
  soup with peas, Chinese, 109
  sticky, 104
  sticky, with mango, 145
  torte, 141
  see also Arborio rice; basmati
    rice; brown rice; congee; rice,
    fried; rice drinks; risotto; wild
    rice
rice, fried, 113
  brown, with gizzards and beets,
    114
  Chinese, 113
  Filipino garlic, 114
  glutinous, 116
  Thai (Khao Pad), 117
Rice Book, The (Owen), 118, 224
rice drinks:
  agua de arroz, tea, 252
  boza, with bulgur, 253
  horchata de arroz, 252

wheat (*continued*)
    Rømmegrøt, 153
    types of, 13, 15
    see also bran; buckwheat; bulgur
        wheat; couscous; noodles;
        orzo; pasta; wheat berries;
        wheat germ; whole wheat
wheat berries, 4–5, 7, 147
    basic recipe, 150
    in bay scallops with eggplant,
      163
    cabbage stuffed with lamb and,
      166
    kebabs, 162
    in kutia, 193
    peppers stuffed with, 164
    peppers stuffed with ground
      meat and, 165
wheat flakes, in familia, 85
wheat germ, 147, 148
    in familia, 85

whole wheat:
    and barley bread, 42
    in dark bread, 180
    in Karen Karp's Banana Bread,
      229
wild rice, 12, 239–46
    basic recipe, 240
    and blueberry muffins, 246
    brisket with apricots and, 241
    cabbage stuffed with lamb and,
      242
    "dirty," 245
    pancakes, Judith Jones's, 240
    salad, 244
Wolfert, Paula, 150, 154

Yan-kit So, 116
Yesuff Fitfit, 238

Zohary, Daniel, 8, 12

A NOTE ABOUT THE AUTHOR

Raymond Sokolov was born in Detroit, Michigan, in 1941. He graduated from the Cranbrook School, Bloomfield Hills, Michigan, and from Harvard *summa cum laude* in the Classics, having also served as an editor on the *Harvard Crimson*. He attended Wadham College, Oxford, as a Fulbright Scholar and later returned to Harvard for graduate study. He has worked as a foreign correspondent and book critic for *Newsweek* and as the Food Editor for *The New York Times*. Mr. Sokolov wrote a regular food column for *Natural History* magazine for twenty years. And for the past thirteen years he has been the Leisure and Arts Editor for *The Wall Street Journal*. He lives in New York City with his wife.

A NOTE ON THE TYPE

The text of this book was set in a digitized version of Fournier, a typeface originated by Pierre Simon Fournier *fils* (1712–1768). Coming from a family of typefounders, Fournier was an extraordinarily prolific designer both of typefaces and of typographic ornaments. He was also the author of the celebrated *Manuel typographique* (1764–1766). In addition, he was the first to attempt to work out the point system standardizing type measurement that is still in use internationally.

The cut of the typeface named for this remarkable man captures many of the aspects of his personality and period. Though it is elegant, it is also very legible.

Composed by North Market Street Graphics,
Lancaster, Pennsylvania
Printed and bound by Quebecor Printing,
Martinsburg, West Virginia
Designed by Brooke Zimmer and Virginia Tan